The University of Michigan
Center for Chinese Studies

Michigan Monographs in Chinese Studies

Volume 56

Citizens and Groups in Contemporary China

edited by Victor C. Falkenheim

Ann Arbor

Center for Chinese Studies
The University of Michigan

1987

*Open access edition funded by the National Endowment for the Humanities/
Andrew W. Mellon Foundation Humanities Open Book Program.*

Library of Congress Cataloging in Publication Data

Citizens and groups in contemporary China.

Includes bibliographies.
1. Pressure groups — China — Addresses, essays, lectures. 2.
Political participation — China — Addresses, essays, lectures. 3.
China — Politics and government — 1949-   — Addresses, essays,
lectures. I. Falkenheim, Victor C., 1940-   .

JQ1514.P7C58 1985   322.4'3'0951   85-114987
ISBN 0-89264-065-0
ISBN 0-89264-066-9 (pbk.)

Cover by Eric M. Ernst

ISBN 978-0-89264-065-2 (hardcover)
ISBN 978-0-89264-066-9 (paper)
ISBN 978-0-472-12788-7 (ebook)
ISBN 978-0-472-90184-5 (open access)

CONTENTS

LIST OF CONTRIBUTORS

JOHN P. BURNS is Associate Professor of Political Science at the University of Hong Kong.

LOWELL DITTMER is Associate Professor of Political Science at the University of California at Berkeley.

VICTOR C. FALKENHEIM is Associate Professor of Political Science and Chairman of the Department of East Asian Studies at the University of Toronto.

MERLE GOLDMAN is Professor of History at Boston University.

HARRY HARDING, JR. is Senior Fellow in the Foreign Policy Studies Program at the Brookings Institution.

RICHARD P. SUTTMEIER is Henry Bristol Professor of International Affairs at Hamilton College.

ANDREW G. WALDER is Assistant Professor of Sociology at Columbia University.

LYNN T. WHITE III is Professor of Politics at Princeton University.

PREFACE

Victor C. Falkenheim

This volume began with two symposia held in 1977 and 1978. The first, a workshop on "The Pursuit of Interest in China," was held in August 1977 at the University of Michigan, and was organized by Michel Oksenberg and Richard Baum. It was supported by a grant from the Joint Committee on Contemporary China of the Social Science Research Council and the American Council of Learned Societies, using funds provided by the Andrew Mellon Foundation. Its principal goal was to use detailed case studies to explore the relevance of interest group approaches to the study of Chinese politics. The second, a panel organized by the editor for the 1978 Chicago meeting of the Association of Asian Studies, sought to apply participatory approaches to the role of social groups in the Chinese political process. The striking degree of overlap in the focus, methodology, and participants in both meetings suggested to a number of the paper writers that there was a need for a more eclectic approach which would focus simultaneously on individual and group actors. The recognition that a volume based on such an approach might serve the needs of students and scholars seeking to examine the dynamics of informal influence and power in China was the stimulus for publishing the studies presented here in book form.

Three of the chapters in the current volume were originally drafts prepared for the 1977 workshop; two were initially presented at the 1978 meeting in Chicago. Three other chapters were commissioned later as the volume took shape through our correspondence and meetings of 1980 and 1981. All have been revised to take account of the dramatic revelations of the post-Mao years.

CHAPTER 1

Citizen and Group Politics in China: An Introduction

Victor C. Falkenheim

The first systematic exposition of interest group approaches to the study of policy-making in Marxist-Leninist polities appeared almost two decades ago. Since that time, periodic challenges notwithstanding, such approaches have become almost universally regarded as essential tools of substantive policy analysis, reflecting the increasing importance of group activity in modernizing socialist systems.[1] Although many conceptual and methodological issues remain unresolved, "pluralist" perspectives have gained wide acceptance. Dahl's recent call for comparative study of the distinctive forms of "organizational pluralism" within "hegemonic regimes" is suggestive of the extent of that acceptance.[2]

Paradoxically, interest group approaches, though first applied to the post-Stalin U.S.S.R., quickly took root in Chinese studies, despite the significant gap between China and the Soviet Union in stage of revolutionary development and in economic structure. Early scholarship on the post-1949 period in China tended to favor totalitarian or mobilization paradigms, reflecting the vigorous transformative programs being undertaken by the youthful post-revolutionary regime. But, as interest group approaches gained influence in the broader field of communist studies, developments in China prepared the ground for their ready acceptance. The collapse of the Great Leap Forward (1958-60) and the state's subsequent retreat in the face of grass roots opposition to radical initiatives revealed the limits of monolithic models of state power. The sharp intra-elite political cleavages that subsequently emerged shattered images of a unified senior leadership. In response, scholars moved toward the use of a variety of conflict models, a shift which was accelerated by the onset of the Cultural Revolution in the late 1960s. The extent of the open

1

elite factional conflict and violent clashes between mobilized social
interests at the lower levels of society revealed during this period
revolutionized scholarly perceptions of the political order. Franz
Schurman, revising his landmark study, *Ideology and Organization
in Communist China,* called for a more society-centered approach,
acknowledging that events had called into question his stress on the
political potency of "ideology and organization" which he now saw as
vulnerable to individual and societal challenges to state power.[3] Similarly, James Townsend, who in his classic study of political participation in China had expressed skepticism about the utility of group
politics approaches, later concluded that his analysis had
understated the potentialities for group formation and pressure.[4]
Michel Oksenberg's pioneering effort to delineate the resources,
strategies, and influence of China's principal occupational groups
opened the way for a growing number of specialized studies of groups
in Chinese politics.[5]

Three kinds of studies resulted from these changing perceptions
and approaches. One focused on the policy-making process and
sought to explore the impact of intra-elite cleavages on policy
continuity and change.[6] A second focused more on policy implementation than on formulation and hypothesized that significant issue-
area variation exists in the policy-making process as a function of
bureaucratic conflict. This literature examined *inter alia* such policy
areas as health, education, commerce, and water policy.[7] The third
examined individual and group political strategies and the policies
that resulted, focusing on occupational groups and social strata,
including workers and managers.[8] These studies confirmed the
importance of focusing on interest politics, established the critical
importance of the bureaucratic setting of policy formulation and
implementation, and clarified the significance of the prevailing pattern of elite conflict in shaping interest politics within the bureaucratic structure and in society. The validity of these insights has been
amply confirmed by the explosion of interest politics in the 1980s in
response to the reform initiatives of Deng's modernizing coalition.

Despite these advances, no real consensus has been reached on
the role of interests in the policy-making process. In particular, considerable skepticism persists regarding the influence of broad social
groups. Though most analysts agree that focusing on elite participation at higher levels in the political system was useful, they disagree
on the question of how such individual, factional, or organizational
interest articulation is structured. Nor has agreement been reached
on how best to describe or conceptualize the pattern of state-society

interaction, either in terms of corporatist or more traditional "directed society" metaphors.[9]

Finally, little agreement has been achieved regarding the most appropriate models for discussing the long-term transformational and development processes underway. What models best take account, for example, of the changing pattern of group politics today? It seems clear that the current more visible and vigorous advocacy of social and economic interests and the more accommodating posture of the regime are in part a reflection of short-term liberalizing trends, but are equally linked to the major generational and systemic transition ahead. As the Chinese seek to devise new institutional forms to accommodate the changing pattern of group and individual demands in the context of eroding doctrinal allegiance, comparative and long-term perspectives are needed to understand those changes.

The authors of the following chapters seek to examine these questions and explore how demands at the grass roots are brokered into the policy process, how choices are shaped at the middle level, and how competing demands are reconciled at the top. While differing in our concepts and frameworks, we agree that the analysis of interests, influence, and policy requires a historically textured, multi-level focus, exploring not only activities of social groups and aggregates, but also focusing on the vertical links which tie grass roots participation by individuals to the strategies of middle-level administrators and to the critically important policy and loyalty groups at the apex of the system. Skilling and Griffith, in their pioneering volume on interest groups in the U.S.S.R., deliberately eschewed a direct concern with social groups and elite factions.[10] We, however, prefer to emphasize the role of social aggregates, professional groups, and bureaucratic interest groups at the base and intermediate levels of the structure, exploring the interactions among them.

Interest Politics at the Basic Level:
Individuals and "Social Aggregates"

Students of comparative communist systems have generally been reluctant to assign any great significance to interest-oriented participation by broad social, occupational, or generational aggregates. Workers, peasants, and youth, among others, are credited, at least hypothetically, with having distinct sets of common interests. However, they are seen as lacking the cohesion and organizational capability to pursue them on a collective basis.

This impotence is partly attributed to the state's hostility to open and organized interest advocacy, and partly to the size and diversity of these interest communities. The mechanisms provided by the state to accommodate or channel citizen interests (e.g., work unit or local elections, mass campaigns, trade unions, or peasant associations) are almost universally seen as preempting rather than facilitating autonomous interest articulation. Operating within these institutional constraints citizens must express their interests on an individual basis at the worksite or communal level. The result is a diffuse and localized pattern of participation, which is viewed as lacking in broader policy impact. Thus, Brzezinski and Huntington, in their early and influential formulation, labeled the social aggregates at the base of the policy-making hierarchy "amorphous social forces," on the grounds that they lacked the structure necessary for the organized pursuit of their own interests.[11] A similar logic underlies Skilling and Griffith's exclusion of social groups from their study of interest politics in the Soviet Union. These views do not deny the reality of intense and regular citizen involvement at the residential and worksite level in socialist systems. They simply assert that this activity constitutes an isolated realm, only tenuously linked to the policy-making chain. A recent expression of this view can be found in Bialer's contention that in the U.S.S.R. seldom do the low politics of individual participation and the high politics of state policy formulation intersect.[12]

There is obviously merit in these views of participation as atomized and limited. The chapters by Burns and Walder show that the bulk of non-ritual interest-oriented participation by workers and peasants in China takes place at the work unit or residential level. It seems clear that the scope of that participation is narrow, with individuals concerned principally with seeking remedies for individual grievances concerning specific local applications of general policy. Moreover, citizens tend to be skeptical of the worth of formal petitions or official organizations and channels and are fearful of the sanctions that often accompany open and direct interest advocacy.

On the other hand, as these same studies also suggest, Chinese citizens do in fact regularly pursue their interests with a repertoire of tactics tailored to these constraints. Though they often disdain formal modes of participation, citizens use a wider range of informal strategies which range from individually buttonholing officials to reliance on informal networks of friends and associates, or passive resistance. Moreover, this participation is informed by a keen consciousness of the context in which participation takes place.[13]

Peasants, as John Burns shows, are keenly sensitive to shifts in policy, alterations in the balance of elite factions, and the potential for policy change, to which they respond quickly.

It is important, then, to recognize that participation can frequently be both constrained and effective. This paradox reflects significant structural and normative features of the Chinese political system. First, as Lowell Dittmer shows in chapter 2, state ideology accords a central legitimacy to the expression of individual and class interests. The state is committed on the basis of mass line theory to accommodate self-interested local or class-based interests. The Party's mobilizational style of leadership often relies on explicit appeals to the interests of specific segments of society and recognizes the importance of class and interest politics in its style of governance. Thus, despite the primacy assigned to the interests of the whole in formulating policy and the monopoly claimed by the Party in mediating and aggregating interests, local and partial interests have an enduring, if contingent, legitimacy. Moreover, in the structure of the Chinese state both party and state hierarchies extend down to the village, neighborhood, and shop level, so that individual actions at the unit level are transmitted directly to local agents of state power. This provides an important way of measuring local response to national policies. That the system is constructed to consider this response in policy-making can be seen from the structure of the policy-making process, in which policy formulation and implementation are merged in a sequence of local experimentation, testing, adaption, and synthesis. The role of local units in policy-making calls into question the conventional distinction between low and high politics, between local and central politics, and between occupational and civic politics.[14]

To a certain extent these realities have always been recognized. Brzezinski and Huntington, though deprecating the importance of "amorphous social forces," noted their ability to "exert pressures which over a long period of time cannot be altogether ignored."[15] Further, though lacking the attributes of groups, these aggregates were capable of influencing policy indirectly, by compelling the Party to anticipate their collective reactions; in effect, treating them as groups. David M. Lampton, in his study of Chinese health policy has, in fact, argued that "the cumulative impact of individual acts at the bottom of the system" can be "as effective as conscious articulation in setting the leadership agenda."[16]

The discussions in this volume then, support a definition of group action that takes account of the influence that groups of individuals with similar attributes and interests, acting separately, can have on government decisions.[17] However, only moving up the vertical hierarchy to examine interest articulation at the intermediate levels of state administration can show the mechanisms through which individual interest advocacy shapes government policy.

Intermediate-Level Participation

Most interest group analyses of hegemonic regimes are based on the premise that effective pressure can be wielded only from within the party-state structure and that effective participation therefore takes the form of "organizational politics." But, which is the most useful level on which to focus within the vertical power structure? Griffith's analysis of "intermediate participation" in the U.S.S.R. emphasizes focusing on "politically relevant individuals who occupy intermediate positions" between the "leadership and the masses of the led." However, Griffith's own analysis is concerned with specific functional elites and his use of the notion of intermediate participation leaves open the question of which levels are most critical for analysis.[18] Most analysts envisage the floor of the policy structure in China as composed of a large number of grass roots factory and farm cadres who, as a crucial gate-keeping sub-elite, selectively broker mass demands into the policy system. Although their official functions are directed toward policy implementation, their role in transmitting local response to intermediate levels is of such critical importance that some scholars have gone so far as to suggest that communal or unit participation in policy-making might be the critical starting point of any analysis.[19]

Yet, the characteristics of unit participation and their links to national-level policy conflict need to be spelled out. As the chapters in this volume by Burns, Walder, and White suggest, basic- and intermediate-level production and accounting units tend to acquire a relatively stable conception of their corporate interests, shaped by such objective factors as the composition of the work force, the unit's resource endowment, and its production and marketing opportunities. These in turn define a unit's needs and ultimately its policy preferences. The ability of lower-level organizations to pursue and defend unit interests stems in part from the legitimacy accorded by the state to unit autonomy (zizhuquan), which entails the right to adapt policy to local needs and realities. This right can be invoked by unit leaders and their constituents to resist excessive administrative pressure under the rubric of what Mao called in 1958 the "right to resist."[20] The system's capacity to use flexibility at the local level, like its use of local response, reflects the consciously experimental character of the policy-making process in China, in which central-level policymakers process initiatives and choices generated at the basic level. The bubble-up character of policy-making hinges significantly on local diversity and revolves around a communications and reporting system which identifies typical or advanced "models."[21] When central policies shift, public media and bureaucratic reporting systems are directed to refocus their attention and praise to those units which best exemplify the benefits of the new policy. For example, when a moderate line emerges at the center, model "advanced" units will tend to be drawn from the reservoir of successful "conservative" units whose resources and experience make their performance suitable for popularization and emulation. When policy shifts in a radical direction these units will either disappear from the press or will be attacked as "black models" while their "progressive" counterparts will acquire visibility as "pace-setting units."

A noteworthy aspect of this system is the tendency for entrepreneurial bureaucrats to search for confirming experience to buttress their policy preferences. Administrative policy-making in China in part pits competing vertical policy coalitions against one another, with bureaucrats at various levels aligning with like-minded producing units in an effort to tilt the reporting process in favor of the preferred policy outcome. In periods of low-intensity policy conflict, these informal clusters are quasi-legitimate but in periods of high-intensity conflict they crystallize into factionalized, patron-client relationships enmeshing affected units in a highly politicized policy struggle.[22]

There is ample evidence to show that many industrial and agricultural units that benefitted from Great Leap Forward initiatives managed to stave off conservative pressures in the early 1960s. During the Cultural Revolution such units were lauded for managing to "resist the sinister wave of contraction" of those years. Andors has documented the significant post-Leap continuity of many organizational and management reforms in industrial enterprises.[23] One of the most closely studied examples of unit independence in the rural sphere in the 1960s is Dazhai brigade. Meisner has shown clearly how Dazhai resisted both left and right policy initiatives in the early- and mid-1960s, building on community solidarity and a variety of horizontal and vertical alliances. His term for the process, "political self-advocacy," captures an important aspect of the reciprocal links between policy groups in the middle administration and producing units at the base.[24]

A parallel process at work during the Cultural Revolution era which insulated enterprises and farming units from what is now described as a decade of coercive ultra-leftism is clearly shown in the chapters by Burns and Walder.[25] In spelling out the reasons why "agriculture had maintained a certain degree of development" despite the Gang of Four's "rabid sabotage" of rural policy, *People's Daily* noted the heroic role of "vast numbers of rural basic-level cadres," who "kept to their posts" and withstood the "perverse acts" of the Gang.[26] The extent to which cadres and farm communities were able to derail the "Learn from Dazhai" Movement in the early 1970s is vividly illustrated in John Burns' discussion of the fate of this program in South China.

The extent of unit independence and continuity is particularly well illustrated by the histories of the new model units which have come to the fore since 1978. For example, Xiashitang production brigade, located in the former radical stronghold of Yipin prefecture in Sichuan, has become an exemplar of rural diversification, its success beginning with a 1964 decision to increase farm cash income through diversification. Strikingly, the "secret" of its prosperity was held to be its "courage to stick the policy of encouraging agriculture and industry to be combined" and *"refusing to yield even when held up by the Gang as a 'sinister' model"* (emphasis added).[27]

Intermediate-Level Participation and Organizational Interests

Moving up the policy-making hierarchy from the unit level, the dynamics of interest conflict become progressively more difficult to analyze. This stems equally from the secrecy that shrouds the policy-making process and from the greater complexity of interest articulation at intermediate levels. As Harding and Suttmeier show in the cases of the military and scientific communities, intra-organizational interest cleavages make questionable the possibility of identifying a homogeneous, corporate organizational interest. In addition, the limited, largely documentary evidence allows us at best to discern broad opinion clusters associated with individual actors and advocates, not with organizations. In response to these analytic and empirical constraints, most researchers have embraced Griffith's tendency analysis perspective, which stresses the importance of gauging the broad thrust of elite policy preferences. It is seen as the best way to capture the myriad parallel individual articulations which constitute the core of organizational interest politics. In elaboration of this perspective a number of scholars, including Suttmeier in this volume, have found useful economic or rational choice models of administrative behavior. Of particular importance are Hirschman's notions of "voice" and "exit," economic terms which posit two main choices for dissatisfied bureaucrats seeking change, either to leave the organization or fight for change from within.

But, if researchers accept the need to center research on the individual administrator or policy specialist, it remains important to identify and analyze the larger policy networks within which they operate. One approach is tailored to the evidence supplied by open policy debates, seeking to identify contending policy groups or opinion clusters without drawing conclusions as to their underlying structure or source of solidarity. A more complex, though inevitably more speculative, conception of intermediate-level participation draws upon the bureaucratic politics model, emphasizing the fusion of organizational loyalty and personal interest as the main cement of policy networks. An alternative that challenges the pure bureaucratic politics model and in the view of its advocates is better tailored to China's cultural context, urges the merits of clientelist approaches with their explicitly personalistic perspectives on group formation and maintenance. This perspective receives strong support in Walder's analysis of working class politics in this volume.

The most forceful challenge to the bureaucratic politics model has been issued by Lucian Pye.[28] Pye contends that China, though indisputably "a bureaucratic polity," lacks bureaucratic politics in the conventional sense of institutional conflicts over resources, authority, and budget allocations. Instead, the principal pattern of conflict discerned by Pye is intra-elite factional strife fueled by concerns over security and power. He also asserts that factions rarely, if ever, represent clearly defined institutional, geographic, or generational interests. Rather, they are best seen as networks of individuals tied together by personal loyalty and common interests, and hence not "strongly motivated to assert generalizable political interests." China is thus, in Pye's view, characterized by a disjunction between "policy and administration," resulting in a generally "weak articulation of institutionalized and specialized interests." Pye singles out the paradoxical identification in the 1970s of the Chinese air force, the most modern segment of the military, with the anti-technological goals of the radicals as perhaps the best illustration of this divorce between institutional interests and policy stance. He explains the

postulated lack of bureaucratic politics in terms of China's under-
development, consensus-seeking traditional values that deny conflict,
and traditional dependent orientations expressed in clientelist form.
His main emphasis however is on structural constraints. China's
policy-making system, in Pye's view, is structured to suppress
conflict and deny the legitimacy of bureaucratic interests. The great
effort to prevent identification of bureaucrats with institutional
interests and the corollary attack on specialization has the effect of
stifling conventional organizational politics, precluding interest
politics at the bottom, and fragmenting and diffusing interest alignments at the top.

Pye's conception of a faction-centered policy-making process is
overstated, but has merit at least as a description of policy-making in
the early 1970s. It is hard to deny the importance of the visible and
damaging forms of factional strife which have erupted at every level
since the Cultural Revolution and which constitute one of its most
intractable legacies. The Cultural Revolution attack on the organizational norms of the 1950s and early 1960s generated defensive
responses which took clientelist forms. However, it is certainly true
that informal organizational networks based on reciprocal interests
and personal loyalties antedate the Cultural Revolution.

The extent to which factional alignments can result in the damp-
ening or suppression of conventional bureaucratic politics, as Pye
claims, is far less clear. Tang Tsou challenges Andrew Nathan's
neutral metaphor depicting formal organization as a "trellis" on
which factions cultivate "an extended network of personal loyalties
and relations." He suggests that the relationship between such
informal loyalty groupings and existing organization is more complex, claiming that when factions inhabit organizations their independence is constrained by their tendency to acquire some of the specialized ideology of the host organization. The policy stances they adopt
thus come to reflect the needs of the constituency in which their
formal power is rooted.[29] During his visit to China in 1981
Oksenberg found a strong example of such organizational ideology
operating in inter-agency management of economic policy, suggest-
ing the limits of a faction-centered perspective.[30]

Whatever the virtues or failings of a factionalist approach, a
principal strength is that it calls attention to the impact of central-
level cleavages on the character of organizational participation at the
intermediate levels. Gordon Bennett's study of the politics of commercial policy in the 1950s and 1960s has shown that elite factions
mobilize their bureaucratic constituencies and resources on a

continuing basis, a process which involves the middle levels, willy-nilly, as direct participants in conflicts over policy.[31] The character of that participation, however, clearly varies over time in relation to the nature and intensity of intra-elite strife. In periods of sharp conflict when the stakes of struggle are high, or even a matter of political survival, faction leaders will try to exact more rigid conformity from their networks of supporters, compelling them to subordinate their organizational needs and interests to the tactical requirements of political struggle. In less polarized periods, some limited policy advocacy and debate commonly occurs, with organizational spokespersons articulating genuine policy preferences with relative freedom.

Lowell Dittmer's interesting study of leadership politics in the 1970s makes a good case for the importance of simultaneously focusing on formal and informal organizational ties.[32] He suggests in a study of the Gang of Four that the influence of leadership rests on formal and informal networks of connections. In routine, non-divisive policy conflict, leaders tend to mobilize only those networks which are part of their formal base of power. But, in times of crisis they attempt to activate informal networks, principally because the weaker ties of the formal network preclude their effective use in vigorous clashes in which survival is at stake.[33]

Organizational Politics: The Vertical Dimension

The chapters in this volume strongly support the conception of organizational politics set forth in Skilling and Griffiths' *Interest Groups in the Soviet Union*. The defensive strategies of managers described by Lynn White and the policy alignments of China's scientific administrators studied by Suttmeier leave little doubt that even during periods of intense policy conflict at the center, much of the activity of middle-level administrators can only be satisfactorily accounted for in terms of a narrow organizational interest approach. Further, contrary to Pye's analysis, there seems little in the structural context of policy-making that inhibits interest advocacy. A distinctive feature of the Chinese institutional setting, however, is the extent to which policy is forged within functionally segmented vertical structures known as "systems" (*xitong*). Within these specialized hierarchies policy conflict crosses both vertical and horizontal divisions. Suttmeier's delineation of the conflict between competing scientific constituencies over different concepts of science and consequently different organizational prescriptions for the management of science policy reveals both types of conflict simultaneously. Harding similarly suggests the complexity of cross-cutting cleavages in his analysis of intra-service and inter-generational conflicts over policy-making for the military and security system. Yet, within this compartmentalized vertical structure, close reciprocal links exist between higher- and lower-level agencies down to the unit level. For example, there are close links between writers and the educational and propaganda organs which supervise their work. In making policy, the two-way flow of information and influence is important. Lynn White's discussion of "low power" documents the importance of managerial activism in the interest politics of Shanghai's industrial and commercial systems.

The complexity of interest articulation within these systems strongly affirms the validity of tendency analysis of intermediate-level participation. It also, however, shows the need seen by Harding, Suttmeier, and White to distinguish between core interests, which are likely to form the basis of corporate institutional advocacy, and less encompassing interests which generate intra-organizational competition.

Power and Policy: A Look to the Future

Who wins and who loses in the competition for scarce resources and which interests are most effectively represented? Although budget and policy data allow some charting of policy outcomes, the studies in this volume largely highlight some of the paradoxes of power. Harry Harding's study of military influence reveals the irony of an interest constituency with enormous access and direct representation at the top whose needs and interests have been given consistently short shrift. Defense since 1978 has ranked fourth in priority among the four modernizations—with agriculture, science and technology, and industry preceding it. The general pattern of holding down defense expenditures has not altered since 1978. Similarly, under the radical pro-peasant coalition of the late 1960s and early 1970s agriculture tended to stagnate, not simply because of deficiencies in the incentive system, but because it was starved of resources. Budgetary data released after the purge of the radicals in late 1976 show that despite Mao's personal advocacy from the mid-1950s of increased allocations for agriculture and light industry, their budgetary shares remained virtually constant. It was only under the allegedly pro-urban conservative coalition in power since 1978 that agriculture has made major strides. Notably, those strides were made not simply as a result of the relaxation of controls over rural trade and commerce, but as a consequence of the readjustment of procurement prices and the terms of trade in favor of agriculture.[34]

In part, these outcomes reflect divisions within the large interest communities which prevent articulation of other interests. In the case of the army, the very factors which place it at the center of the political system, i.e., the extraordinary scope of its involvement in civil economy and polity, make it incapable of acting as an interest constituency. Since most conflict takes place within specialized functional systems, it tends to be resolved *within* those systems, resulting in relatively minor reallocations of a limited pie. Where *inter*-system conflict is involved, the tradeoffs will be calculated at the very top, within the State Council and the Politburo of the Party, where generalists dominate the policy debate. Here the task is to reconcile competing demands on the basis of resource availability, fiscal constraints, and the performance records of competing programs and constituencies.[35] How these are reconciled also depends on the political conflict at the top and the factional and ideological composition of the top-level leadership. When a rough balance exists between sharply opposed groupings, as in the 1970s, policy paralysis or stalemate is the main result. But, recent analyses suggest that the growing complexity of China's economy and administration and the resulting web of policy interdependencies mean that incremental adjustment is the most likely future pattern of policy evolution. Tom Fingar's study of the 1969-76 period suggests that the issue clusters that define and shape coalition building have been growing in size since the late 1960s, contributing to a pattern of trade-offs that maintain policy continuity over time.[36] Reinforcing these long-term secular changes in China's political economy are equally important changes in the norms of policy conflict since 1978. The leadership has abandoned mobilization-style politics, probably for good, in favor of a highly institutionalized system of direct and indirect representation of interests. Although some of the more sweeping 1980 proposals for political reform have been rejected, for example, a bicameral legislature with a House of Producers on the Yugoslav model, the current reforms specify an expanded consultative role for unions, associations, and specialists groups in the formulation of policy.[37] National policy-making is now far more hospitable to diversity and the pragmatic articulation of interests. The effect should be to dampen factionalism and increase the openness and sophistication of policy debate.

The impact of these changes on patterns of intermediate-level participation should be substantial, with conventional bureaucratic politics increasingly becoming the norm. How this will affect the interests of particular constituencies is unclear, but one might surmise, for example, that the People's Liberation Army (P.L.A.) will find it easier to effectively assert its interests as it professionalizes, modernizes, and narrows its involvement in the political system. The character of interest politics at the unit level, on the other hand, is not likely to change, though it should be less constrained by doctrinal limits.

The critical factor shaping the long-term character of interest politics will be changes in the Party's role. The redefinition of that role is, of course, a central and perennial problem in maturing socialist systems. Party organs inevitably find their functions altered by administrative changes, and there has been ongoing debate over the optimal role for primary party organizations within enterprises, for regional party organizations in relation to ministerial organs, etc. But, put in larger context of the transition to developed socialism, the process is extraordinarily complex, with interdependence of economic and political reform bearing critically on the issue of party role. As Richard Lowenthal has characterized the process of transition, it involves a fourfold challenge to single party regimes: to adapt structurally to the requirements of an efficient and rational industrial order; to develop political forms capable of responding to shifting group interests in an increasingly differentiated society, permitting interest articulation while monopolizing the arbitration of those interests; to develop new and credible forms of legitimation; and, finally, to develop the capacity to cope with the unintended consequences of the adjustments in party structure and methods of governance.[38]

In Lowenthal's view there are only two viable reform alternatives, each with an economic component and its political counterpart. The first, and most prevalent, is limited reform, involving some economic decentralization, rejecting free price formation on the market, and retaining a considerable role for direct physical central planning. This rationalized form of command economy is designed to be compatible with a slightly softened form of single party rule, which Lowenthal (following Skilling) labels "consultative authoritarianism." The other alternative is radical reform which, in the economic sphere involves full marketization, free price formation, and competitive independence for managers. But successful radical reform that meets "requirements of technical efficiency and rationality" can take place "only at the price of political changes . . . that raise the problem of redefining the role of the Party itself." Lowenthal suggests on the basis of the Yugoslav record that "radical reform" requires political changes that occur in tandem with, or precede radical economic change—otherwise the powerful vested interests in the central and regional economic and party bureaucracies will block reform. The power of this latter group accounts for the resistance to this kind of reform throughout most of Eastern Europe.

The dilemma is clear: the Party must be strong enough and disciplined enough to preside over reforms which undermine its corporate influence. Yet the fact that initiating the reforms requires a prior circumscribing of the party's role may negate even the hope of reform. The long-term nature and difficulty of the coming institutional transition in China is indicated in Lowenthal's summation of this dilemma:

> If the ruling party clings to a minimal type of consultative authoritarianism, permitting only informal and bureaucratic interest articulation, it will remain without an effective counterweight to its own bureaucracy and unable to break its inertial resistance to major economic reform. It will also run the risk, sooner or later, of a major political crisis caused by poor political feedback. If, on the other hand, the Party chooses a bolder form of pluralistic or participatory authoritarianism, it may avoid those dangers but will find itself perpetually trying to balance the highly heterogeneous elements of a potentially unstable system that combines the existence of quasi-democratic institutions with the authoritarian nature of ultimate power. Though the conditions of stability for such a system—strict leadership solidarity "above the battle" and renunciation of mass mobilization by all groups—may be clearly defined, they are difficult to preserve in the political climate created by pluralistic and participatory institutions.[39]

CHAPTER 2

Public and Private Interests and the Participatory Ethic in China

Lowell Dittmer

The purpose of this chapter is to elucidate the Chinese Communist concept of the proper political role of participation as it has been formulated in classical and contemporary ideological texts, particularly as this relates to the pursuit of political interests. The democratic concept of participation, based on such ideas as the contract theory of the state in political theory, a free market guided by a benevolent "invisible hand" in economic thought, and the adversary tradition in legal theory, has consistently assumed the existence of distinct and explicit private interests. These interests may appear to conflict with the perceived public interest, which has usually been formulated so abstractly as to obscure the issue. Nevertheless, their advocates should steadfastly pursue them, secure in the knowledge that such independence and enterprise will ultimately redound to the public weal. This idea seems never to have taken root in Chinese political thought, and conceivably never will. In China there is a corporate concept of interest. Group or individual interests may be acknowledged, but the public interest occupies a position of sacrosanct priority, and other interests may be tolerated only within the latitude of some plausible interpretation of the public interest.[1] This means that political participation as it is understood in the West, in which individual participants make autonomous political decisions based on their own interests, is rather difficult to accept or even to comprehend.

The tendency in Chinese political culture is for the public interest to subsume all private interests to the extent that the two may hardly be seen as separate or in conflict. This results in two characteristic patterns in Chinese political participation. The first is the tendency for those with power to use it to reconstrue the public

17

interest so that it conforms with their own interests, either to indulge in private luxuries, vain self-glorification, and so forth, or to pursue grand designs of no immediate benefit to the masses. Under these circumstances, the masses, who sense they are contributing more to the common project than they are benefitting from it, tend to ritualize their participation: that is, to render *pro forma* compliance while withholding authentic cooperation. The second, weaker, tendency is for the masses to usurp claims on the public interest when there is weakness or division at the center, whether to seek economic self-aggrandizement or to form factions in pursuit of local self-interests through demonstrations, criticism of troublesome officials, or strikes. Under these circumstances the leadership finds its claims on the public interest so attenuated that it must temporarily subordinate its ideological objectives to public demands or risk falling from power. Thus behind the linguistic veneer of common purpose there is a constant tug-of-war over legitimating symbols which may be used in subtly nuanced ways toward very different objectives.

The Ideological Context of Participation in Classical Maoism

In affirming the overriding importance of service to the public interest in legitimizing popular participation, Mao stood squarely in the mainstream of classical Chinese political philosophy, but in a somewhat awkward relationship to Marxism. For the mature Marx denied the existence of a public interest, attributing interest rather to classes, which were based on the set of relationships surrounding the process of production. He considered the "public interest" an ideological delusion purveyed by the ruling classes in order to manipulate subordinate classes to act contrary to their own interests, specifically to work for a fraction of the true value of their labor while allowing the ruling classes to appropriate the rest. To sacrifice one's own interest in service of the public interest was to betray one's class interest, which had the sole legitimate claim on one's loyalties.

Given the "semicolonial, semifeudal" class structure of China and the diminuitive size of its industrial proletariat, political expediency dictated an eventual departure from an exclusively class-based criterion for determining whose participation should be encouraged in the Chinese revolution. As early as the Second Comintern Congress in 1920 it was conceded that revolutions were less likely in industrial countries with large working classes than in less-developed countries without a large proletariat. In the latter, the participation and cooperation of relatively progressive bourgeois reformers should be solicited in a united front strategy during the preliminary, "bourgeois democratic" phase of the revolution. The principal class enemy during China's first such united front (1923-27) was defined rather abstractly as "imperialism," and corresponded to China's "semi-colonial" status. The chief enemies were the warlords who stood in the way of national unity (and who were said to be aligned with various imperialist powers). Because very little united the participants in this united front beyond their common commitment to national unity, as soon as a semblance of unity was achieved the dominant partner in the coalition, the Guomindang (GMD), jettisoned the CCP. Consequently, in the period immediately following the disintegration of the first united front the returned student leadership turned again to a more narrowly class-based criterion for deciding who should be encouraged to participate. This "closed door" mentality, however, failed the test of political expediency by dogmatically excluding potential allies among other classes and by focusing party efforts on those urban areas where the GMD enjoyed overwhelming superiority via its military and police forces.[2]

During the late 1930s and early 1940s the ideological touchstone for legitimate participation seems to have shifted from class to nation. The Japanese invasion so clearly threatened the survival of the Chinese nation that service to national salvation transcended group or class interests. The CCP still insisted that it was a proletarian party leading the exploited classes, but the interests of the latter now merged with those of the nation at large. Thus the Central Committee in June 1938 declared that "the highest interests of the Chinese working class are identical with the highest interests of the Chinese nation and the Chinese people." If in some cases it seemed that the national interest conflicted with the interests of the working class, the Party demanded that the latter be sacrificed, claiming that the "long-term" interests of the workers coincided with those of the nation so that only "false" or "narrow" interests were being abandoned. Once the Party had identified its ultimate objectives with the national interest, it began to assume a paternalistic responsibility for national salvation and to assert leadership over anyone else who claimed to support this objective.[3]

It was also during this period, not by chance coinciding with the rise of Mao Zedong and the consolidation of his leadership, that the two patterns of participation that were henceforth to characterize Chinese Communist politics took coherent theoretical form. The first of these arose on the foundation of a multi-class united front. From the Party's point of view, the key problem was how to exert party leadership over the other classes included in the united front, thereby enhancing the power of the CCP vis-à-vis the Japanese and the GMD, without allowing the non-proletarian classes to exercise reciprocal influence over the Party. To achieve this objective the Party proceeded to construct a series of front organizations in which representatives of other classes or parties were given nominal leadership roles, meanwhile retaining the substance of power within the party apparatus. For example, in 1940 the Party introduced the "three-thirds system," in which left, right, and middle groups were represented in equal ratios. Because the "left" under the CCP was the only part of the coalition with clearly specified objectives and strict organization, it was able to exercise guidance even though party dominance was played down.

The concept of the united front went hand-in-hand with a propaganda emphasis on democracy designed to appeal to the intellectuals, a stratum whose support has traditionally been considered indispensable for the success of any Chinese government and who were most disenchanted with the conservative, repressive tactics of the GMD. In 1940 Mao placed the united front concept in the central position of the projected "New Democracy," abandoning the "dictatorship of workers and peasants" of the soviet period for a more inclusive formula in which political rights to participate would be given to anyone willing to cooperate with the CCP on certain broad national objectives. During the war the most important of these goals was obviously the expulsion of Japan; afterward it became the success of the revolution.[4]

The fate of the united front apparatus in the post-Liberation years was one of increasing formalization and ritualization. The mass organizations which had specialized in the mobilization of specific political strata (e.g., women and youth) were now explicitly subordinated to the Party in a neocorporatist arrangement. The Party established the Chinese People's Political Consultative Conference (CPPCC) as the core institution of its New Democracy, expanding its definition of the allies allotted representation there to include bourgeois democratic parties, democrats without party affiliations, national minorities, intellectuals, religious groups, and overseas Chinese. The Party also made the principle of alliance consultation the theoretical foundation of the CPPCC. Most representatives of non-proletarian classes, from the CPPCC at the national level down to the people's conferences at the local level, were selected on the basis of their ability to cooperate with broad party objectives. By

September 1952 "people's governments" and "people's representative conferences" had been established at all government levels in China. In 1953-54 the CCP conducted elections throughout China and established a uniform system of representation based on geographical units and administrative levels. This created a hierarchy of increasingly indirect democracy with the National People's Congress (NPC) at its apex, and a people's congress and an executive body called the people's council at each level. The CPPCC was based on representation of groups rather than individuals, based on their contribution to the functioning of the whole. It was retained despite the establishment of the NPC in order to serve as a symbol of the united front and "play its part in mobilizing and rallying the whole people."

The vicissitudes in the status and influence of the CPPCC in the post-Liberation era have reflected the Party's assessment of the functional importance of the intellectual, bourgeois, and professional middle classes whom it represented. This is to say that its influence tended to decline from 1954 to 1976, corresponding to Mao's steadily mounting radical (and anti-intellectual) proclivities, though this tendency did fluctuate from time to time. In 1956-57 the bourgeois democratic parties (BDPs) were invited to criticize the CCP in the context of a campaign to mobilize the support of managers, engineers, and other intellectuals for China's modernization projects. After initial caution, the leadership of the BDPs joined enthusiastically in such criticism. As a result, when the Hundred Flowers Movement was curtailed and followed by an Anti-Rightist Movement the ranks of BDPs were decimated by purges. This resulted in a decline in the fortunes of the CPPCC from which it was not soon to recover, and even those BDP leaders who survived now made haste to join the CCP.

The intellectuals enjoyed a resurgence in the early 1960s when the Party sought their support in the effort to revive the economy after the Great Leap Forward. However, after 1957 they had to make their influence felt from their positions as coopted members of the party apparatus rather than from the more vulnerable united front organs. Those with constructive contributions to make usually participated in one of the state council ministries or commissions, or in any of the numerous "work conferences" or "expanded party meetings" that were convened during the post-Leap recovery period to solicit the advice of functional experts without high standing in the Party. Those with more damning criticisms (i.e., those directed against Mao, the Great Leap, or other unassailable fundamentals) made them through Aesopian historical or literary satires, but still from their positions within the Party—usually the cultural, educational, or propaganda organs. These developments spelled the provisional failure of a system of functional representation designed to mollify non-party elites by granting them status without real political influence.

Whereas the pattern of participation based on the united front paradigm was always an ambivalent arrangement designed to invite cooperation and support while foreclosing influence, the pattern of participation known as the "mass line" was from its inception designed to include the party's core constituency, and the CCP therefore went to some pains to facilitate feedback. The mass line, as expostulated in Mao's classic 1943 essay "Some Questions Concerning Methods of Leadership," proceeds "from the masses, to the masses," and "linking the general with the specific."[5] In contrast to the indirect democracy characteristic of the united front organs, under the mass line elites were expected to keep in constant contact with the people, said to be the motive power in history and the source of great creative energy. After observing the "scattered and unsystematic views" of the masses, the cadres were to summarize them in reports to their superiors. The highest committee responsible for the area covered by the reports should receive the reports, together with comments from lower echelons, and issue authoritative directives and instructions on how to deal with the problem. These directives would then be sent back through the apparatus to be popularized among the masses "until the masses embrace the ideas as their own, stand up for them, and translate them into action by way of testing their correctness." Should some of the masses fail to achieve this enlightenment they must be educated through persuasion and discussion until they correct their errors; should errors occur among the leadership they may also be pointed out through mass criticism and corrected. The circular flow pattern emphasizes direct, open channels of communication from the highest to the lowest levels of information and opinion and implies some degree of reciprocity. Though the masses are thus assured some input into the policy process, they remain essentially passive: the cadres come to survey their opinions and summarize the issues in upward-bound reports and the party leadership preserves a monopoly of decision-making power. And, the party leadership may disagree with the masses' subjective perceptions of their own interests. If the "partial and temporary" interests of the masses should come into conflict with their "total, long-range interests," then the latter must take priority.[6] By dint of the interest-aggregating process of the mass line the Party alone is capable of arriving at a correct synthesis of scattered and unsystematic opinions and defining the public interest.

The hallmark of the mass line concept, according to John Lewis, is its flexibility within the limits of firm operational principles; that is, it provides an aura of consistency and stability during periods of rapid policy shifts. In contrast to the tendency of the returned students and other pre-Mao leaders to rely on the traditional principle of leadership prestige to issue doctrinaire commands, the mass line focuses leadership attention on cultivating the receptivity of its constituency.[7] Uniquely favorable circumstances allowed the Party to come closer to realizing the theoretical ideal of the mass line during the Yenan period than at any subsequent time. There was an identity of interest between the Party and its host population in expelling the Japanese, and the Party was obliged to solicit cooperation from the population and less able to coerce or remunerate it than it would be after it had captured the state.[8] The mass line does not entail reciprocal influence between elites and masses, but it does require that circular flow be maintained.

There are two major types of deviations from the mass line which can be extrapolated from the public polemics that have in recent decades made such a significant contribution to the definition of ideological orthodoxy. The first is "revisionism," which consists of an asymmetry of influence and communication to the advantage of elites. The second is "radicalism," which tends to permit too much latitude to the "revolutionary masses" in the exchange. Although in the following accounts I emphasize the differences between them, the reader should be aware that both deviations are rooted in and justified by elements of Mao's classic formulation, differing from it more in interpretation than in principle.

The Revisionist Version of Mass Participation

According to Maoist criticism during the Cultural Revolution, the basic flaw of the revisionist construal of the mass line was that it gave too much play to the pursuit of self-interest. To the revisionists, just as the untrammeled pursuit of interests under capitalism endowed that system with an internal dynamic that would burst its integuments and usher in socialism, so under socialism the continued pursuits of interests would propel that system toward the realization of communism. Revolution would emancipate the economic system

from an economically irrational set of production relationships, and
with the introduction of socialism the interests of the proletariat
would truly coincide with the public interest. Indeed, inasmuch as
class was defined in terms of economic criteria, once the means of
production had been socialized there would be no reason why everyone in society should not become members of the proletariat, making
class struggle inapplicable. To those identified with the "proletarian
revolutionary line," on the other hand, self-interest was inherently
venal, a bourgeois mode of thinking that should, with the advent of
socialism, make way for general dedication to the public interest and
to universalizable values. The slogan "Fight self, champion the
public" (posi ligong) is typical of this view.

The revisionist concept of the economic origins and political cultivation of interests gave rise to a pattern in which participation was
essentially confined to the leadership. The masses would by no
means be excluded from politics, but would participate in a form of
mass line in which their performances would echo themes first
articulated by the party leadership. Political participation could be
likened to a long procession, led by the party vanguard and the
progressive classes and docilely followed by the relatively backward
classes. The logic of this sequence was dictated by the assumption
that the party leadership was the most altruistic in the pursuit of the
public interest, an assumption which was in turn predicated on the
existence of a natural hierarchy of values.

This idea is perhaps most elaborately formulated in the works of
Liu Shaoqi. According to Liu, the aspiration for higher values was
normally reached only after the base physical appetites had been
sated. The satisfaction of material interest was but the basic foundation in a long process of "raising the level," whereby people would be
brought to an understanding of the interdependence of their interests
with those of others in the same circumstances. Although the
political organization was the highest form of organization because it
dealt with the public interest, the economic organization was thus the
most important because everyone had economic interests. Therefore,
"all the economic demands of the masses must be integrated with
political or cultural demands. When the masses begin to take action
on one simple demand, they can understand better a series of problems and further push their actions to a still higher stage." Thus by
"raising the economic demands to political demands, raising partial
and temporary demands to whole and permanent demands, and
raising local demands to state and national demands," the masses
would be elevated to a higher concept of their interests.[9] Self-interest

would never be renounced or transcended in any quasi-religious sense, but it would gradually become more inclusive and enlightened.

This concept of the transformation of self-interest into public interest through "cultivation" was premised on the assumption that under socialism the interests of the individual and those of the collective were always in principle compatible—that is, they merged. Merging took place by tacit reciprocal agreement: the individual performed certain services for the collective and the collective in turn provided for the individual's welfare.[10] Consistent with Liu's belief in a hierarchy of values, this transaction involved the exchange of such tangible assets as labor and commodities on a *quid pro quo* basis among the uncultivated masses, but among the cultivated party cadres it involved the exchange of increasingly symbolic or deferred values. The good party member, having attained the insight that the inexorable course of historical development assures that his or her interests will ultimately merge with those of the working class and the party, would be willing to perform services disregarding immediate subjective interests.

Liu's general concept of the role of interests in the socialist transition was allegedly manifested in the early 1950s in the theory of productive forces. According to this theory, the pace of the revolutionary transformation of the relations of production was limited by the capability of the forces of production to provide the wherewithal for that transformation. This would mean, for example, that the collectivization of agriculture should wait until China had sufficient industrial capacity for the mechanization of agriculture. Based on this theory, Liu is said to have opposed the accelerated collectivization of agriculture in the early 1950s and he admitted having approved the 1955 decision dissolving 20,000 (200,000, according to an erroneous rumor) cooperatives for which the material preconditions were considered immature.[11] Though the evidence relevant to decision making during collectivization is still incomplete, the theory of productive forces is entirely consistent with Liu's views on the appropriate role of interest in motivating participation. Because the satisfaction of material interests has basic priority, the expansion of productive forces must keep pace with the transformation of the relations of production. As productivity expands, the greater efficiency (and profitability) of the larger units will become evident and people will eagerly pool their resources to join them. Thus individual self-interest and the interests of the collectivity will merge.

During the Cultural Revolution the Maoists criticized this theory from two different but closely related perspectives. First, they argued that the hierarchy of values bore a negative relationship to the social stratification pyramid rather than the positive one asserted by the revisionists. The picture of a materialistic mass and an ideologically motivated party leadership may have been roughly accurate during the thirty-eight years that the Party was an itinerant pariah group; those who persevered and rose to responsible positions under such trying circumstances could hardly have been motivated by material advantage. But it began to acquire a hollow ring once the Party occupied the state apparatus and became the main distributive network for the nation's resources. At this point the hierarchy of offices fell into correspondence with the allocation of material rewards to implement policy. Individual and public interest merged so perfectly that the motives of the most well-rewarded officials were ambiguous. Through organization, altruism became compatible with the pursuit of self-interest, permitting revolutionary heroism to atrophy from functional redundancy. Because in this system of bonuses and graduated incentives those who worked hardest and most effectively were most bountifully rewarded, it was plausible to argue that they were in fact motivated by these rewards and not by the ideology of moral elevation that legitimated the structure of incentives.

The whole notion of a public interest had become a self-serving ideology for the elites, the Maoists suggested, whereas the actual relationship between moral and social stratification was quite the reverse. It was not the "cultivated" party leaders, but the workers and peasants and soldiers at the basic levels who were most likely to approximate communist ideals. They were more intelligent, because their work brought them into closer touch with empirical reality; more selfless, because their acquisitive and possessive instincts had not yet developed; more revolutionary, because they had less to lose and more to gain from radical change. It was the elites who were most in danger of falling into revisionist ways, with their responsibility for the disposition of social resources tending to give them delusions of high status and inspiring them to act like bosses rather than public servants. Thus it was the elites who should "go down" (xia fang) and learn from the masses rather than vice versa. This tended to discredit the upward-striving achievement ethic that motivated officials and spurred them to seek absolution in self-criticism and other forms of self-abasement.

The second Maoist criticism follows from the first. This is to dispute the compatibility of public and private interests, the doctrine of merging. The Maoists believed that altruism required self-sacrifice and so it followed that the graduated system of incentives arranged by the Party to coincide with moral efficiency could not possibly motivate genuine altruism. Those who managed to acquire prestige and high position were suspected of having been motivated by these mercenary values, and because they were so motivated they were categorized as "bourgeois," "revisionist," or "party persons in authority taking the capitalist road." The tendency to assume a compatibility of self-interest with the public interest was discredited by a number of arguments.

In a revival of Marx's critique of the notion of a public interest, it was argued that in a class society there was only class interest and no public interest and that throughout the phases of socialism and even full communism, classes and class struggle would persist. In addition, the motives of the leadership as a group became suspect because their supposedly altruistic careers had also brought them power and prestige. This point was dramatized by vignettes of the luxuries and vanities with which high officials allegedly indulged themselves, such as good food, mahjong parties, filter cigarettes, pearl necklaces, and chauffeured limousines. Finally, the integrity of the institutions in Chinese society that had been responsible for reconciling public and private interests — viz, the Communist Party, the mass organizations — was seriously compromised by allegations that they were staffed by "capitalist roaders" and afflicted by "bureaucratism." For example, during the Cultural Revolution such tenets of democratic centralism as majority rule within committees, the segregation of party and public affairs, and unquestioning obedience to superior authorities were discredited in the name of substantive justice as defined by Mao's thought. The incompatibility of private interests and the public interests as defined by these corrupted institutions was effectively illustrated by indignant accounts of the manipulative and coercive techniques employed by the work teams dispatched by the Central Committee under Liu Shaoqi in June to July 1966. In the name of promoting the Cultural Revolution, these work teams imposed such stringent demands for conformity on the masses that their own leadership could never be questioned, although that was the whole object of the Cultural Revolution.

The Radical Version of Mass Participation

Whereas the revisionist deviation from the mass line was essentially practical, the radical deviation was primarily theoretical. The revisionists made only slight modifications of doctrine while in practice interpreting that doctrine to the advantage of compliant officials and economically productive citizens. This was quite effective in furthering their own motivating assumptions and developmental objectives. The radicals, on the other hand, made a substantial contribution to the development of theory. However, they failed conspicuously in the application of theory to practice, with the destructive aspect of their program succeeding to a considerable degree while the constructive aspect failed. Part of the reason for this is that even after they acquired high party positions the leading radicals continued to comport themselves as if they were an opposition group outside the established leadership, devoting most of their attention to "continuing the revolution." By repeating and continuously refining their powerful criticisms of erstwhile patterns of participation and interest articulation without presenting viable alternatives they also disrupted the effort to reconstruct the organizational structures within which the mass line had previously been conducted. Mass participation therefore took place in somewhat chaotic fashion outside these structures. Their oppositionist revolutionary stance and consistent opposition to any form of organizational suppression left them with no instrument to impose unity but ideological criticism of deviation, which gave rise to an incessant stream of polemics. But factional groups were skilled in construing polemics for their own interests and the radicals failed to restore unity. The leadership finally had to fall back on the public security apparatus. In the following sections I will examine the radicals' practical failures and then turn to their critical contributions.

During the Cultural Revolution the radicals introduced original patterns of participation. These included such populist innovations as the unsigned big-character poster, the independently published tabloid newspaper, the freedom to travel and exchange experiences (*quanlian*), which arose in the midst of the almost complete breakdown of provincial and local civilian political authority. Prior to the Cultural Revolution the articulation and aggregation of interests had been monopolized by the Communist Party apparatus and its ancillary mass organizations. Interests were articulated by the masses in mass campaigns or the mass line and aggregated into univocal statements through the arrangement of meetings convened in well-established sequence.[12] The radicals attacked this system on the grounds that it allowed the revisionist organization-men who controlled the apparatus to define the public interest based on their own interests and then to use the organizational and propaganda resources of the Party to manipulate everyone else to support this interpretation. While Mao supported their criticisms, the radicals were able to bring this system to a standstill. Thereafter, the party organization was eclipsed by quasipluralistic voluntary associations, or factions, more or less spontaneously assembled on the basis of long-standing ideological and social cleavages.

These associations, cited by some radical publications as a model for the ultimate reorganization of the state itself, lacked internal structure and rested on the assumption that concurrence on a set of abstract universals entailed concurrence on various concrete particulars. But just as ideological agreement constituted the basis for inclusion in these associations, disagreement became sufficient grounds for exclusion or schism, as few procedural mechanisms were acceptable means of reconciling internal contradictions. "Struggle" was the constitutive principle and *raison d'etre* of these associations, and it proved difficult for them to cooperate in more peaceful and constructive endeavors. Thus the factions were forcibly disbanded in 1968 and were repeatedly condemned whenever they reconstituted themselves. The central leaders who survived the Cultural Revolution seemed to have reached a consensus that henceforth participation should proceed through more formal institutional channels.[13]

The central leaders who had incited the Cultural Revolution then attempted to cage the more spontaneous pattern of mass participation that emerged in its course within some institutional setting that would permit economic growth and other essential social processes to resume normally. First they sought to construct new and more revolutionary organizations under their own aegis. Second, they sought to infuse existing institutions with a more revolutionary spirit.

In their attempt to foster the construction of new and more revolutionary organizations, the radicals were prolific indeed. Beginning with their rise to influence in 1973 following the death of Lin Biao, the civilian radicals introduced a series of models in rapid succession: the Fanghualian Model Army Unit in Zhejiang, the Xiaojinjiang Brigade's Political Night School, the Chaoyang Model Agricultural College, the July Twenty-first Worker Colleges and May Seventh Peasant Colleges, the armed workers' militia, etc. Although these organizations have not yet received full attention from western scholars, they seem to have been launched with minimal preparation and little follow-through, and none of them achieved the status accorded Dazhai brigade or the Daqing oilfields. The organizations usually offered few intrinsic rewards—they did not seem to improve productive efficiency or augment unit income, and in fact usually imposed sacrifices on their participants. They could rely only briefly on the extrinsic reward of publicity, after which their news value would decline and radical attentions would shift. If a radical-sponsored organizational venture did prosper, on the other hand, it faced problems of a different nature. In that case, the party establishment would seek either to coopt it or to impede its further development. There is evidence that the radicals sought to construct a base for themselves in the trade union movement, armed workers' militias, and mass organizations, for example, but there was no precedent for organization building outside the auspices of the CCP. When these organizations were linked to the Party (after the latter's reconstruction from the top down in 1971) the radicals found they lacked the inner-party support at the provincial and local levels to maintain their influence among responsible cadres at those levels. Shanghai was the only exception, and even there their control ultimately proved much more limited than had been expected.[14]

The attempt to infuse existing institutional structures with a more revolutionary spirit began with the introduction of many ideas designed to enhance mass participation. Some of these were "open-door rectification" of the Party, which involved the non-party masses in the purge and reconstruction of the Party; the regular rotation of leaders between front-line labor and desk jobs; replacement of the branch principle with the committee principle for unified leadership at regional and local levels, implying more influence by "reds" and less by functional specialists; a general simplification and decentralization of the bureaucracy; and so forth.[15] Although here again additional research would be required to reach a definitive verdict, it would seem that many, perhaps most of these changes proved shallow and ephemeral, few of them surviving the first, conservative phase of the movement to criticize Lin Biao (1972-73). One reason for their lack of viability was that by obscuring the boundaries between party and masses, organizational control over both was attenuated. The public security and police system had already been damaged by the Cultural Revolution, and the legitimacy of various intra-party disciplinary techniques remained controversial. Inasmuch as the salient problem in the immediate aftermath of the Cultural Revolution appeared to be the restoration of economic production, these democratizing tendencies could be curtailed on the grounds that they contributed to disputes among factions.[16]

A second reason for the short life-span of the Cultural Revolution innovations—one that the radicals at the center probably found easier to countenance than the allegation that they were incompatible with economic growth—had to do with the accelerated rehabilitation of purged civilian cadres that began after the purge of Lin Biao.

Despite the criticism and self-criticism that they had endured at the hands of the Red Guards and later in the May Seventh Cadre Schools, resulting in their purported transformation to a revolutionary viewpoint, these veteran officials tended to revert to the pre-Cultural Revolution policies with which they were most familiar. According to Jiang Qing, "More than 75 percent of the old cadres inevitably turn from members of the democratic faction into members of the capitalist-roaders' faction."[17] The vacancies left by the purge of the followers of Lin Biao precipitated a competition between rehabilitated cadres and representatives of the "revolutionary masses" that exacerbated the ideological and policy differences between them. The radicals were at a disadvantage in this competition because as early as February 1967, when the revolutionary committee replaced the Paris Commune concept, it was generally acknowledged that their lack of bureaucratic experience disqualified them from executive leadership positions. The most they could hope for thereafter was a quasi-apprenticeship under the "three-in-one" formula, which tacitly allotted them a third of all plenary seats. The radicals did, indeed, achieve visible gains under this arrangement. For example, the percentage of mass representatives increased from 26 percent in the Ninth Central Committee to 34 percent in the Tenth, and young Shanghai radical Wang Hongwen, a petty factory cadre before 1966, became a vice chairman of the Party.

Yet these gains were more apparent than real. With the reconstruction of the Party at the provincial and local levels the radicals found themselves unable to take advantage of Lin's purge to make significant inroads: none of the mass representatives at the Tenth Congress were first or second party secretaries of their provincial party committees and twenty-eight of the forty-eight did not have positions on the standing committees of their provincial party committees. The general tendency at all levels was to confine radicals to symbolic and easily expendable positions on the plena while reserving most executive positions and key committee assignments for veteran party officials. The plena had only nominal power in the policy process and their chief function was to form a pool for the recruitment of members of the executive and functional committees, but the radicals were rarely able to rise from the plena to influential positions at the Central Committee level or below it. For example, in preparation for the Fourth National People's Congress (NPC) in 1975, the radicals managed to place ninety of their members on the Presidium (whose only apparent function is to

elect the NPC Standing Committee), yet only thirty-one of these
were elected to the NPC Standing Committee and only one of the
twelve vice premiers on the State Council (Zhang Chunqiao) was a
radical, while three others could be considered radical sympathizers.
In general, the radical struggle for power and position succeeded only
in those areas under Mao's immediate jurisdiction (particularly the
Central Committee Politburo), and only as long as he was still alive.
This put the radicals in the position of an imposing head and torso
without arms or legs.

The summarize, the radicals' failure to institutionalize the more
spontaneous patterns of participation that emerged during the Cultural Revolution resulted from the weakness and vulnerability of
their own constituency, the unrelenting and increasingly skilled opposition of the veteran bureaucrats who emerged to regain control, and
their inability to acknowledge and remedy the problems of the new
patterns of participation they had introduced. Of course, the chief
weakness of the radicals at every level was their lack of administrative experience. Most of them had become involved in politics
through the Cultural Revolution, an experience that did not dispose
them to be patient with old rules of the bureaucratic game that would
consign them to a long apprenticeship before acquiring real influence.
This revolutionary impatience in turn inclined them to be disruptive,
for example, to split from the committee and denounce their
colleagues publicly if outvoted, or to retain their links to factional
constituencies and use them to lobby for specific policies. This
exacerbated the mistrust between veteran cadres and radical
sympathizers and hastened the weakening of the latter. The veteran
cadres, since the fall of Liu and Deng under the leadership of Zhou
Enlai, avoided direct confrontations with the radicals and managed to
blunt the most potentially dangerous themes in their polemical
offensive by reinterpretation and to ignore the rest.

The greatest problem of the new participation pattern was of
course its disruptive, anarchic quality. Although the radicals agreed
to the suppression of factionalism whenever it became a serious
threat to production, they were unable to discover a forum or
medium whereby their constituency might acceptably articulate its
support for radical policies. They remained suspicious of the tendency of institutionalization to impose procedural constraints on participation and exclude the young and inexperienced. Their lack of a
base of bureaucratically eligible supporters and general ineptitude in
intra-organizational infighting severely limited any attempt to
cultivate a constituency by offering patronage or other official

rewards. Their constructive programs also came to naught (as noted above), and so the only way they could mobilize their supporters was by leading them in criticism *against* certain policies and personnel, with the implied promise of seizing power if a sufficient number of cadres could again be toppled. Under these circumstances mobilization tended to be very brief and destructive, resulting in an on-going two-line struggle that oscillated from left to right with increasing frequency.

The Radical Contribution to Theory

The radicals formulated no positive theory of participation and their ideas can only be inferred from their criticisms of others. These ideas fall into three categories: the relationship between public- and self-interest, appropriate criteria for participation in politics, and methods of participation.

The Relationship between Public- and Self-Interest

The radicals assumed that public- and self-interest were inexorably in conflict, so that to serve the public meant to sacrifice oneself, to serve oneself to betray the public. Their purpose was to foreclose the comfortable assumption that selfishness was objectively compatible with the public interest and force people to make a clear-cut choice. Although this was intended to preclude the expression of self-interest altogether, the open-textured quality of most ideological formulations of the public interest permitted private interests to be expressed in altruistic rhetoric, which in turn discredited such rhetoric and fostered a certain amount of apathy and even cynicism about the public interest. All the same, by severely damaging the sanctimonious reputation of the Party the radicals at least temporarily succeeded in liberating the public interest from the CCP's exclusive definition. The non-party masses learned to manipulate altruistic rhetoric for their own purposes, resulting in a more frequent incidence of original big character posters (such as the famous Li Yizhe poster in Guangzhou), in strikes, slowdowns, factional strife, and other autonomous political activities.

The Party strongly discouraged such activities, both because they were disruptive and because they were autonomous, attempting to reassert the merging of public and private interests under the

auspices of the Party. Once again it was claimed that correct procedures enabled the Party to define this fusion. The radicals periodically protested this subordination of ideology to organization, for
example in the 1973 campaign to "go against the tide." But because
they could find no acceptable alternative, they concurred in suppression of the movement whenever the disruption it precipitated
threatened production.

Participation in Politics

The radicals repudiated dependence on bureaucratic rules and
procedures to determine who could participate. They supported inclusion on the basis of a correct ideological stand. This begged the
question of how to determine who was correct. Obviously class was a
decisive factor, but how should class membership be determined in a
society in which the means of production had been socialized? Prior
to the Cultural Revolution this question was answered by ignoring
the individual class composition (geren chengfen), or current occupation, of the individual in question and relying on family origin (jiating
chushen), the occupation of the person's parents' three years before
Liberation. This proved to be an increasingly inaccurate indication of
current socioeconomic status, including among the proletariat the
children of both poor peasants and high-ranking cadres, for example.

During the Cultural Revolution the radicals were inclined to substitute ideology for family background as a criterion for class membership, but this gave rise to much ideological posturing and over-
blown rhetoric, not to mention factional schisms and fights. In their
search for an objective economic basis for the determination of
classes in a socialist society, radical theorists fastened on two criteria: ownership and distribution.

With regard to ownership, the radicals emphasized that socialization of the means of production was not simply a matter of state
appropriation, but a long process requiring ongoing struggle. There
is a contradiction between collective ownership (by members of the
unit only) and ownership by the whole people (as represented by the
state), according to Mao, and this manifested itself in China in the
form of the "three great differences": between city and countryside,
manual and mental work, and workers and peasants. To permit
collective ownership to consolidate too long without pressure for
further transformation to "whole-people" ownership would be to
threaten further progress toward communism and raise the spectre

of Soviet-style revisionism.[18] In the People's Republic of China (PRC), while whole-people ownership held sway in industry and commerce, collective ownership still predominated in agriculture because the production team had been the unit of accounting since the early 1960s.[19] This implied that workers (in state enterprises) were more progressive and advanced than peasants and their participation was therefore valued. The distinction further implied that participation aimed at movement toward a higher level of ownership was preferable to participation within the parameters of existing property arrangements, presaging a future drive to raise the unit of accounting from the team to the brigade or the commune.

By extending the definition of ownership to include the form of distribution the radicals were able to extend their critique to challenge the basic principle of distribution in the People's Republic: "From each according to his ability, to each according to his work." This exemplified the principle of exchange of equivalents, or "exchange between a given amount of labor in one form and a similar amount of labor in another form," and as such was part of the "commodity system," a relic of capitalist productive relations. Differences in market conditions, conditions for production, and levels of technology, mean that equal rights in the exchange of equivalents in socialist society (in the form of competition between collectively-owned enterprises or production units, or individuals in the rural free markets) is still unequal in reality. As Marx put it in his *Critique of the Gotha Program,* "Equal right here is still in principle – a bourgeois right."[20] In terms of participation, the implications were to narrow the range of politically acceptable behavior to preclude the further commercialization of social relationships which, if permitted to continue, would have a spillover effect on the distribution of political power:

> If we do not follow this course, but call instead for the consolidation, extension, and strengthening of bourgeois right and that part of inequality it entails, the inevitable result will be polarization, i.e., a small number of people will in the course of distribution acquire increasing amounts of commodities and money through certain legal channels and numerous illegal ones. Capitalist ideas of amassing fortunes and craving personal fame and gain, stimulated by such "material incentives," will spread unchecked; such phenomena as turning public property into

private property, speculation, graft, and corruption,
theft and bribery will rise; the capitalist principle of
the exchange of commodities will make its way into
political life and even into party life, undermine the
socialist planned economy and give rise to such acts
of capitalist exploitation as the conversion of commodities and money into labor and labor power into a
commodity; there will be a change in the nature of
ownership in certain departments and units which
follow the revisionist line; and instances of oppression
and exploitation of the working people will once again
occur.[21]

In short, while the definition of *political* participation was expanded,
the criteria for *acceptable* participation were contracted. "The
socialist economy must function in accord with the correct ideological
line," as defined by the CCP leadership: "The historical experience of
the dictatorship of the proletariat at home and abroad tells us that
whether the socialist system advances or moves backward is closely
linked with whether or not we correctly adjust the relationship,
whether Marxism or revisionism is practiced, and which line is
implemented."[22] As in Calvinist Geneva, participation would be
rigorously screened to sanction only those whose values coincided
with those of the leadership. The correctness or incorrectness of the
ideological line and the control of the leadership by one class or
another determine which class actually owns a factory.[23] In the
context of the prevailing political situation, this criterion for participation may be seen not only as a response to those "revisionists"
within the leadership who wished to restore material incentives, but
as a counter to mass factions who were taking advantage of the
breakdown of discipline in the Cultural Revolution to agitate on
behalf of their own interests.

Method of Participation

The radicals tended to distrust formal institutional arrangements, whether those of democratic centralism within the Party or
the forms of electoral democracy that survived the era of the united
front. Thus at various times they sanctioned violation of such canons
of democratic centralism as majority rule, obedience to the higher
level, and obedience to the Central Committee, arguing that

ideological correctness superseded procedural criteria, and ideological correctness had to be determined by the masses. Electoral democracy was a sham in a class society, and the radicals dispensed with elections in favor of an informal procedure they called "democratic consultation." The principal reason for the radical rejection of formal institutions seems to have been the tendency of the latter to degenerate into "bureaucratism," i.e., empty formalism.

Having therefore abandoned due process, the radicals placed their faith in a radicalized concept of the mass line as the sole realistic way for the masses to influence their leaders. According to this concept, the leaders must remain in constant (or at least frequent) physical contact with masses and be intent upon serving their interests; only through such intimacy and concern on the part of the leadership can authentic mass involvement in political decisions be ensured. If a given leader should fail in this obligation, that leader is apt to develop his/her own distinct and even alien interests. Thus in 1965 Mao said: "The bureaucrat class on the one hand and the working class with the poor and lower-middle peasants on the other are two classes sharply antagonistic to each other."[24] He reiterated this point of view about a decade later.[25] A leader who undergoes such a process of embourgeoisement is no longer a Marxist-Leninist and has forfeit the legitimate support of his constituency. "When we judge whether a person is a true or false Marxist, we need only find out how he stands in relation to the broad masses of workers and peasants, and then we shall know him for what he is," Mao decreed. "This is the only criterion, there is no other."[26] During the Cultural Revolution Mao introduced the notion that the masses might spontaneously criticize and demonstrate publicly against leaders who were travelling the "capitalist road." Such tactics had a devastating psychological effect upon their targets, sometimes resulting in physical injury or even suicide.

According to refugee informants I interviewed in Hong Kong, the Cultural Revolution was in fact quite successful in inducing leaders to cultivate a closer relationship with their constituents, hoping thereby to conform with this radicalized notion of the mass line and forestall future criticism from an activated mass. Most informants felt that this gave them somewhat more control over local policy implementation and improved their chances of attaining political demands or redressing grievances. But intensified elite-mass fraternization also brought problems in its train, which involved both the demands of the masses and the motives of the leaders.

The first problem lay in the possibility that the masses might take advantage of the more conciliatory posture of the leadership to escalate their demands or to thwart policies to which they objected, thereby promoting their own interests at the expense of the public interest (as the Party saw it). The use of this more fraternal relationship to attain demands was apparent in the proliferation of the "back door" phenomenon, the use of privileged official access to scarce goods or services to allocate these in exchange for reciprocal favors rather than according to universalistic criteria of need. Previously this form of corruption had been limited to party cadres and their families. Aggressive escalation of demands was also apparent in the proliferation of industrial strikes and slowdowns in 1975-76 and the Tian'anmen incident of April 1976, an almost unprecedented case of major mass protest without demonstrated elite collusion. Originally touched off by a refusal to allow a memorial to Zhou Enlai, this incident symbolized mass resentment of radical censoriousness.

The second danger inhered in the possibility that elites might cater to the subjective interests of the masses as a way of cultivating personal constituencies beyond the ambit of the formal mechanisms of control. This tendency appeared in its most virulent form at the highest levels of elite politics and in the Lin Biao case in particular. While the reasons for the rift between Mao and his erstwhile heir apparent still remain obscure, most analysts agree that it was precipitated less by ideological or policy differences than by Lin's attempt to exploit his patronage and other official powers in order to consolidate his own political base.

Thus, after the Lin Biao episode the radicals found themselves in the paradoxical position of criticizing the intensified elite-mass fraternization they had only recently hailed as a panacea for optimally effective mass participation. To be sure, they did not attack fraternization *per se*, but only fraternization that was badly motivated. The radical argument, as it appeared in its most theoretically sophisticated form in Zhang Chunqiao's 1975 article on "bourgeois right," held that classes were defined not merely on the basis of economic attributes but in terms of particular "relations among men." Those relations that resembled the instrumental relationship between men and commodities in a capitalist system were *ipso facto* bourgeois.[27] Thus Lin Biao was accused of "handing out official posts and making promises, inviting guests and giving them presents, wining and dining, and traffic in flattery and favors."[28] His private notebooks were found to contain telltale mention of "inducement — official post, emolument, favor," stripping bare the manipulative intention behind Lin's service to his constituents. This was "bourgeois," according to Yao Wenyuan, because it transformed the relations among people into "relations of buying and selling commodities."[29]

The problem with this criticism, justified though it might be in Lin's case, is a problem endemic to all such attempts to draw a clear line of distinction between public and private interests: there are numerous situations in political life in which the motives of the actor remain ambiguous. The services that a "revisionist" official might render his constituents — the adjustment of policy to suit local circumstances, the provision of protection, funding, patronage, etc. — are not essentially different from those that his more "revolutionary" colleague might provide; the main difference is in the motive behind the action. The difference between an official who acts for the public welfare and one who hopes for reciprocal benefits is difficult to maintain when some form of reciprocity is likely in either case, and attempts to draw such a distinction begin to seem hair-splitting and inquisitorial.[30] This imparted a note of caution to what cadres might safely consider "serving the people," which was reinforced by the official media in their exegetical commentaries during this period. These emphasized that serving the people meant serving the "overwhelming majority" of the people,[31] which might well involve temporary deferment of the interests of their immediate constituents.[32] Those who seemed to "show concern for the masses" and "work for the well-being of the public" might well be actually "divorcing themselves from the broad masses" if they defied party directives. Implicitly, the independent ideological judgment of the local masses and cadres about what was in the interests of the masses had been invalidated, and in its stead the infallibility of party procedure had been resurrected.

In sum, the weakness of the radical critique of Liuist practice was that it took two contradictory positions. First, it challenged those aspects of the mass line which led to a public policy that ignored vital mass interests. Then it criticized the pursuit of self-interest altogether. The result was to place the radicals at odds not only with mainstream Marxism, but with mass aspirations. This fatally alienated them both from the bureaucrats and from the masses.

The Emerging Synthesis

The primary goal of the successor government since it came to power in 1976 has been to restore pre-Cultural Revolution practices and theories of mass participation, although this restoration has necessarily been incomplete. The result of the redefinition of public interest during the first, mobilizational, phase of the Cultural Revolution was a quasi-pluralism of group interests masquerading as the public interest. The Deng government seems to have been quite successful in discrediting the autonomous organization and factionalism of the radicals even before the fall of the Gang of Four, at least partly because even the radicals at the center found it impossible to use the potpourri of competing interest groups for their own programs. This is not to say that the problem was solved immediately; indeed, during and even after the succession crisis there were widespread reports of strikes and factional violence that still followed organization patterns originally set by the radicals during the Cultural Revolution. But these were no longer ideological problems, for the legitimacy of the radicals had already been destroyed; it was sufficient to link them with the Gang of Four to bring the latter into disrepute. And during the initial phase of the post-succession consolidation the new regime took draconian punitive measures against persisting outbreaks of factional conflict, including a wave of executions. Clearly a subjective conviction of ideological correctness is no longer sufficient to legitimate dissenting or disruptive forms of participation.

During the second phase of the radicals' ascendancy, they attempted to institutionalize the Cultural Revolution innovations in participatory behavior, thereby allowing them to survive in somewhat more innocuous form. Rather than "housebreaking" the radical movement and preparing the young rebels to succeed to leadership of a permanent revolution, however, this seems to have introduced factionalism and ideological polarization to the councils of party and state. Largely because of the radicals' lack of administrative experience, the veteran officials were for the most part successful in confining them to showcase positions without significant leverage.

Much more dangerous to the new regime were the theories devised by the radicals to legitimate spontaneous mass activism. These critical theories exerted considerable power and cogency, as evidenced by the care taken to refute them. The radical premise that the relationship between public and private interest is contradictory has given way under the successor regime to an emphasis on the

merging of collective, group, and individual interests as interme-
diated by correct party procedure; any apparent incompatibility of
interests is only temporary.[33] Whereas radical theory encouraged
self-sacrificing nonconformity for altruistic ends, this new interpretation identifies altruism with organizational conformity and the satisfaction of legitimate self-interest (e.g., earning salary bonuses by
working harder). The emerging pattern of participation should be a
less disruptive one, more compatible with the functional needs of
economic modernization as well as with the material interests of the
vast majority of the citizenry. At the same time it may have costs,
tending for example to discourage negative feedback or innovative
behavior.

On the question of who should be permitted to participate, the
radical critique of "bourgeois right" implied that classes should be
redefined on the basis of substantive rather than procedural criteria.
For the polity, correct socialist orientation was defined at any time
by the ideologically correct line. For the individual, correct socialist
orientation was defined by the preeminence of pure motives. These
were assumed to coincide. Any behavior, any motive not consistent
with socialist ends should be criticized until it is dispelled. The
commodity system and the distribution of unequal pay according to
labor performed were still indispensable at the present stage of
socialist development, but they should be criticized and eventually
superseded. "We must not say, 'Long live distribution according to
work.' The fact that we recognize it and allow it to exist at the
present stage does not mean that we should extend or develop it."[34]

Once they gain currency, key polemical catchwords tend to
survive in the passive vocabulary of their users long after their
repression from public discourse. This is particularly so when the
post-Mao regime elects to soldier on under the ideological masthead
of "Mao Zedong Thought." No matter how it may try to reconstrue
and domesticate that thought, its radical implications are apt to
linger like a ghost. The existential questions so confidently (and
disastrously) answered by the radicals — What should we do? What is
the purpose of life? Where are we going? — have generally been
begged, or answered superficially ("seeking truth from facts").
"Modernization," to the Maoists a dubious means, has become the
all-justifying end. Aside from *tu quoque* arguments,[35] only the
juridical distinction between capitalist and socialist ownership spares
the reformers from the haunting reproach, "capitalist roader."[36] By
so unreservedly embracing the gospel of development, the Deng
Xiaoping leadership risks becoming hostage to an economic machine

which it cannot fully control. Its growing awareness of the danger
has become clear since the Sixth Plenum of the Eleventh Central
Committee (June 1981), when the Party suspended further criticism
of Mao's Thought and launched a campaign for "socialist spiritual
civilization," which is defined somewhat independently of the
economic base.

Whatever the posthumous career of radical sentiment, it is
worth bearing in mind that radical politics was practically bankrupt.
On the key issue of mass participation, for example, the radical position went through an initial extreme phase and a subsequent
moderate one. During the first phase leadership claims to represent
the public interest were validated on the basis of their intimacy with
the masses and their satisfaction of constituent interests. During the
second, the radicals backed away from this criterion and criticized
certain forms of elite-mass fraternization, now using substantive
correctness as the sole legitimate determinant of the public interest.
In its attempts to criticize the radical version of the mass line the
successor regime has focused on the first, radical phase, when
leadership claims to represent the public interest were evaluated on
the basis of their intimacy with the masses. This seems to have
exerted broad popular appeal despite its later abandonment by all
contingents of the leadership (including the radicals). The critique
takes the form of an *ad hominem* attack: the radicals divorced themselves from the masses and "used a portion of the power they
usurped to 'happily' loot the national coffer and live extravagantly—
in a manner even more ruthless than landlords and capitalists."[37]
This line of criticism harbors a certain degree of ambivalence,
masking an unresolved problem. In the first two years of the
succession the new regime permitted a form of mass participation
ironically redolent of the Cultural Revolution, permitting those who
had been repressed during the various phases of the Cultural
Revolution to press their criticism of the Gang of Four toward the
logical outcome of a critique of Maoism and all those who had
benefitted from it (ultimately including Hua Guofeng himself). But
after the ascendancy of Deng Xiaoping in the winter of 1978-79 the
attitude toward mass participation became more reserved. The mass
activists were suppressed, first with quasi-judicial measures and
then with the full force of the law. Even the famous "big-character
poster" was eliminated for its association with the irresponsible and
chaotic polemics of the Cultural Revolution.

Although the Deng Xiaoping regime seems to have turned the
clock back to 1962 (or even 1956), like all restorations this may be

viewed as a synthesis of selected aspects of the idealized bygone era with inadvertent or unavoidable components of the immediately repressed past. The radical phase, after all, lasted ten years and cannot simply be effaced from participants' memories. The highly prejudicial Maoist conceptualization of bureaucracy lingers on in the resentment of the masses as well as the literati, as does the marked xenophobic and populist strain in the recent campaigns against bourgeois liberalization or spiritual pollution. The democracy movement manifested again a conviction that there is a contradiction between public- and self-interest which justifies dramatic self-sacrificial gestures on behalf of the former. In spite of all attempts to enhance respect for authority, the pervasive attitude seems to be far more irreverent than before 1966. The current era seems to represent an uneasy synthesis of disparate participatory traditions.

Conclusion

The bourgeois democratic concept of participation, in which individual participants make autonomous political decisions based on their own interests, is rather difficult to assimilate to Chinese political culture. The Chinese revolution has if anything reinforced the indigenous corporate concept of interest. This is not to say that private interests do not exist in Chinese politics, and in fact there is a great deal of evidence in the critical literature of their ubiquity and ineluctability. But they may only be expressed in euphemistic, public-spirited form.

Under these circumstances political participation takes a somewhat different form than it does in the West. Rather than the explicit confrontation of sharply diverging interests and ideologies, we find each side trying to lay claim to the same legitimating symbols, while at the same time using the same demonology to denounce their opponents. Wang Ming's denunciation of Mao Zedong employed many of the same themes that Mao used against Liu Shaoqi; the official denunciations of Liu, Lin Biao, and the Gang of Four have also been thematically similar. This means that political conflict in China does not result in a clear-cut delineation of alternatives unless one side can monopolize communications, in which case the opposition is grotesquely caricatured. Instead it is expressed in esoteric allusions and tirades against anonymous opponents. This gives rise to an Aesopian language of "holding high the Red Flag to oppose the Red Flag" that is difficult for outsiders to comprehend. It fosters an iterative rather than an adversarial form of participation in which self-interest may be pursued only through subtle modification of consensually acceptable themes; the adversarial form of participation is used only against absent or powerless targets. Although this form of participation pays a price in terms of public clarity about political issues, it does ensure that all policy proposals make some attempt to accommodate the public interest. And the "mass line" paradigm stipulates that such proposals be circulated among a broad range of elites and masses before being generally implemented.

CHAPTER 3

Communist Social Structure and Workers' Politics in China

Andrew G. Walder

When asked about the place of a social group in a political system, the first impulse of the political sociologist is to assess its relative strength or weakness according to its ability to organize, mobilize, articulate its interests, and enforce its preferences in the political arena.[1] The standard measure of political strength and influence is the ability of the group to enforce its preferences, even against the resistance of other groups. The standard independent variables are those which help or hinder the group's ability to organize itself and mobilize whatever political resources it may possess: its degree of internal homogeneity, geographical proximity and ease of communication among members, control of resources valued by other groups, the availability of coalition partners, disposition of the state or other powerful organized forces toward the group's activities, and so forth.[2]

This standard imagery of group politics — interests, organization, mobilization, and political action — yields few insights in political systems where social groups outside of official power structures are systematically demobilized. In a polity where independent efforts at collective action are readily detected and contained with great effectiveness by well-organized political forces, and where there are no institutional mechanisms for the articulation and enforcement of group interests, any social group is by most liberal political standards politically weak and ineffectual, a dominated group dependent on the orientations of the powerful.

This, however, is a starting point, not a conclusion. A social group may be completely demobilized as a collective political force, but this does not mean that members of the group are unable to pursue their interests, have no influence individually or collectively,

and therefore are not a factor in national affairs. To the extent that
the political environment is hostile to collective group activity, members of the group will turn to other means to pursue their interests.
This is true not only in communist political systems, but in all
political systems where independent group activity is tightly
restricted or generally ineffective in influencing the making of
government policy. If group members are unable to enforce their
preferences in the making of policy, they will attempt to influence its
subsequent implementation. If interests cannot be pursued openly in
public institutions, they will be pursued privately outside of them. If
groups cannot enforce their interests collectively, many group members may decide to pursue their private interests individually.[3] The
predominance of non-public, non-institutional political activity, aimed
at influencing the implementation rather than the making of policy,
presents a challenge to those who wish to understand the political life
of such societies: to uncover, describe, and analyze the informal political system.

Among those who study communist political systems, use of the
interest group approach has been one popular response to this
challenge. Its proponents, while fully aware that the group politics
described in the first paragraph of this chapter are not a feature of
communist systems, insist that a modified group approach accurately fits informal political processes, especially among elite occupations inside the circle of bureaucratic power. According to this view,
many social groups defined by common occupational, educational, or
other characteristics come to share similar attitudes on matters that
relate to their group. Especially in the post-Stalin years in the Soviet
bloc, they have had increasing opportunities, in the words of Gordon
Skilling, to "express their views collectively" and make a "common
claim."[4] Group politics, as described by well-known analysts of
pluralist systems, takes place in communist systems as well,
although in quite restricted and usually hidden forms.[5]

Many have challenged the application of group theory to communist polities, even in this tentatively-stated and modified form.
These critics do not dispute that communist societies encompass
different social groups with different interests, and that this fact is
essential for understanding the formulation and implementation of
government policy. However, they deny that the hidden politics of
these regimes is group-based. According to this view, "groupness"
entails not only common interests and views, but mutual
communication, interaction, and coordination of activities, whether
public or informal. There is very little evidence that this is a

characteristic of interest groups in communist systems.[6] There are identifiable groups and shared interests, but no "interest groups" that act as such. Divergent groups and interests enter into the political system, in Franklyn Griffiths' words, through countless "parallel individual articulations" of interest at all levels of society.[7] In place of a hidden, informal "group politics" beneath the monolithic facade of communist society, this interpretation offers the image of a highly fragmented and random pattern of interest articulation and hidden bargaining, through which social groups almost imperceptibly influence the political system without engaging in common group activity.[8]

The analysis of Chinese industrial workers in this chapter provides detailed support for the critics who argue that common group activity, even of an informal nature, is highly restricted in a stable communist system. But our analysis of the social structure and political culture of the Chinese factory leads us to a picture of workers' politics quite different from even the modified "tendencies of articulation" approach offered by Griffiths and applied by many others. First, our research shows that the "articulation" of interests is not the primary activity through which individual group members successfully pursue their interests. And second, we find a picture of worker political activity that is much more highly organized in regular patterns than the fragmented and random pattern suggested by Griffiths.

Our study points to a different model of the participation of non-elite social groups in communist political systems: clientelism. A clientelist system is one in which individual members of subordinate social groups pursue their interests not by banding together for coordinated group action, but by cultivating ties based on the exchange of loyalty and advantage with individuals of higher status and power.[9] In China's large state enterprises, the party organization and its associated managerial hierarchy control the distribution of a near-complete array of needed goods and services, as well as career opportunities, and they distribute them preferentially to loyal clients of the party organization. As a result, the most active and able of workers are often drawn into loyalties that make them favored clients in a stable political network that cuts across group boundaries. This common route for the pursuit of interests requires that selected workers become coopted into articulating the Party's interests rather than those of the workers. This permanently splits workers as a group and makes group activity, even of an informal nature, very difficult. In other words, to understand how workers

pursue their interests in China, we must study the formation of
stable vertical ties in the social structure, as well as the horizontal
cleavages and group loyalties pointed to by group theories.[10]
Clientelism is a concept that focuses attention on these vertical
networks and the political activity associated with them.

This survey of workers' politics is divided into three parts. The
first is an analysis of the position of the industrial labor force in
China's broader social structure and network of political institutions.
Before we can talk about "workers' politics," we need to recognize
that industrial workers in China are divided into distinctive
subgroups according to their terms of employment, the degree to
which they have vested interests in their enterprises, and their
relationship to local political institutions. In this first part, we will
identify and describe several subgroups among China's industrial
workers, and show how their positions in broader social and political
structures endow them with different interests, orientations, and
capacities for influence.

The second part of this survey is an analysis of the small-scale
social structure in which state factory workers pursue their interests. It is made up of vertical ties of loyalty that stretch from party
committees to their client activists on the shop floor; loyalties that
are cultivated and reinforced through small group organization and a
system of political surveillance and record-keeping. The factory
controls the distribution of an enormous array of material benefits,
and the party and management use this control as part of a reward
system that favors loyal clients and penalizes the expression of
opposition to party policy. As a result, formal meetings in which
workers participate are emptied of genuine political content and
workers' exercise of voice often becomes ritualistic. Interests are
instead pursued informally, by becoming a client-activist, through
personal connections and petty corruption, or through such
unorganized, passive resistance as work slowdowns and absenteeism. So embedded are these strategies and orientations in the minds
of workers that they shaped patterns of open group conflict during
the Cultural Revolution of 1966-68.

The task of the final section is to illuminate the obscure and
complex paths of worker influence on national policy. Workers are
not a collective force in national politics, but they do affect policy
implementation at the local level and, indirectly, policy-making at the
local and even national level. No matter how thoroughly the expression of group interests is restricted and the active workers coopted by
the Party, workers as a group still exercise the one group strategy

that workers everywhere employ: the conscious withdrawal of efficiency and passive resistance to the designs of management. Chinese workers have employed this residual strategy with varying success over the past thirty years. The strategy is designed to influence the implementation of national policy regarding wages and work discipline and it has been most successful in those periods in which industrial efficiency was a major national priority, and managers were allowed some flexibility in implementing policy. In this last part we will examine a period (1978-82) in which workers were able to influence the implementation of wage and incentive policy so successfully that they helped alter the effects of a new industrial reform program and force national policy-makers to adjust their course. While an unusual case, this example illustrates the ways that even unorganized and dependent workers can have a large impact on policy implementation at local levels, and thereby become a hidden factor in national policy-making.

The Social Structure of the Industrial Work Force

There are roughly 76 million people currently employed in some form of manual labor in the industrial branches of China's economy.[11] Their employment benefits, standard of living, and future opportunities vary enormously. Some work as day laborers or seasonal workers and move from job to job; others remain permanently in a single enterprise. Some receive little more than a small cash wage for their efforts; others receive nearly all of their needs, including wage supplements, supplementary rations, housing, hospital care, insurance, and retirement benefits. Some work in small workshops which employ a few dozen people and have very little fixed capital investment, all of it locally-generated. Others work in massive industrial complexes which may employ over 10,000 and absorb large investments of capital from the national treasury. These are very different worlds of work, both socially and economically.

Four variables, to a large extent, determine the degree to which workers are oriented toward their workplaces for the pursuit of interests, have a vested interest in their enterprise, and are involved in national politics. The first is the extent to which workers depend on the enterprise for the satisfaction of needs. The degree to which workers derive their income from their wages and their housing, hospital care, meals, and other public goods from the enterprise determines their vested interests in the workplace as an institution, and the influence of the social and political structures of the workplace on their orientations and behavior.

The second variable is the duration of worker attachment to an enterprise. Vested interests in the enterprise, and its importance as a locus of political behavior and influence on future opportunities increase with the permanency of employment.

The third variable is the amount of state capital resources which are fixed in the enterprise and the amount of funds budgeted to it annually by planning bureaus. In many small enterprises, the amount of capital is quite low, and funds are budgeted by lower-level government units. Sometimes the capital is generated largely by local units themselves—communes, brigades, or small enterprises in urban districts and neighborhoods. The activity of workers in these kinds of enterprises is of little direct consequence for the national economic plan and they are far removed from national politics. In the largest enterprises, on the other hand, vast sums have been invested in fixed capital equipment and large sums are budgeted each year by national ministries or industrial bureaus for expansion, renovation, and new operating expenses. The performance of the workers in this sector is of crucial importance for the fate of the national economic plan and for the political battles that revolve around budgeting, investment, and development strategy at the top levels of government. The directors of these large enterprises, further, may have bureau or ministerial rank.[12] Not only are there fewer levels of administration between them and the top levels of government, but the factory director's rank and status greatly increases his informal capacity for communication and influence in resource allocation decisions at the highest levels. For all of these reasons, the performance of workers in large state enterprises has the most direct impact on national affairs and any influence such workers may exert over their factory leadership may affect the behavior of enterprise directors in their informal lobbying at the highest levels of the national bureaucracy.

The fourth and final variable is the extent to which national political institutions—and the reward systems that accompany them—are formally organized within the workplace. The Communist Party, Communist Youth League, Trade Union, and associated organizational life of group meetings and political study, are spread very unevenly through China's industrial enterprises. The more completely organized and active these workplace institutions are, the more their systems of surveillance, evaluation, reward, and promotion influence worker orientations and political behavior, and the more completely workers are drawn into the rhythms of national political life.

These variables allow us to distinguish five major categories of workers which form a hierarchy of industrial labor — rural workers in collective enterprises, rural temporary workers, urban temporary workers, urban workers in collective enterprises, and permanent workers in state enterprises. Permanent workers are themselves stratified into a secondary sector of small enterprises and a primary sector of large ones. Only this last group is fully oriented to a workplace social and political structure, and occupies a position in the industrial bureaucracy which lends it some importance in national affairs. After a brief examination of the social and economic conditions which differentiate the political experience of each of these segments of the labor force, we will turn in the rest of the chapter to a detailed analysis of the political orientations and behavior of this last, most important group.

Rural Workers in Collective Enterprises

At the bottom of China's hierarchy of industrial labor are some 19.8 million residents of rural communes who receive wages in cash or in kind for their work in small collective enterprises operated by brigades, communes, and rural towns. All of these small enterprises are under a form of collective ownership outside of the state sector. While there are over 700,000 such enterprises, they are usually quite small (an average of twenty-four people) and as a group produce only one-tenth of national industrial output.[13] They may enjoy a regular sales or subcontracting relationship with state enterprises and commercial agencies and in some cases receive small grants from county budgets, but the resources invested in these plants are locally generated. Their products are usually geared to local needs — agricultural machinery, water pumps, chemical fertilizers, cement and building materials, processed food, or cash crops — or to nearby urban markets for handicraft items and consumer goods. Drawing minimal resources from state budgets at the lowest levels, producing items that are usually tangential to state plans in relatively small quantities, this industrial sector does not weigh heavily in national affairs.

Workers in these enterprises are still closely integrated into the agricultural economy. Peasants who work in enterprises run by their brigade or commune usually receive some form of cash wage. However, local customs vary widely. In brigade-level undertakings workers sometimes receive work points, which will determine the amount of cash and grain he or she will receive at the end of the year. Sometimes they receive a combination of cash and work points. In any case, arrangements must always be made to ensure that the worker continues to share in basic grain rations and in collective distributions of the harvest. This may be done by deducting an amount equal to a set number of work points from a worker's wage.[14] Those who find jobs in collective enterprises organized by nearby rural towns (*zhen*) receive a cash wage for their efforts, but they must usually pay part of their wages back into production team coffers in order to continue receiving rations of grain and other foodstuffs for themselves and their families.[15] In either case, the workers' family members continue to live in the village and earn work points for agricultural labor.

These jobs are among the least desirable forms of industrial employment in China, yet they are highly valued by rural residents. Employment in a collective enterprise is a release from the drudgery of field labor (which is still largely manual) and exposure to the elements, and can often excuse the rural laborer from the heavy physical labor that often marks the commune's earth-moving and capital construction projects of the slack season. In addition, jobs in these enterprises greatly multiply the cash income of a rural family, which is usually much lower than an urban worker's, in part because commune income is paid partly in kind.[16]

Even with the extra cash income generated by factory work, in most cases the majority of the rural family's needs are still met by its private sidelines (livestock, vegetables), the grain and other food rations distributed by the production team, and the cash income distributed to team members at the end of the year.[17] And employment in the small collective enterprises is often temporary or seasonal, depending on the decisions of brigade and team leaders, seasonal labor demands in agriculture or in the small enterprise, and business trends for the enterprise's products. A minority of such rural workers in small enterprises may be able to stay year-round on a near-permanent basis, but most continue to work in agriculture at least part of the year. Rural residents cannot be released to work in these industrial concerns without the permission of their team leaders (and sometimes brigade leaders), and often this permission is obtained only with the understanding that the worker will return during the peak harvest season if needed.[18]

In part because of the tenuous links of rural workers to these small enterprises and in part because of the weakness or absence of party organization, these workers rarely engage in any organized political life at their workplaces. The lowest administrative level at which party branches are organized is the brigade headquarters in the countryside, and they are rarely present even in the largest of county-level collective factories.[19] Political meetings and study sessions at the workplace are rare. It is in the team that most of the worker's needs are met and the decisions are made which affect his or her livelihood. Therefore it is the leadership of the team and brigade which rural workers must attempt to influence, and they remain oriented largely to the politics of the village.

Rural Temporary Workers

In addition to employment in local collectively-owned enterprises, roughly nine million residents of rural communes are able to find legal or covert temporary employment in urban collective or state sector industrial enterprises.[20] The paths they take to find these jobs and the terms of their employment vary enormously. Workers find jobs individually or through village officials; are paid in cash or in some combination of cash and work points; have fixed individual or group contracts, or no contracts at all; work in a single place for a week, or stay on for years. This bewildering variety of temporary jobs stems from the informal, and sometimes quasi-legal nature of the arrangements, which are largely outside of state regulation and planning. The unifying features of this category of employment are that the workers' official household registration remains in the countryside and the workers are not included in official plant employment rosters regulated by state plans.

One common form of temporary labor is seasonal work (*jijie gong*) or casual labor (*san gong*) found by individual peasants in nearby state-run county or municipal enterprises. This often occupies the peasant during the slack agricultural season in places where there is a large demand for seasonal labor in enterprises that process food or cash crops—especially cotton ginning, sugar and paper production, the processing of oil-bearing plants, and grain milling. Generally the worker must get permission from team leaders to be absent from the team during this period and arrange to pay part of the wages into team coffers to pay for basic grain rations.

A second common form of temporary work, contract labor
(*hetong gong*), is more common in the areas that surround urban
centers. State enterprises occasionally have short-term labor needs
which exceed their planned labor allocation. They will then make
arrangements with nearby rural officials to allocate them a fixed
number of workers for a contracted period, usually from one to six
months. These job opportunities are distributed among various
production teams, with the commune, brigade, or team (depending on
which level of leadership arranged the contract) taking a cut of the
contract worker's wage. These workers usually do heavy physical
labor — excavation, construction, moving, and hauling — which the
permanent employees of the enterprise cannot be spared to do. A
variation of this is "rotation labor" (*lunhuan gong*), where a contract
is established to maintain a specified number of rural workers in an
urban enterprise by a brigade or commune which assigns the
workers on a rotating basis.

A third common form is a type of outside contract work (*waibao
gong*), in which a state enterprise contracts with a construction team
made up of rural workers to complete a job — usually construction,
excavation, moving and hauling, or road-building. The enterprise or
the team may organize the work and provide materials and tools.[21]
The head of the construction team is paid and either distributes the
cash to the workers (often after paying a percentage to team or brigade officials, in some cases as bribes), or turns all of the money over
to a brigade or team, which then pays the workers entirely in work
points.

The varied forms of this temporary labor all have certain common features. While rural workers can greatly increase their cash
income through this outside labor, they and their families are still
tied to the production team's agricultural economy and its year-end
distributions. They depend on team or brigade leaders for permission
to engage in outside work and usually turn over portions of their
wages to team coffers in return for grain rations. Their connection
with the state enterprise is tenuous and usually brief. They are not
usually eligible for any of the fringe benefits permanent state
employees normally receive. Often they have little contact with
permanent workers, since they usually take part in common labor
outside the production process. If the enterprise has a well-organized
political life, temporary workers are usually excluded from participation. Their political orientation is still toward the leaders of the rural
agricultural unit, where permission to work is received and where
most material needs of the worker's family are met. If the rural

temporary worker tries to exert influence on the enterprise, it is usually through diligence and obedience in an effort to extend the period of employment or, in rare cases, to be hired on a permanent basis.[22]

Urban Temporary Workers

There are roughly four million residents of towns, county seats, and cities of various sizes who work on a temporary basis in state enterprises.[23] Unlike rural temporaries, these people do not have rural households, and therefore do not have the alternative sources of income and other support that agriculture provides. They must work continuously in state enterprises and their income rises or falls in almost direct proportion to the amount of time they are employed. But in other respects their position in the state enterprise is similar to that of rural temporaries: they are outside of the enterprise's planned official roster and are paid with excess plant funds; they are ineligible for many of the fringe benefits available to permanent employees; and they are usually excluded from organized political life.

Urban temporaries are allocated, hired, and compensated in a wide variety of ways which reflect the semi-regulated nature of the activity and wide variations in local practice. They often work under oral or written contracts that range up to one year in length, although some work as casual day laborers with no fixed term of employment. Many, especially in the larger cities, are allocated through a bureaucratic system whereby they register at labor service stations in their neighborhoods and municipal labor bureaus serve as clearinghouses, making assignments to enterprises which file requests for workers. Some workers, however, find temporary jobs through casual inquiries or personal connections, especially in the smaller enterprises. Urban temporaries are usually paid a fixed wage which is set by custom generally at the rate of grade two permanent workers — slightly below the average pay for manual workers. But veteran, skilled temporaries may be classified at much higher rates which are fixed in their files at labor bureaus.

Because urban temporary workers tend to be more continuously employed in industry and more dependent on their wages than rural temporary workers, they are more likely to be skilled and integrated into the core production process. For example, one major source of demand for urban temporaries is in heavy industrial plants during hot summer months, when absenteeism soars and fill-ins are needed. Such workers do not have periodic obligations to return to communes to work, and often have informally-acquired skills valued by enterprises. Therefore the more diligent and obedient among them are more likely to have their period of employment extended indefinitely. It is not unusual for urban temporaries to work for many years at the same establishment. And, because they have an urban household registration and can maintain their families in urban areas, these temporaries are far more likely to be hired eventually by an enterprise as part of the permanent labor force.[24]

Unlike rural temporaries, urban temporaries are not exploiting an opportunity for greatly expanding their cash income, but have somehow fallen outside the secure state employment sector and to the bottom of the urban labor force.[25] More dependent on industrial wages, more likely to be skilled and integrated into the production process, and more likely to be long-term employees, they tend to feel the inequities of their position more keenly. They compare their lot with the permanent employees who often perform the same work and yet enjoy many fringe benefits and opportunities for increased salaries and standard of living that the temporaries do not have. As a result, they usually attempt to extend their employment, and eventually attain permanent status, something to which they feel entitled as urban residents. This is usually pursued by exhibiting diligence and obedience in work.[26]

Because of the features of their social position, it was urban, not rural, temporaries who fueled the active movements of temporary and contract workers in large cities like Shanghai during the Cultural Revolution.[27] Their demands, usually targeted at municipal authorities and their labor bureaus rather than enterprise officials, were summarized as "the abolition of the corrupt system of temporary and contract labor." In practical terms, this meant simply that they be granted permanent status and the security, fringe benefits, and enhanced opportunities this would entail. The system was not abolished, but the grievances of long-term, skilled temporaries were addressed in 1971 when those who had built up several years of seniority in a single enterprise and who were *de facto* permanent employees, were granted formal permanent status.[28]

While urban temporaries are more completely integrated into their enterprises than their rural counterparts, they are still marginal. Generally excluded from the network of formal political organization that binds permanent employees—party, union, youth league, political study—they lack the status to press claims in the political world of the state enterprise. Constituting a very small minority of employees at any given time (usually less than 2 percent), and except for a privileged core of skilled veterans, experiencing continual turnover, they have virtually no capacity for influence within the enterprise.[29] Making a living on the margins of the state plan, they are also of little consequence in national affairs.

Urban Workers in Collective Enterprises

Another 15 million urban residents make a living as regular employees of collective enterprises which are administered by towns (*zhen*), counties (*xian*), or municipalities (*shi*).[30] There were 111,000 such enterprises in 1981, ranging in size from small handicraft collectives employing a few dozen people to factories manufacturing fabricated metal parts or small machines that may employ as many as 1,000.[31] As a group, they have an average of 134 employees. These enterprises, especially the larger ones, are often subsidized in some way by local governments, but their workers are not paid according to official state pay scales and they are not covered by the regulations which give labor insurance and welfare benefits to state workers. The result is a complex patchwork of payment systems and benefits—but in general, wages and benefits are lower than those of permanent state employees. The average annual wage in collective enterprises was 622 *yuan* in 1981—less than three-fourths the average wage of a permanent worker in a state enterprise.[32]

Unlike rural residents who find industrial jobs, workers in urban collectives have no alternative to the income provided by industrial employment. While these workers are therefore wholly dependent on industrial employment, their enterprises can satisfy few of their needs beyond a wage. The small collectives rarely provide more than a small wage and relatively stable employment. This is especially true in the smallest one-third that are run by urban street committees (*jiedao*) and rural towns and counties.[33] Larger collective enterprises run by county or municipal governments, which typically employ between 100 and 200 people, pay higher wages and sometimes provide the worker with some limited forms of accident insurance, sick leave, and retirement benefits. The largest of these, which typically enjoy a stable relationship with a large state enterprise and are integrated into municipal industrial systems, may begin to provide some of the benefits of state workers—a meal hall with subsidized food, a medical clinic, and various kinds of wage supplements. But this situation is rare. A medium-sized enterprise is generally able to provide little more than a wage, somewhat stable employment, and basic labor insurance for the worker.

In part because of the limited benefits of employment in this sector, worker attachment to the enterprise is not as strong as that of permanent workers in state enterprises. They are likely to change jobs several times in the course of their lives and many are youths for whom state sector jobs could not be found. They generally maintain a semi-active search for work in other collective enterprises or small state enterprises where conditions and benefits are more desirable, and may drift in and out of temporary labor, or in and out of the labor force altogether. In larger enterprises the work force exhibits much less of this kind of turnover because benefits are more desirable and often linked to seniority. Another cause of weak worker attachment to the enterprise is that some enterprises, especially the smaller ones, may periodically disband because of a lack of funds or markets for their products. Only the larger collectives can offer stable employment.

The small size of urban collective enterprises and the nature of their products mean that they are marginally important to the state plan. The entire sector produced only 14 percent of the nation's gross value of industrial output in 1981.[34] The small collectives that produce handicraft items and small consumer goods may be important to the economies of the towns, county seats, urban neighborhoods, and districts that run them, but their performance has little impact beyond these local areas. Larger industrial collectives often make spare parts, small machines, and other products used in the manufacturing and assembly processes of small- and medium-sized enterprises. In some cases this supply and sales relationship is so stable that the collective may be a *de facto* branch factory of a state concern. In these cases enterprise performance has an indirect impact on the state plan and their output is crucial as a source of supply for the state enterprise involved. But the state enterprises they supply are themselves rarely the largest and most important. In either case, state investment in these enterprises is small. Even in the larger plants the capital equipment is often outdated or worn out, obtained from state enterprises that no longer need it. Production processes are generally labor intensive and use low cost labor at that.[35] When they receive subsidies from the state, it is in small amounts and the funds are never budgeted at a level higher than a municipal government, usually coming from towns, counties, neighborhoods, and urban districts.

Urban collective enterprises are as marginal politically as they are economically. Small handicraft collectives usually have at most a single party member stationed in them and often have none at all. Larger collectives, which are of some importance to local governments, generally have a party member placed in a leadership position who is responsible to the party branch in the local government agency that oversees it. The very largest of the collectives, usually those which are virtually branches of larger state factories, may have enough party members to warrant a party small group or branch. But even in the largest collectives, formally organized political life is a pale imitation of that in larger state enterprises. Such common features of political life in large state enterprises as regular group meetings, political study, active youth league organization, and the recruitment and preparation of potential party members through periods of activism and candidacy, are largely absent in the collective sector.

Permanent Workers in State Enterprises

By far the largest and most important subgroup among China's workers are the 29 million who work in the nation's 84,000 state-sector industrial enterprises.[36] These workers, only 42 percent of the industrial labor force, produced 75 percent of the country's gross value of industrial output in 1981.[37] Their average annual wage in 1981, 854 *yuan*,[38] was almost 40 percent higher than that of the average collective worker and well over twice the average of the 33 million rural and temporary workers. Just as important, however, are the many fringe benefits, wage supplements, and welfare and insurance provisions which the state provides. Their cash value averaged 526 *yuan* per worker per year in 1978, 82 percent of the average wage.[39] These workers obtain jobs through assignments made by local labor bureaus, enjoy virtual lifetime tenure unless they commit a crime or a political offense, and are paid a basic wage according to an eight-grade scale which allows them increasing salaries through the life cycle. Their enterprises, in addition, are often able to provide subsidized meals, housing, and medical care.

Because of the increased capacity of state enterprises to provide for worker needs in addition to wages, workers in this sector come to depend on their enterprises more completely. Yet this dependence is spread very unevenly among state sector workers. Many state enterprises are quite small, employing from 100 to 500 workers, and are run by towns, counties, small cities, and district governments of larger cities. Their ability to subsidize meals, provide medical care, housing, and other services is usually quite limited, and is sometimes no greater than that of the largest collective factories. Workers at the bottom of the state sector hierarchy are often provided with little more than a wage, job security, and basic state labor insurance, retirement, and welfare benefits. They must still rely on family and on municipal services for many of their needs. At the other end of the spectrum are the workers employed in China's large enterprises of over 1,000 employees, run directly by municipal governments, provinces, or national ministries. They are often able to provide for almost all immediate and future needs of workers and their families, including added rations and foodstuffs, meal halls, housing, medical care, factory clinics and hospitals, kindergartens, and nurseries.

These differences between the "primary" sector, consisting of large state enterprises, and the "secondary" sector, consisting of smaller ones, leads to differences in duration of worker attachment to the enterprise. Workers in large primary sector enterprises tend to stay in an enterprise throughout their lives. Because the state will provide a worker with only one job assignment and because transfers are very difficult to arrange, workers in these enterprises almost never quit their jobs. To do so would mean taking a job as a temporary worker in a collective factory or a smaller state enterprise, and this would inevitably entail a major decline in standard of living and future life chances. Workers in the smaller enterprises, on the other hand, are more likely to move to other factories one or more times. Since their enterprises do not provide for a large portion of their non-wage needs, it is less costly for them to change jobs and easier to find comparable alternative terms of employment at other small enterprises.[40] Turnover in these enterprises is still very low by international standards, but compared with workers in China's primary sector it is significant.

This marked stratification of enterprises according to their ability to provide for workers' needs is matched by differences in their contribution to the national economy. The largest 6,000 enterprises in 1980 produced 60 percent of the gross value of industrial output of the 42,000 state enterprises included in the central budget.[41] This small number of large enterprises is of crucial importance in the national economy, representing the majority of the state's fixed capital investment in industry, and absorbing the lion's share of the state's annual budget for industrial production.[42] Top executives hold high ranks in the national bureaucracy and travel regularly to high-level meetings and to ministries in Beijing to lobby for their annual allocations of state resources. The position of large state enterprises in the industrial economy makes the performance of their workers of central interest to national policy-makers, an important variable in national affairs.

The party's network of political organization is also spread unevenly across state sector enterprises: the larger the enterprise, the more fully developed its formally organized political life. The very smallest state enterprises may not even have a party branch, or have a more active organized political life than large collectives. Small enterprises employing from 200 to 500 people usually have a party branch, but party ranks may be very thin on the shop floor and not all leadership positions are filled by party members or committed activists. The result is a relatively weak organized political life in which shop floor production groups are not well integrated into the party's systems of surveillance, control, and reward.

The larger enterprises, on the other hand, usually have a full general branch or party committee, branch committees with headquarters in workshops, and small groups which discipline the rank-and-file party members on the shop floor. In this situation the party branches are usually able to place members or activists in all leadership positions on the shop floor—especially the crucial production group leaders, workers who supervise small groups of eight to twelve workers. Organized political life is well developed in these situations. Workers participate regularly in after-hours production and political meetings; the leaders of these meetings are loyal to the Party and responsive to its policies, and the organization has the resources to reward the politically active. These large enterprises are the places where workers are the most likely to take part in the full range of grass roots meetings and activities that many have come to associate with mass political life in China. They alone among China's industrial workers are drawn completely into participation in national political life.

Summary

The four structural features we have used to differentiate the political orientation and potential of China's workers vary in unison (see figure 1). Those who work in enterprises marginal to the national economy (or who are marginal to their enterprises) also tend not to be highly dependent on the enterprises for the satisfaction of needs, work in them for briefer periods, and do not normally have opportunities to participate in officially organized political life. These workers do not see their enterprises as institutions which will provide for them throughout their lives, or as a locus for political activity. This situation characterizes well over half of the industrial workers in China.

Politically Important Characteristics of Labor Force Subgroups

	Rural-Collective	Rural-Temporary	Urban-Temporary	Urban-Collective	State-Secondary	State-Primary
Worker dependence on the enterprise for the satisfaction of needs	low	low	low to medium	low to medium	medium to high	high
Duration of worker attachment to the enterprise	weak	weak	weak	weak to medium	medium	strong
Impact of enterprise performance on national planning and budgeting	marginal	varies	varies	marginal to indirect	indirect to direct	direct
Formally organized participation in enterprise political life	low or none	low or none	low or none	low	medium	high

At the other end of this spectrum are those who work permanently in medium and large enterprises. This relatively small group of enterprises is crucial to the performance of the economy as a whole. Workers tend to be highly dependent on their enterprises for the satisfaction of their families' needs, and it is difficult to transfer within the sector. As a result, they are strongly attached to their enterprises and usually expect to remain in them throughout their lives. Such workers participate in the full range of party-organized political activities which bind citizens to national political life. They therefore see the enterprise as the place in which their future life chances will be determined and, as a result, their political activities are centered there.

If any workers in China exert influence in the national arena, it is these permanent workers in large state enterprises. Producing the majority of the nation's industrial output and fully integrated into the official party network of political participation, they would seem well placed to do so. Yet the other features of their position in China's social structure—that they are highly dependent on their enterprises for the satisfaction of their needs and that they continue to work in them throughout their lives—have profound implications for their political behavior in the enterprise. These workers are fully encapsulated in an enterprise-level social structure which includes a system of surveillance, evaluation, and reward that has often been missed by observers of China. Yet it completely defines the ways in which these workers attempt to pursue and preserve their interests in a system of officially-supervised political participation.

Large State Enterprises: Life Chances and the Vested Interests of Permanent Workers

The Chinese communist system for administering labor markets and distributing goods and services among the population makes legal attachment to an official work institution (or *danwei*) a primary determinant of a worker's current standard of living and future life chances. Institutions, not markets, are the primary mechanisms through which goods and services are distributed. Legal attachment to an institution provides entitlement to these distributions. The marked scarcity of goods and services typical of a poor, overpopulated country, coupled with the stark absence of comparable alternatives outside the state sector, further magnifies these vested interests.

Much of the social stratification in China is therefore accounted for by the social institution with which a person is formally connected. The rest is determined by status within the institution, which determines relative entitlement to distributions. Pay differentials are not the most important part of this picture. As a consequence, state enterprises are in one respect communities of fate, with resources available which all employees can potentially share, if not at present, then in the future. Since these resources are too scarce to be distributed to all, employees must remain sensitive to the way leaders make decisions about distribution.

The multifaceted opportunities for increased income and access to public goods which state employment affords workers weigh heavily in their consciousness, life plans, and behavior. These include subsidies and allowances, regional supplements, insurance, distribution of goods and services, and opportunities for employment offered to relatives. Subsidies and allowances (*butie, jintie, buzhu*) provide for additional non-wage income in a number of circumstances. In some regions, state enterprises provide a winter heating supplement to be used to buy the coal used in small furnaces in factory dormitories and apartments. For employees who live a considerable distance from the enterprise, a transportation supplement is

provided for train or bus fare, or simply to compensate the worker
for expending the physical energy to bicycle or walk the extra
distance to work.[43] Workers whose job assignments take them away
from their family can receive annual paid leave and a transportation
supplement to subsidize their train ride back home.

Special regional supplements are added to the wages of workers
in high cost of living areas. Workers who take part in arduous or
potentially dangerous work — underground mining, certain types of
construction, or in such high temperature areas of a factory as the
front of blast furnaces — receive wage supplements that may total up
to 15 or 20 *yuan* a month, or some one-third of the average base pay
before bonuses are calculated. Yet another important supplement is
the grain subsidy that protects state workers against rises in state-
set grain prices.[44] This list, by no means exhaustive, begins to indicate the ways in which permanent workers in state enterprises
receive supplements to a base wage which is already considerably
higher than that of other workers in the industrial labor force.

Another set of benefits, only partially available to workers in the
collective sector, ensures the security of workers and their families in
a variety of life circumstances. Workers are provided with illness or
injury leave for up to six continuous months at 60 to 100 percent of
their salary, depending on seniority. While in the hospital, not only
are all major expenses paid, but they are given a convalescence
supplement at a percentage of their regular wage which varies by
seniority. All state enterprises pay half the medical expenses of
dependent family members, some pay more. Retired workers receive
pensions which equal 60 to 90 percent of their former salary, again
depending on seniority. If a worker dies due to illness or injury, the
enterprise pays funeral expenses and a monetary "death benefit" to
the family, and will support the worker's children through monthly
payments which continue until they finish their schooling. Female
workers are given fifty-six days of childbirth leave at full pay. When
a worker finds himself in dire financial straits due to low per capita
family income, if the enterprise cannot arrange employment for
another family member, it provides regular welfare supplements for
as long as the problem persists. Or, in some cases it provides the
worker with a short-term loan.[45] China may indeed be a welfare
state, but only the state employee is a full-fledged member of it, and
the benefits generally grow with seniority.

In addition to income supplements and this impressive system of
social security, state enterprises provide public goods and services
directly to their employees. While supplements and labor insurance

are available in all state enterprises, these public goods and services vary considerably with the resources of an enterprise, which, in turn, are often directly related to the size of the enterprise. The most important of these public goods is housing. Residential overcrowding is endemic in China and per capita urban housing space actually declined some 20 percent in the twenty-five years after 1952.[46] Over the same period state enterprises have been the most active builders of new dormitories and apartments. Workers attached to large state enterprises therefore have a considerably better chance of obtaining larger or better housing quarters than the rest of the population—if not in the short run, then in the future as the enterprise expands its housing stock. In addition, rents for enterprise housing are subsidized, rarely exceeding 2 to 3 *yuan* per month for the average family.[47] Employees who do not live in factory housing can receive money grants to repair their housing.[48] Large enterprises also run their own medical clinics or hospitals, and refer employees to them directly, sparing them the long queues at overcrowded municipal facilities. In addition, medium and large state enterprises provide meal hall services, kindergartens, and day-care nurseries. Child-care services are especially valuable where, as is now common, both spouses work.

There are, in addition, significant distributions in kind to the employees of state enterprises. These distributions also vary according to the resources commanded by the particular enterprise. State enterprises, for example, often provide ration coupons to workers engaged in taxing physical labor or pregnant women which supplement state standards for grain and other foodstuffs. Enterprise general affairs departments can also obtain ration coupons for scarce consumer items from state commercial agencies and distribute them to selected employees. This increases the ability of the worker to buy the higher quality consumer items. In addition, enterprises often maintain their own farms on spare tracts of land in their possession. A total of 1.15 million acres were cultivated by state factories and mines in 1980, producing a total of 500 million kilograms of grain and 1.5 billion kilograms of vegetables.[49] This food is outside the urban rationing system and is distributed solely to state employees through subsidized meal services, or sometimes direct holiday distributions. Factory general affairs departments also procure fruits and meats from distant regions for factory meal halls—foodstuffs which may not be available locally.

Large enterprises also have the capacity to provide employment and education for relatives and these have become important mechanisms for increasing family income and even transmitting state employment status across generations. Many state enterprises, for example, commonly hire the spouses and children of permanent employees as temporary workers, which increases family income considerably. This is especially important when children delay marriage into their late twenties and continue to live in the parents' household, a common situation. Others have even formed subsidiary collective enterprises for the primary purpose of providing long-term employment for the dependents of permanent employees. There were 6,766 such collective enterprises in existence in 1979.[50] Further, large enterprises often run middle-school level technical schools for the children of employees. Completion of this kind of education instead of a more academic middle school education generally guarantees permanent state employment as a skilled worker or assistant technician in the parent's enterprise or elsewhere. Finally, in recent years state employees have been allowed the privilege of designating a son or daughter to replace them when they retire—a practice known officially as *dingti*. These practices have always been highly valued by workers, not only because the traditional orientation to the family remains strong, but because family members are economically compelled to pool their income and share common housing even after children are grown. The progressively acute shortage of jobs after the mid-1960s, which has recently reached near crisis proportions in many large cities, has made these practices increasingly valued.

Political Surveillance and the Control of Labor

The party organization and its system of political surveillance and record-keeping is a crucially important feature of large state enterprises, enabling party committees and branches to control the distribution of rewards and appointments to leadership positions. The patterns of surveillance and control weigh heavily in workers' consciousness, restrict their capacity for collective action and open expression of interests, and set the ground rules for the pursuit of their interests within the enterprise.

Every party member in the enterprise is part of a system of organization which is parallel to, yet separate from, the administrative structure of the enterprise. In a large enterprise with an active, well-run party organization, as many as 20 to 30 percent of the employees may be party members.[51] In the biggest enterprises there is at most one worker-member on the shop floor in any single production group. These workers are organized into party small groups which span several production groups. The heads of these groups are members of the party branch committees, which are organized in workshops. The heads of branch committees, party branch secretaries, are members of the party general branch or party committee at the top of the enterprise hierarchy. Party branch secretaries, in turn, are under a full-time party secretary, the top party official in the enterprise. This network of interlocking committees and groups forms a chain of communication, command, and discipline which is separate from the enterprise administration. The meetings of these party small groups and committees are separate from others held in the factory; they can be attended only by party members, who are given information and allowed to read documents which they are forbidden to reveal to non-members.

Surrounding this kernel of party members is a layer of "activists" (*jiji fenzi*) and "backbones" (*gugan fenzi*) through which the Party extends its influence on the shop floor. These are people who are positively oriented to the Party and its policies and who actively do its bidding. Many are members of the party's subordinate organization in the enterprise, the Communist Youth League. These activists are a small minority of the work force, roughly as numerous as party members themselves, whom the party organization is grooming for eventual party membership, and often for later promotion to positions of leadership.

The Party's power derives from its control over promotions and other rewards and its ability to apply sanctions and punishments. Party committees and their branches review all promotions to positions of leadership, all transfers, and all nominations for wage raises. Its control over promotions allows the Party to reward members and activists for their execution of party policy, and has resulted in a near-monopoly of leading positions in the enterprise administration. With very few exceptions, production group leaders are either party members or trusted activists. If there are no party members in a production group, one will be transferred in if available. One of the reasons for the weaker political organization in small enterprises is the scarcity of trusted activists and party members on the shop floor. At higher levels of the leadership hierarchy the Party's monopoly of leadership positions becomes more complete.

To screen candidates for promotion and other rewards the Party must have accurate intelligence on the disposition of workers toward its policies. The Party employs two institutionalized means of intelligence-gathering and record-keeping to help this task. The first

is a system of surveillance having both formal and informal components. "Study reports" are regularly filled out by production group
leaders based on the results of political study sessions. In addition,
group leaders continually give oral "small reports" (xiaobao) on the
situation in their groups, including the disposition of individual workers. It is likely to be reported if, during political study or the work
day, a worker offers a heterodox opinion that requires criticism or reflects an unyielding attitude with regard to party policy. The report
makes its way up the party hierarchy and will sometimes come to
rest in the personnel department, where it will become part of the
worker's permanent record if the person in charge judges the matter
to be serious. More informally, workers, and especially activists, are
encouraged to report utterances and actions of their coworkers which
reflect dissent or "incorrect" attitudes. Some factories maintain a
network of informants on the shop floor that report on a regular
basis directly to the plant security department. In political meetings,
especially criticism and self-criticism sessions, workers are also
encouraged to report on their own actions and thoughts. This
occasionally results in the worker revealing new information,
because workers can never be sure what informers have reported
and self-confession usually enables them to escape any sanctions.

The second such institutionalized mechanism is the system of
political dossiers (dang'an), the files kept by the party staff in the
personnel department on each enterprise employee.[52] These records
include a complete political history of the employee and immediate
family members: class background, occupational status, political
punishments, and allegiances before 1949. Reports of informers,
evaluations of superiors, serious criticisms, warnings, and other
punishments are all recorded here. The dang'an will stay with the
worker throughout his or her life. If there is a transfer or job change,
the dang'an will be transferred also. Workers have no right to see
their files and there is a high degree of uncertainty over the eventual
consequences of detrimental materials. The files are regularly
consulted when reviewing candidates for promotion or wage raises,
and they can even influence applications for housing, the severity of
punishments for transgressions or political offenses, and the
selection of targets in political campaigns. Workers, quite understandably, are acutely concerned to keep detrimental reports out of
their files, especially since the effects of such information are so
unpredictable and a black mark can haunt an individual throughout
his or her life.

One of the functions of the plant security department is to act as the enterprise political police. It acts in those rare cases where open resistance to authority is offered by a worker or workers, or when other political or criminal offenses are committed. Security departments are not usually staffed by workers who have been promoted from the shop floor, but by demobilized soldiers, often party members, disciplined through years of military indoctrination and regimentation.[53] They are often from rural areas and their social backgrounds, experiences, and their outlooks differ from those of the rank and file worker. They organize their own investigations of suspected workers, have powers of interrogation, and question friends, coworkers, and relatives about a suspect's behavior, often maintaining their own network of informants on the shop floor. Connected with municipal public security bureaus, they can trace workers' movements outside a factory and put their homes under surveillance. They are empowered to enact a wide range of administrative punishments for which there are no trials or legal appeals, ranging from putting workers under a form of control similar to parole to sending them to prison or labor reform camps.[54] These measures are not routinely taken and few workers ever become involved with the security department, but all workers have seen security personnel at work.

The most important consequence of this system of political surveillance and control is that it makes it almost impossible for workers to organize themselves to formulate their own proposals and agendas of issues outside of party auspices and without the organization's knowledge. The communication among workers so crucial for effective political action cannot take place without the Party detecting it and applying sanctions to those involved. One activity that has been treated with consistent severity in China is political organization outside the Party; it is by definition counter-revolutionary. Where this system of surveillance is intact, workers are demobilized as a political force. If they are to participate in workplace politics and exercise voice, they must do so as isolated individuals in formally organized meetings where the Party sets the agenda and defines the issues. Once in these meetings, a formidable array of incentives are brought to bear on their behavior.

Reward Systems and Leadership Authority

The system of political surveillance and control just described can prevent organization and opposition among workers and channel their political activity into officially sponsored forms, but it cannot by itself stimulate active compliance with authority. This is accomplished through the organization of reward systems, the marriage of the enormous economic potential of the enterprise with everday patterns of party surveillance and evaluation.

Reward systems in Chinese industry encompass far more than wage and incentive practices designed to motivate work performance. Rewards are regularly linked not only to work performance, but to other realms of worker behavior as well. This has been true no less during periods when the Party has stressed production and bonuses, than during highly politicized periods. Bonuses, promotions, and wage raises have all formally involved behavior and attitudes outside the workplace. The many other rewards the enterprise has to offer are often linked informally to these behaviors and attitudes. This close connection between non-work behavior and rewards has been a distinctive feature of reward systems in Chinese industry, though it tends to be present in any real-world organization. The party's presence and surveillance function, coupled with the workers' marked economic dependence on the enterprise, move Chinese enterprises far beyond the forms of particularism which exist in most modern industrial systems.

The notion that the worker's behavior is evaluated and linked to rewards is so firmly implanted into the worker's consciousness and is such a common, accepted part of enterprise life, that there is a short-hand term used in everday language to refer to it: *biaoxian*. The word means, literally, to manifest, display, or show something that is an expression or manifestation of an underlying quality. This term applies to the vaguely-defined realm of worker behavior that is subject to leadership evaluation: behavior which indicates underlying attitudes and orientations worthy of reward. In practice, it applies to the kinds of opinions, suggestions, and criticisms voiced in meetings, the extent to which a worker exhibits an understanding and approval of party policy, willingness to accept orders without questioning them, and the ability to maintain good and cordial relations with coworkers and leaders. Needless to say, if a worker is criticized for some sort of transgression, or gains a reputation as someone who contradicts leaders and fails to accept direction, this is poor *biaoxian*. Good *biaoxian* is, in effect, compliant behavior as exhibited during participation in meetings and in day-to-day relations with leaders.

There are, however, two distinct dimensions of *biaoxian* which vary in importance according to the political climate of the country as a whole. The first is a formal, public one: a political assessment of the worker according to orthodox criteria, strictly interpreted. Has the worker exhibited a correct understanding of the current political line and actively volunteered these opinions in political study? Has the worker actively volunteered for unpaid overtime during production campaigns? Has he or she been an active instrument of party policy, "helping" coworkers comply and making timely criticisms of them if called for? The public behavior of the worker, as measured against the current party line, is the purely political dimension of *biaoxian*, the sense in which it is discussed in official newspapers and journals.[55]

A second dimension of *biaoxian* is a more informal, personal one, and is distinct from the first. This is the extent to which, in the course of the entire array of everyday activities in the work group, a worker is unfailingly helpful, cooperative, and courteous in dealings with group leaders and makes a favorable impression on them. There is more to *biaoxian* than making a public display of political rectitude. A worker must also make a personal impression on the people who evaluate performance and influence rewards. Workers learn quickly that an uncooperative, critical attitude towards group leaders and other supervisors quickly leads to bad impressions, which inevitably influence rewards regardless of positions taken in political meetings. Good evaluations are more likely when the worker maintains an agreeable attitude in the face of authority figures, agrees to run errands, take attendance, put away tools after the shift, and generally builds up good will (*ganqing*). Group leaders and other supervisors are concerned just as much with having workers who are helpful and obedient, making their jobs easier, as they are with having workers who maintain political orthodoxy.

These two dimensions of *biaoxian*, while conceptually independent, are closely related in practice. In everyday situations a devoted political activist cannot achieve favorable evaluation by using orthodox political principles against supervisors. He must express these sentiments in a way that maintains harmony with leaders and he must be helpful to leaders in other areas. By the same token, the helpful, courteous worker must also exhibit an awareness of current political issues and the proper lines to take on them. In highly politicized periods—especially the mass campaigns of past decades—the public, "political" dimension of *biaoxian* is more closely linked to rewards. In more quiescent periods, where production is stressed, the personal dimension predominates, since this is what helps leaders to achieve production goals.

Biaoxian is an important determinant of individual rewards of all types in Chinese industry, even those like production bonuses which are usually closely tied to work performance. This is because in almost every area of wage and personnel management, a broad framework of bureaucratic rules are applied quite flexibly, case-by-case, by leaders at every level of the leadership hierarchy. There has been an almost total absence of clearly specified criteria for bonuses, wage raises, and promotions. Instead, there have been general formulas subject to broad interpretation by people who apply them—for example, "good work, good politics, and high skill level." Biaoxian therefore becomes a general behavioral yardstick that leaders at every level can use personally to enforce the compliance of their subordinates, rewarding the cooperative and penalizing the uncooperative, almost without regard for their actual level of production.[56]

Wage levels, for example, are attached to individuals, not simply to job classifications, as they are so often in the United States. A worker is affixed to a wage grade and can be given a raise in grade only during a national "wage readjustment." At such times, worker performance is assessed in small groups and nominations lists are drawn up. The lists travel up the leadership hierarchy, where they are pared down and revised by committees at each level. Evaluations of workers' biaoxian play a crucial role in the process (during which dossiers are routinely consulted), especially since those who revise the lists at higher levels must rely heavily on the personal evaluations made by the workers' supervisors. The final list of workers given raises often diverges from the workers' own perceptions of the most diligent performers. This is not thought of as unusual. It is generally understood that it is just another indication of the importance of biaoxian, part of the accepted rules of the game.

The same considerations apply even to ostensibly work-related bonuses. For the most common form of bonus used in industry since 1956, workers are evaluated in small group meetings and nominated for a monthly bonus at one of three grades. The evaluations are of work performance (as measured by attainment of quotas) and biaoxian. A favorable evaluation in both areas is necessary to achieve the highest bonus consistently. Group leader evaluations play a guiding role in these cases, especially since the nominations are revised by higher-level committees who make sure that the total expenditures for bonuses do not exceed planned amounts. Because excessive reliance on *biaoxian* in the past has contributed to declining work performance, as part of the current economic reforms national policy has called for a closer link between production level and reward. This, however, is not likely to result in an elimination of *biaoxian* as a factor in determining rewards, because it is impossible to derive completely objective standards for skill and effort in different work settings, and because leaders at all levels have an active stake in using *biaoxian* to buttress their personal authority.

Biaoxian plays an even greater role in other areas of enterprise reward systems. For promotions into leading positions or office jobs or transfers to lighter kinds of work, *biaoxian* is perhaps the most important factor. Applications for enterprise housing, requests for optional supplements, and requests for employment for family members are not generally influenced by work record, but by leaders' personal impressions of workers. When a worker commits a mistake in his political or personal life and receives group criticism for it, the group leader's assessment of his attitudes and general pattern of behavior are the crucial determinant of whether or not the case will be referred to the plant administration for further action. Even in everyday work routines, assignments to the easier and more desirable jobs in a group are distributed as a function of the employee's non-work behavior.

The importance of *biaoxian* allows leaders to manipulate rewards to a considerable extent. Whether or not they choose to exercise their authority in complete accord with orthodox political criteria, their power stems from their responsibility for evaluating the non-work behavior of employees. In the past, when factories were more politicized and there were strong pressures on leaders to conform to orthodoxy, the public political behavior of workers was measured against orthodox standards and weighed more heavily in workplace evaluations. As this politicization has subsided, the more informal, personal aspects of *biaoxian* have increased in importance. However, in either case, rewards are applied according to the behavior and attitudes of workers at meetings and in personal dealings with authority figures.

Strategies of Participation and Orientations to Authority

When western social scientists use the term participation, they usually have in mind a concept that includes the articulation of interests, the bottom-up influence of decisions by individuals who pursue interests by trying to shape the decisions that affect their lives. In China, however, worker behavior in the course of participation is monitored, evaluated, and linked to a very broad array of rewards available in the enterprise. Tied into reward systems in this way, worker participation is central to the exercise of leadership authority. When leaders initiate a meeting and solicit worker participation they have clear goals in mind: the resolution of production problems, an increase in shop productivity, or the communication of a political message or new policy. Workers are aware of this and know that their behavior at the meeting will be evaluated.

This process requires workers to develop strategies of how to manifest properly compliant attitudes and behavior. There are a wide variety of individual strategies which range from active and committed compliance to the ritualistic recitation of the proper lines, as if in a dramatic performance. In some respects, it is misleading to label these behaviors strategies, because this would imply a degree of rational calculation that is not always present. These behaviors become habitual, almost second nature to employees. However, workers do sometimes plan the best way to repesent themselves.[57] The strategies they develop have many fine degrees of variation, but generally fall into two groups: competitive or activist strategies, and defensive or non-activist strategies.

For the first group of workers, participation in factory meetings represents a positive opportunity to be seized, an arena in which they can display the desired behavior that will lead to favorable evaluation and reward. Independently of whether they are genuinely committed to the ideas they espouse in such situations, and there is considerable variation in this regard, their activism is a form of competition. It tends to split workers by coopting activists to the power structure, further undermining the potential for worker solidarity in resistance to authority figures.

The competitive strategy of participation requires the employee to be positively oriented toward authorities. The hallmark of an activist is that he attempts actively to interpret leadership messages and respond in orthodox ways. In routine political study, this means not only reading articles or listening to people recite them, but trying to think of ways to comment on them, to apply the messages in them to the situation in the small group. During a campaign, this means listening closely to the speeches of enterprise officials when the tasks of the campaign are explained at mobilizational meetings (*dongyuan huiyi*). Then, in the meetings which follow during the "period of fermentation" (*yunniang qi*) in small groups, activists will be the first to respond to the party's message. This greatly aids the group leader's job of enforcing compliance. In a production campaign, the one or two activists in a group will be the first to suggest ways to increase output, to volunteer for unpaid overtime, or to exceed their quotas by large percentages, thus putting pressure on other employees to do the same. If self-criticism is required, activists will be the first to make a speech about their own shortcomings and how they will reform in the future. If an individual in the group expresses an incorrect opinion, activists will usually criticize the view without being prompted by the group leader. The rewards for activism thus prompt behavior that moves participation in the direction desired by the leadership.

For the large majority of workers, on the other hand, participation does not represent an opportunity, but a hurdle which must be negotiated to avoid losing out in the system of rewards. For these people, participation is a game in which risk-taking must be avoided. This means that safe responses must be ascertained before venturing to speak out. Non-activists usually respond to messages after seeing how the activists in the group respond, or by watching the reaction of leaders to initial worker responses. Once the desired response is clear, the non-activist will try to stay as close as possible to the orthodox version and try to avoid a deviation that could draw disapproval. This applies equally to volunteering extra efforts in production campaigns, in making self-criticisms, or expressing opinions on current political trends.

Non-activists exhibit a marked hesitancy toward expressing opinions unless they are in the presence of close and trusted friends.[58] Since the attitudes manifested during participation are continually evaluated, these workers learn through experience that carefully managing their emotions and keeping contrary opinions locked deeply inside is the safest stance to maintain. But the subjective experience of participation varies considerably according to the specific content of the meeting and the tenseness of the political atmosphere. During a campaign in which this atmosphere is tense and there are indications that the leadership may be preparing to single out individuals for criticism, participation can engender considerable anxiety and non-activists listen very attentively for indications of appropriate responses. In other periods, however, the experience is much more relaxed, with the chief difficulty being boredom and the main objective staying awake.

The heart of the non-activist's defensive strategy of participation is to avoid standing out from the rest of the group. If others in the group, usually beginning with the activists, volunteer to put forth greater efforts, the non-activist will follow suit to avoid standing out. If others in the group are criticizing a targeted group member, the non-activist joins in to avoid having his silence interpreted as dissidence. If others in the group are volunteering to spend their only day off at a mass public rally to celebrate the anniversary of the founding of the Party, the non-activist follows the tide. If a worker becomes isolated from the rest of the group he is aware that not only will social pressures be applied, but rewards will be withdrawn as well.

The caution that marks habitual defensive strategies tends to empty political participation of genuine political content by muting the articulation of interests and ideas outside the bounds of what is perceived to be acceptable. What is distinctive about worker partici-pation in Chinese industry is that individual interests are pursued precisely by *not articulating them;* by burying them in shows of compliance. This effect is not achieved through the regular application of coercion or terror, but through the routine organization of rewards and the institutionalized patterns of behavior that grow out of it. In many subtle ways, employees are consistently rewarded for manifesting active support for leaders and they are systemati-cally penalized for failing to do so. Activists compete to manifest the most outstanding support, while the rest are careful to avoid isolation from the rest of the group. Dependent on their enterprises for a very broad range of needs, and dependent on their superiors for the continual evaluations which lead to the satisfaction of these needs, workers in state enterprises comply habitually, sometimes ritualistically, with authority to preserve or pursue their interests.

Informal Networks, Patronage, and the Substance of Workplace Politics

Worker participation in formally-organized meetings, which has so captivated many observers of China, is not a mechanism for the bottom-up communication of ideas and articulation of interests. Instead, it is a mechanism for routinely mobilizing a politically-neutralized labor force toward leadership ends. As such, "mass participation" of the type that distinguishes Chinese institutions is only ephemerally related to the pursuit of workers' interests. The real decisions about who gets what and when are made elsewhere. Workers understand this clearly and it is one of the reasons they routinely restrict their exercise of voice in this public arena.

Informal relationships are the real arena for the pursuit of interests in a Chinese enterprise. In marked contrast to the bureaucratized systems of labor relations that have grown out of labor-management contention in the West, there is a distinct absence of formal rules and regulations that restrict the discretion of factory leaders. As a result, officeholders have considerable personal control over the distribution of resources and they naturally become the main targets for workers' attempts at influence.

These features of workplace social structure make the Chinese enterprise an exceedingly rich ground for the growth of informal networks of patronage. Throughout the enterprise hierarchy, the relationship between leaders and led is one in which the exchange of active loyalty and personal good will for promotion and reward has formed a well-developed system of patronage. Activists tend to work very closely with the leaders who are cultivating them. They not only actively support leadership initiatives but, as "backbone elements," they are the ones on whom group leaders habitually rely to help with other tasks: filling out reports and order forms, taking attendance, working long hours after the shift on propaganda posters, and so forth. Their help is crucial in enabling shop leaders to perform their jobs well enough to obtain favorable evaluations from their own superiors.

The activist, in turn, receives consistently favorable evaluations of *biaoxian*, which result in larger bonuses and eventual raises. Just as important are the oral and written personal recommendations that shop-floor leaders send to higher offices which may eventually provide the activist with an opportunity for promotion.[59] Admission to the Party itself is based on these personal relationships. The process requires detailed personal recommendations from two party members, one of whom must have a certain level of seniority and rank. These will often be the activist's immediate superior and a higher-ranking party member who has become acquainted with the candidate through that superior and who will personally assure the candidate's worthiness.[60] Such ties of patronage attract and bind activists to the power structure.

Just as there are both formal and informal dimensions of *biaoxian*, there are ways for non-activists to participate in these patterns of patronage and there are rewards other than those of promotion and party membership. The first rule of the game is not to alienate any leader or anyone else who is in a position to affect the distribution of rewards in the workplace. Defensive strategies of participation are one outgrowth of this rule. Another is the ceremonialized mask of politeness which many present to power-holders. But the rank-and-file worker, if so disposed, can also engage in a number of activities designed to win the personal good will of officeholders in a position to affect their lives. These activities usually involve personal favors of some sort, including attentive helpfulness, willingness to run errands and assist beyond the normal call of duty, or such work for the cadre's personal benefit as making repairs to his home and furnishings for free. The favors more commonly involve small gifts presented directly to the cadre, or allowing the cadre to share in some special "connection" the worker may personally enjoy—for example, a friend who works in a store who is willing to set aside scarce consumer goods when a shipment arrives.[61] The cultivation of relations with such officials as the immediate superior, the union staff, the staff of the general affairs department, or factory doctors can affect a broad range of decisions outside the normal realm of promotion and pay. Decisions regarding the assignment of factory housing, the distribution of supplementary wages or ration tickets, the granting of paid sick leave, the hiring of family members, and even punishment for disapproved behavior, can all be influenced by these purely personal ties.[62] Since workers in large enterprises tend to stay with their enterprises throughout their working lives, time and expense invested over the years cultivating these personal ties can bring significant benefits later on.

The importance of the pursuit of interests through informal networks is reflected in the language used to describe workplace politics. Any tie between two unrelated people of different social status having behavioral consequences of the sort described above, is described by the term *guanxi*. But such a connection can be strong or weak and can vary in emotive content. When it is strong and is overlaid with personal feelings of consideration and affection, there is said to exist *ganqing* or *renqing*, "feeling" or "human sentiments." These are the most powerful types of *guanxi*. These personalized patterns of pursuing interests by forging ties between people of different social status are identical to those practiced traditionally in pre-revolutionary economic situations,[63] and the terms *ganqing* and *guanxi* are those used most often when contemporary factory employees describe the pursuit of interests. Quite justifiably, Chinese workers tend to see the formal hierarchy of offices as a hollow shell overlaid with informal networks that determine how the organization actually operates.[64] Attempts to pursue interests or exercise influence necessarily involve these informal relationships.

The chains of patronage, which stretch from the top of the enterprise hierarchy to the bottom, are commonly referred to as "factions" or "cliques" (*paibie*). They form informal power structures which employees tend to see as the "real" political arenas in the enterprise. At the same time, they form ladders of career advancement. Very often there are two such cliques in an enterprise (if not more) which continually jockey with one another for power. The source of this kind of factionalism varies considerably according to the particular circumstances and history of the enterprise. It may result from long-standing competition between a party secretary and a plant director; generations of leaders with different backgrounds absorbed by the enterprise at different periods; commonplace struggles between departments with different claims to authority and different priorities (for example, production and technical departments versus the party apparatus and its propaganda and security departments). To the extent that there is political contention within an enterprise, it is among these kinds of informal factional networks. The contention is often subtle and subdued, but it can be overt and bitter.[65] Workers participate in these struggles as the lowest-ranking clients in a network.

The significance of these informal networks for the formally-organized political life of the enterprise is that a worker-activist who enjoys close ties with a factional network is able to speak out more boldly in meetings. When an activist speaks out in a forthright manner on political topics, or initiates criticisms of others, it is generally understood by other workers that the person must have personal backing, that "someone behind the scenes" (*houtai ren*) is sponsoring the performance. A worker has to be aware of the ebb and flow of factional undercurrents before venturing to speak out in this way. Members of the factory leadership or staff who have been criticized and punished during the political campaigns of past years have tended to be members of staff offices which are not aligned with any party factions and thus fall outside their protection,[66] or people who were leading rivals of the dominant faction. In either case, the targets of campaigns are chosen as a result of informal political considerations and well-connected activists venture such criticisms only with the political backing of their patrons. The mass criticism of formally-organized political life is only an epiphenomenon of these deeper-seated informal patterns of political contention.

While informal patterns of the pursuit of interest are central to the political strategies of workers, they do not represent "workers' politics," a crucial distinction. Workers can pursue their interests through these networks as individuals, as clients of people who occupy positions of influence and may be able to make their own lives more secure and prosperous. The overall effect of these informal patterns is to humanize and personalize a rather authoritarian system of labor relations, and in so doing further stabilize it by providing a parallel web of personal obligations. Yet workers pursue their interests as clients, not as workers. The crucial social ties are vertical, spanning the social hierarchy, rather than horizontal, among workers. Workers pursue their interests in these networks as isolated individuals oriented to people of higher status, rather than as a group defined by common social characteristics and pursuing group objectives. These informal networks therefore allow workers to pursue their interests only in ways which serve to divide them internally and bind them closely to authorities.[67] Of the entire range of political behavior, the closest thing to a workers' politics is the activity of workers who organized themselves into groups during a brief period at the beginning of the Cultural Revolution.[68] Even then, as we will see presently, the resulting patterns of collective action bore the indelible stamp of the social structure we have so far described.

Collective Action in the Cultural Revolution

Factionalism is the immediately striking feature of worker involvement in the Cultural Revolution, one which is in marked contrast with the Polish workers' movement of 1980-81. Workers formed many organizations which had different political orientations and actively opposed each other, in some instances fighting armed street battles. The origins of this mass factionalism, determinants of individual orientations, decisions whether to participate, targets of collective action, and style of collective action were straightforward outgrowths of the social structure of the work force and the informal social structure of the workplace.[69] This extraordinary episode of politics was a direct outgrowth of ordinary workplace politics, which alone makes intelligible the behavior of workers during the Cultural Revolution.

Our analysis of the social structure of the work force yields some predictions about where workers organizations of different orientations are most likely to emerge. "Conservative" organizations of the period were protective of the party hierarchy and the economic status quo. We would expect them to arise most often among permanent workers in the larger state enterprises, where vested interests in the enterprise are great, the party organization is active and well-organized, and workers are more fully oriented to a workplace social structure where patterns of patronage and reward are closely interwoven with the official party hierarchy. The "rebel" organizations were critical of existing political and economic arrangements and were anxious to pull them down. We would expect them to arise more often among other segments of the labor force, where vested interests in the enterprise are less compelling or negligible, the party organization is less active and well-organized, workers are less fully oriented to workplace social structures, and patterns of patronage and reward are not well integrated with the official party hierarchy.

These structural divisions in the labor force do indeed seem to explain a good part of the variation in worker orientations, or at least where specific orientations are more likely to predominate. Hong Yung Lee has found that conservative worker organizations took the names of large state factories much more frequently than did their rivals. His documentary evidence from movement newspapers in Canton also indicates that conservative allegiances predominated among workers in the large state enterprises there.[70] In Shanghai, not only does the evidence indicate that members of the large conservative organization, the *chiwei dui* ("scarlet guards"), were predominantly permanent workers in state enterprisee, but it has been fairly well established that the organization had close ties with the Party and was headquartered in the city's official labor union office building.[71] Segments of the work force outside of this core group of permanent state workers, on the other hand, appear to have gravitated more often toward radical organizations. The role in rebel organizations of workers marginal to state industry, especially various kinds of urban and rural temporaries, is already well-known and need not be elaborated here.[72] They were among the first to denounce local authorities and demand that the economic systems affecting their work status be reformed. Lee also finds some documentary evidence to suggest that workers from small state enterprises and collective factories were more active in rebel organizations than in others.[73] The evidence is still fragmentary, but the broad patterns uncovered so far clearly suggest that the social structure of the workplace conditioned worker political activity precisely in the ways one would expect.

These broad divisions in the workplace explain some of the variation in worker orientations, but by no means all of it.

Workplace social structure is another dimension which powerfully shaped worker orientations. Among permanent workers in state enterprises, participation in the Cultural Revolution was an outgrowth of routine patterns of participation in workplace politics. Those who previously had practiced "competitive" and "defensive" strategies of participation tended to do the same during the Cultural Revolution. The movement also opened up a new role for workers: the rebel activist dedicated to criticizing and pulling apart the old power structure.[74] But those who chose this role did so for reasons which were rooted in routine patterns of workplace politics.[75]

Conservative workers, or "royalists" (baohuang pai, literally "protectors of the emperor"), were the workers who had been closely aligned with informal networks of party-sponsored patronage before the Cultural Revolution. They were prototypical "activists," group leaders and assistant group leaders, rank-and-file party members, model workers, youth league members, and other recognized "backbone elements" who were generally able to mobilize other workers in their factories into a "quasi-active" participation which resembled the defensive strategies activists employed before the Cultural Revolution. Among the non-activists in a factory, veteran workers with the higher wage grades and vested interests that came with their seniority tended more often to align themselves with conservative groups in this quasi-active way.[76] The criticisms these groups made of the party officials who had been their patrons were generally mild and politely stated. Instead, they tended to target non-party factory administrators and staff, especially those with questionable class backgrounds and personal histories. These were precisely the kind of targets typically chosen in party-sponsored campaigns in the past, and the activity of conservative workers was an outgrowth of these standard patterns and their associated mentality. Conservative groups had no desire to pull apart existing structures of power, since their leadership core benefited directly from it.

Rebel workers (zaofan pai) were not always uniformly outside informal networks of patronage. Rather, the active core of rebel groups came precisely from those who had tried activist strategies in the past and had failed to be successful at it, and from those who had been victimized, often unjustly, by the official network and received damaging marks on their records at an early age.[77] They were generally able to recruit non-activist workers who had the fewest vested interests in their enterprises or in existing arrangements. These were typically young workers, without spouses or family to support, at low pay grades and with little accumulated seniority, and apprentice workers who were still paid subsistence allowances as part of their fixed training period.[78] These rebel groups generally ignored non-party administrators and experts and were unconcerned with the class backgrounds and political histories of the factory leadership. They moved directly against the core party leadership hierarchy of the enterprise, accusing it of corruption and abuse of power. They raided party offices and pulled officials to mass repudiation meetings where they were subjected to shouted accusations, epithets, and sometimes physical abuse. It was a daring course of action, a gamble that Mao Zedong genuinely supported their actions and that these officials would not be able to take revenge at a later date.[79] Those who took this course were those who had the most to gain and the least to lose.[80]

The majority of an enterprise's workers initially remained either unattached to conservative and rebel activities, or participated in them in nominal ways. Theirs was a continuation of the defensive strategies of participation. Sometimes they formed "moderate" (*wenhe*) groups that wrote wallposters and raised carefully reasoned and restrained criticisms of leadership practices, in part because this activity was expected of them. But more often they were members of what they referred to, tongue-in-cheek, as the "tea drinking faction" (*hecha pai*), or the "carefree faction" (*xiaoyao pai*). These were the many workers who were relatively uninvolved observers of, or lukewarm participants in, the Cultural Revolution. When conservative or rebel groups organized factory rallies they might attend, but only if asked directly. When faction members formed "fighting groups" and went out to participate in public rallies, demonstrations, or street fighting, these workers stayed in the factory and worked as long as their supplies held out. The unmarried ones might travel about the country on "exchanges of revolutionary experience," but primarily with tourism in mind. When factional struggles turned violent inside the factory, these workers stayed home. When pressures were applied by them to participate in one of the two main factions, they joined so as not to be isolated and subject to criticism for "not supporting the Cultural Revolution." Many joined conservative groups as a logical extension of their normal defensive strategies of participation, but quietly left when it became unclear whether conservative groups had the official blessing. As the Cultural Revolution wore on, self-preservation made it necessary to side with one or another group, and they usually chose the side that appeared to be winning. The originally predominant "carefree" faction shrank to a small minority, swelling the nominal ranks of the major factions.[81]

Just as individual worker orientations and patterns of participation were a natural outgrowth of routine patterns of workplace politics, the distinctive targets and style of workers' collective actions were shaped by the features of workplace social structure. One common activity of rebel groups was the storming of factory offices in search of official documents, especially the personnel files containing evaluations of worker behavior (dang'an). The rebel groups sometimes published lists of informers and released materials to other workers to illustrate the kinds of suspicions and undocumented charges that could find their way into personnel files.[82] Sometimes they removed such "black materials" and destroyed them. When rebels raided personnel offices in search of dang'an, they were attacking not just a symbol, but a central institutionalized prop of the enterprise power structure.

Animosities were often directed at enterprise officials personally. When rebels made demands, they were usually accompanied by a denunciation of the targeted official. Factory officials were dragged to mass repudiation meetings where they were publicly humiliated, forced to kneel and bow their heads to the masses, confess their mistakes and beg the masses' forgiveness, enduring insults and sometimes repeated kicks and blows in the process. Some were imprisoned in makeshift cells where they remained for months, writing endless confessions and being made to sweep the factory floors during the day. It is highly unusual in industrial societies for the targets of workers' movements to be personalized to this extent. Collective demands are usually made to institutions or groups. Class hatreds are generalized animosities, but the hatreds of these workers were vented directly at specific individuals. In a very real sense, the ritualistic self-criticisms and personal humiliations endured by these officials were simply a mirror image of the self-effacement workers ritually performed in front of leaders in factory meetings. This personalization of conflict was a direct outgrowth of the system of officially-organized patronage that personalized social control and rewards to an extent unusual in other industrial settings. These aspects of mass worker behavior during the Cultural Revolution, as senseless and irrational as they sometimes seemed, were rooted in a logic derived from the distinctive structure of Chinese work institutions.

Workers' collective action during the Cultural Revolution, in sum, never quite broke free from the premises of routine workplace politics. Vertical ties of patronage that had earlier served to divide workers as a group continued to do so. The result was a crippling factionalism that prevented them from acting as workers rather than as clients of higher political figures. The Cultural Revolution represented less a break from previous patterns of politics than their continuation by another means. As enterprise revolutionary committees demobilized workers' organizations and built new power structures — with a militantly expanded role for *biaoxian*, for investigations, *dang'an*, and officially supervised political activities — the role of personalized patronage increased and workplace politics reverted smoothly into its familiar patterns. New chains of patronage were forged and the forms of administration altered, but the substance of workplace politics and patterns of participation and social control remained the same.

Non-Political Influence: "Hidden Bargaining" in the Factory

For party officials and economic bureaucrats, the political demobilization of workers is indispensable for a planned approach to rapid economic development. It insulates the economy from demands that would inevitably reduce the rate of investment. But no matter how effectively group politics is restricted, the system cannot completely insulate economic decision making from important kinds of non-political influence, especially in periods when economic policy is in flux and national leaders view increases in worker productivity as a major priority. Under these conditions, workers can wield very real non-political influence over the implementation of policies that affect their lives and, indirectly, over the making of these policies, by withholding their cooperation and work effort in a form of "hidden bargaining."

For this kind of non-political influence to be effective, two conditions must be met. First, factory managers must have the autonomy to shape incentive policies flexibly and they must have the ability to determine the size and distribution of incentive pay. If managers have no flexibility in this regard, there is no policy implementation for workers to influence at the factory level. Second, national leaders must place considerable emphasis on industrial productivity in general, and labor productivity in particular. To the extent that increases in productivity are valued highly by national leaders, who in turn put pressures on factory managers, the value of worker cooperation and discipline is enhanced.

Neither of these conditions were met in China for more than a decade prior to 1978. Managers after 1966 were allowed virtually no flexibility in wage matters: incentive pay was prohibited and the factory wage bill was fixed. While the national leadership paid lip service to increasing productivity through discipline and hard work, the weakness of fiscal controls and adherence to output as the only measure of enterprise performance reflected the low priority placed on industrial productivity. The highly factionalized national leadership of that period subsidized industrial inefficiency with continued high rates of industrial investment that caused imbalances in the economy as a whole. Average real wages in industry declined by almost 20 percent, and as a response absenteeism and slack work discipline grew to legendary proportions. Yet management was relatively indifferent to the problem.[83] Industry continued to muddle through in the 1970s thanks to its favored place in the national budget.

Industrial reforms and economic readjustment after 1978 created the necessary conditions for worker influence at the factory level. It gave enterprises greater autonomy in distributing incentives and greatly raised demands for productivity. Wage levels were raised, incentive pay was restored, and managers given considerable autonomy in shaping new bonus systems. New incentive funds were created in enterprises that for the first time allowed total bonus pay to vary with attained profits. Profit was reasserted as the primary measure of enterprise performance and factory managers were offered productivity incentives in the form of a profit retention system. The government began to enforce its new stress on industrial efficiency by redirecting investment to long-neglected sectors of the economy and by gradually tightening loans and credit to inefficient enterprises.[84] In short, worker cooperation and discipline on the job became an increasingly valuable commodity and at the same time wage policies were made flexible at the factory level. More than ever, managers needed the cooperation of workers and they now had financial means at their disposal to encourage this cooperation.

Workers responded to the new situation in a way designed to protect their interests in two areas: first, to ensure the highest wage possible under new conditions, especially in order to offset the declining real wage of past years; and second, to ensure that the new bonus standards were fair both in the amount of work demanded and in the performance measures used. Attendance and performance improved gradually in response to the new incentives. But, workers also regulated the improvement carefully, sometimes withholding cooperation in order to defend their interests.

Press accounts as well as emigré interviews reveal a number of the methods used by workers to influence the shaping of new factory incentive policy during these years. As soon as managers set output quotas, workers returned to the universal strategy of output regulation to maximize income. They shunned quotas set too high and carefully restricted output, in some cases holding back pieces to prevent a revision of norms on jobs that were set at manageable rates. The setting of new quotas after many years of laxness also provoked contention on the shop floor, with whole work sections reportedly engaging in slowdowns. Individual arguments over revisions began to break out with increasing regularity. Group evaluations of worker performance for wage raises and bonuses stimulated arguments about the fairness of the criteria used to assess performance and often delayed final decisions. In some cases workers openly refused jobs for which quotas were felt to be impossibly tight and increasingly harassed activists as "rate busters" who broke informal group norms about restricting output.[85] As workers attempted to act on the shop floor to shape the new incentive policies in accord with their interests they created troublesome new problems for factory managers.

Managers, themselves under new pressures to perform, needed to increase productivity while maintaining harmony in labor relations. Their entirely rational response was to distribute as bonuses the maximum amount feasible under existing regulations (and sometimes more), while maintaining a relatively loose link between reward and actual work performance. The first resulted in widespread overexpenditures on bonuses, with managers sometimes illegally diverting funds from other accounts, and rates of increase in bonus expenditures unrelated to enterprise performance. The second led to practices within enterprises that were quickly criticized as "egalitarianism": the distribution of bonuses on an equal basis, very small gradations in bonus size, or vague bonus criteria that weakened the link between output and pay.[86] These results, viewed as deviant implementation of policy by national leaders, were in large part a response to problems created by workers on the shop floor.

By 1980 national leaders began to adjust their own policies in response. That year marked a loss of enthusiasm for monetary rewards as the sole instrument for increased productivity. Increased emphasis was placed on combining bonuses with invigorated political work by party branches and the enforcement of punishments for violations of labor discipline. In May 1982 a new set of strengthened punitive regulations were passed and widely publicized, which were aimed at problems with enterprise personnel, including management diversion of funds for bonuses and worker restriction of output. New trial policies were announced that allowed the basic wage itself to fall if performance did not meet minimum standards and specified renewable job contracts for newly-hired permanent workers, thus threatening both wage and job security. And tighter restrictions on enterprise expenditures of retained funds were put into effect, thus reducing some of the increased enterprise autonomy that had been the main feature of the reforms.[87]

This example illustrates both the strength and weakness of the largely hidden influence that workers can exercise by bargaining informally with their performance. On the one hand, workers appear to have successfully defended their interests by influencing the implementation of new wage policies. In so doing, they diverted the course of industrial reform from some of its original intentions, requiring adjustments by national policy-makers and no doubt affecting the strength of different opinion groups in the leadership. On the other hand, workers appear to be able to influence policy implementation at the grass roots much more effectively than they can influence subsequent rounds of policy-making. In this case, worker influence at the factory level has provoked an increased stress on punitive measures by the national leadership which, if actually implemented in factories, would represent a setback to their interests.

While the changes that have taken place in China since Mao have opened up new opportunities for workers to influence wage policy at the factory level, they have not fundamentally changed the political rules of the game in other respects. State enterprises remain the central point of distribution for most public goods and services and the Party continues to recruit and favor its clients. If anything, recent changes in economic policy will increase the volume of resources that enterprises are able to distribute, thus reinforcing the broader clientelist patterns described in this chapter. However, by making wage policy more flexible, China after Mao has enhanced opportunities for informal influence over wage patterns.

Conclusions

China's workers are able to pursue their interests in a variety of ways. They are a social group that is divided into five distinct subgroups, each with different standards of living, relationships to political institutions, positions in the national economy, and aspirations and interests. Yet, close examination reveals that despite fairly clear group boundaries based on common economic position, "group politics," even on an informal basis, is barely evident. The only political activity that can be interpreted as having a group basis is the "hidden bargaining" described in the preceding section of this chapter, but even this requires hardly any group organization and involves largely silent obstruction rather than open articulation of group interests.

More important than the absence of group politics is the presence of political activity organized overwhelmingly along network rather than group lines. Workers may enjoy very little mutual communication and organization, but their condition is by no means one of social atomization. The Chinese enterprise, a focal point for the distribution of goods and services, is laden with vertical networks through which individual workers seek protection, advancement, and personal advantage. Some of these ties are strong, enduring ones between the party organization and its loyal activist-clients on the shop floor. Others involve weaker, less stable ties relied on only for occasional exchanges of favors. In either case, the worker seeks a relationship with someone of a different social status, not with other workers. Networks, not groups, provide the crucial structural framework for a clientelist political system.

There is one final implication of this analysis: the study of political participation can tell us much more than simply the degree to which citizens can exercise influence. From the actor's viewpoint, the activity that constitutes participation is designed to attain certain consciously intended outcomes. But the sum total of these activities has an impact independent of the actors' intentions. A political system that successfully channels the political activity of citizens into individual efforts to maintain ties that cut across social statuses is not going to be challenged readily, or effectively, from below. The informal social networks that result from this political activity are perhaps the single most important source of political stability in the Chinese regime.

CHAPTER 4

Political Participation of Peasants in China

John Burns

Introduction

In 1970 a brigade in Taishan county in southern Guangdong, was asked to build a road linking it more directly to commune headquarters.[1] The brigade revolutionary (later, management) committee had to determine through which of several production teams the road would pass — that is, which teams would give up land for the road. In the discussion that followed, during which it became obvious that each committee member was trying to ensure that the road would not be built through his own production team, it was finally decided that the road should pass through the land of three of ten teams making up the brigade (the three teams which were underrepresented on the committee).

Peasants of the three affected teams were, not surprisingly, upset, and demanded compensation from the brigade. When this was refused, the three teams withheld laborers from the road building project. That year they also refused to contribute to the annual levy to defray brigade expenses. In exasperation, brigade officials eventually ordered the remaining teams in the brigade to send laborers to clear new land for the three teams, equivalent to the land taken up by the road. The three teams then resumed provisioning the brigade.

In this example, peasants first attempted to protect their interests from encroachment by the revolutionary committee. When discussions through institutional channels failed to move brigade officials, peasants were prepared to use more informal and illegitimate means to press the brigade for compensation, means which in the above case were successful.

This episode, one of many such instances, offers a vivid illustration of the willingness and capacity of peasants to exert effective

91

pressure on policymakers when their interests are engaged. But if it dispels earlier notions of peasant passivity, it leaves many questions unanswered. Are such cases the norm or the exception? What do such examples imply about the significance of local forms of civic pressure for policy-making? Should they be seen as constituting a form of political action or economic action? What are the implications of such village-based interest articulation for China's developmental needs?

No questions are more important than these in a country still largely rural and poor. Indeed, recent press statements have attributed much of the success of the past several years to steadfast local resistance to bureaucratic pressure, which created grass roots economic democracy for rural development. Instances of failure have been blamed on the periodic ineffectuality of peasant participation in the face of political pressure from above. The unprecedented peasant demonstrations in Beijing in 1978 and 1979, then, were simply a more visible and less orthodox manifestation of a longstanding pattern of peasant activism.

The aim of this chapter is to look at the pattern of peasant participation in the political process, analyzing rural institutions and channels of participation and the characteristic patterns of political action in the 1960s and 1970s. What channels are provided by the regime? Under what conditions, on which issues, and how effectively do peasants participate? And, what alternatives to these channels exist?

This chapter, which uses documentary analysis and interview data,[2] is based on the view that local work and residence unit participation must be treated as an integral form of national participation. There has been some skepticism about the "political" character of this participation or its capacity to directly influence central decision processes. However, it seems clear that in a collectivized agricultural setting where politics reaches down to the village level through a direct party presence and where government intervention in the production cycle is pervasive, participation at this micro level is both political and linked to policy formulation. This is particularly true given the experimental character of policy-making in China, which blurs to a unique degree the distinction between implementation and formulation.

Decisions are taken at all levels in the bureaucracy, depending on the issue at stake. Final decisions taken by duly constituted authority, such as the decision to build a road through particular production teams, are taken locally. To exclude local decision making from the concept of participation, then, would be arbitrary and logically unjustifiable. These decisions may affect fewer people than decisions made at higher levels, and the stakes in them may be smaller, but they are nonetheless policy decisions.

Government directives are implemented by team and brigade officials, who are seen by villagers as at least part-time representatives of the state. Through the public security apparatus, they have the authority of the state to carry out governmental policy. Brigade officials in particular are held accountable by the state for fulfilling state production plans. Most brigade officials are also party members, and thus part of a national organizational hierarchy extending to Beijing, which parallels, overlaps with, and controls the governmental hierarchy. Therefore the brigade should be seen as an extension of party-government authority. To influence party officials in the brigade is to influence public authority. Insofar as production team management committees make authoritative decisions (and they do, on some issues), and are integrated into the national party organization, they also should be seen as objects of peasant influence which can properly be called political participation. Political participation, then, means "activity by private citizens designed to influence governmental decision-making."[3]

Interests and Policy in Doctrinal Perspective

Chinese policymakers themselves have recognized political participation from diverse political and social sectors as legitimate and have sought to accommodate it to consolidate their power and enhance the capabilities of the policy-making system.[4] For most of the past thirty years, the Chinese government has distinguished different levels of interests in Chinese society (individual, collective, and state), and has recognized that they may not always coincide. Official China has also recognized the interests of peasants as a class, with the interests of some strata within the peasantry receiving special attention. Some (landlords and rich peasants) were specifically discriminated against and denied the right of political participation, while the interests of others (middle peasants) were actively protected during some periods.[5]

Finally, the interests of other groups in rural Chinese society, such as those based on the number of skilled workers per household (or labor power), have been officially recognized at least implicitly since the Great Leap Forward. Given, then, the official view which

acknowledges that China is composed of diverse but legitimate
interests, it is not surprising that channels were provided by the
authorities for individuals and groups to influence government
decision making.

The Party has been concerned to protect individual peasant interests even during periods of rapid change, a pattern especially
evident during cooperativization. A 1953 directive on autumn distribution work, for example, stated that: "the individual interests of
co-op members should receive first attention and a guarantee should
be given to members that their actual incomes will not be lower than
the levels they attained before joining the co-ops, but in excess of
such levels."[6] Discrimination against the individual interests of
peasants by mutual aid teams and co-ops was strictly forbidden
during this period.[7] More recently Chinese authorities have stressed
the importance of protecting the interests of peasant households as
new policies which encourage small group and household farming
have been implemented.

The Party's answer to the problem of conflicts between individual and collective interests has been to deny them, at least in the
long-term. "Personal interests are indivisible from the public
interests of the country and society: . . . they are one and the same."[8]
Locally, peasants were encouraged to see their interests in terms of
the interests of their collective production unit. Sayings such as "If
the big river has water, the little ones are sure to be full"[9] and "As
the river rises, the boats go up,"[10] popular in the countryside, clearly
identified individual peasant interests with those of the collective.
Peasants perceived that their welfare, particularly their income, was
at least in part dependent on collective effort. As the propaganda
Bureau of the Fujian Provincial CCP Committee stated in a 1962
report: "Our emphasis on the collective is for the purpose of further
assuring and satisfying the good of each individual."[11]

The Party has officially accepted that the peasants as a group
have interests particular to them,[12] and that within the peasantry
there are conflicts of interests. Indeed, peasants have been
encouraged to see themselves in class categories.[13]

Authorities allowed the different strata within the peasantry,
with the exception of landlords and rich peasants, to pursue their
own interests during cooperativization. The *People's Daily* in 1955,
for example, criticized poor peasant cadres for retaliating against
middle peasants who had excluded poor peasants from their co-op,
and went on to say: "In the leading organs of the agricultural
producer's cooperative there must be upper-middle peasant cadres

representing the interests of the upper-middle peasants."[14] The implication was, then, that upper-middle peasants had interests of their own which could legitimately be pursued and, moreover, that cadres from their own class background could best protect those interests.

During the 1960s and 1970s class designations ceased to be meaningful behavioral categories in the countryside. Class divisions within the peasantry were replaced by a new conflict of interest between labor-rich and labor-poor households and production units, a conflict that has received scant recognition in official sources. The Lianjiang Documents, however, did recognize a "serious polarization" among households based on labor power, particularly when contracting output to the household was practiced in 1960-62.[15] Press reports of "affluent" or "rich" middle peasants also hint at this conflict. It has, however, not been explicitly mentioned in public policy documents.

Recognizing that different occupational groups and strata within various classes have their own interests, the Party has created a wide range of institutions in rural China, some of them organizationally unique, to mobilize and channel rural political participation. Where these channels have not been available, peasants have attempted to influence higher levels in the administrative hierarchy through informal, usually illegitimate and semilegal means, such as passive resistance or open defiance.

Institutions of Political Participation

One of the most dramatic changes in village society since 1949 has been in the organizational life of the peasantry. The party and government have actively sought to organize rural life and institutionalize channels for peasant participation. This has resulted, from 1962 to 1984, in a three-level system of organization in the countryside. Twenty to forty households were organized into production teams, the basic unit of ownership and accounting for most of rural China. Ten or so production teams were organized into production brigades, the seat of most local party branches in the countryside. These were further organized into communes, ranging in size from 20,000 to 40,000 people. By the early 1980s, there were approximately 50,000 communes in China.[16] Meetings of peasants and local cadres; elections of local leaders; work and investigation team activities at local levels; the media; and mass organizations such as peasants' associations, have all served as channels for peasant attempts to influence decision making.

Meetings

Authorities have encouraged peasants to attend a wide range of mass meetings called regularly and frequently at team and brigade levels.[17] Often, especially during campaigns, mass meetings were called to mobilize the peasants for a particular task, or to inform them of a new policy or directive. But officials also called mass meetings during which they asked peasants to make decisions, the outcomes of which were not predetermined, and which depended on peasant action at least as much as on the action of cadres. Such meetings have dealt with a variety of issues, including the distribution of work points and agricultural planning. Meetings of peasants at the production-team level have usually been more effective forums for political participation than meetings at the brigade level. Brigade-level mass meetings are usually very large, with an attendance of perhaps one or two thousand people and have been called infrequently since 1962 (except during the height of the Cultural Revolution).[18]

One illustration of peasant influence over a brigade decision occurred in a 1971 case in Taishan county. The private plot distribution system, in use since 1961, became an issue in the brigade because there had been no readjustment of private plots for ten years to take into account demographic changes.[19] The brigade asked all of its constituent production teams to call mass meetings to give team members an opportunity to express their opinions on the private plot distribution issue.

Each team held its own meeting, chaired by its team leader. According to one participant: "The team members' opinions reflected their own interests. Some said to retain the present system of distribution, others wanted changes." Those with large families in 1961 had been given large private plots and thus wanted the original distribution to be maintained. New households without private plots or households that had grown since 1961 demanded a readjustment. When, one month later, team cadres were summoned by the brigade to report on the meetings, it emerged that there was an overwhelming sentiment for readjustment.

The uncertainties of the 1971 Lin Biao affair made these meetings an effective forum for peasant demands. Although some peasant households had been dissatisfied with the system for many years, they did not raise the issue formally until 1971, when commune and county governments were preoccupied with political instability in Beijing. Before that time even the existence of private plots had sometimes been questioned. The peasants had, however, grumbled and complained in private. By 1971 peasants had considerable support from some local cadres, who were just as eager for the readjustment. Still, the initiative in this case came from the brigade, which put the issue formally on the agendas of production team mass meetings.

Elections

Although village officials have usually appointed team leaders, occasionally village cadres have permitted peasants to elect team leaders directly.[20] Detailed regulations setting out the process of village and production team elections have never been published.[21] Nonetheless, we do know that where authorities have called elections at this level, usually either brigade officials, in consultation with current team cadres, or the current team cadres themselves, nominate candidates for membership on the five- to seven-person team management committee. Local officials call an election meeting during which team members can make further additions to the list of nominees. However, there are rarely more nominees than management committee posts. Peasants usually vote by a show of hands and the resulting list of new management committee members is forwarded to the brigade for review and approval. The team leader, deputy leader, accountant, cashier, and storehouse keeper are selected by the brigade from among the elected committee members. But peasants expect that the candidate with the most votes will become the new team leader.

Many villagers have been unwilling to serve in cadre posts[22] because the work can be time-consuming and because they risk alienating their friends, relatives, and neighbors as they attempt to implement (sometimes unpopular) state and party policies. Still, the benefits have been sufficient to attract many villagers to assume these responsibilities at one time or another. Cadre status brings higher income and better educational and job opportunities that can be passed on to relatives.[23] In addition, the educational system emphasizes service to others and tends to act as a ormative incentive, countering peasant unwillingness to serve.

Production team elections can be used to pressure brigade cadres to make policy changes.[24] For example, in 1968 a new party secretary was sent to a brigade in suburban Guangdong to replace a secretary dismissed for political deviations during the Cultural Revolution. The new secretary adopted a series of "radical" policies. Under his direction, the brigade took over the ownership of fishponds and bamboo groves, which production teams had previously owned and from which they derived a substantial income. There was considerable opposition to this move not only among production team leaders and peasants but among other brigade cadres.

To silence criticism from the production teams, the new secretary cultivated leaders from minority lineages in each of several production teams as candidates for team leadership positions. In 1972 the current leader of one team had opposed the new secretary and received the most votes. Team members therefore expected him to remain in his post, but the new secretary passed over him in favor of the minority-lineage candidate. This infuriated the majority lineage in the team, who had backed the original team leader, and they retaliated by refusing to follow the directives of the new team leader. Output and incomes declined as a result, a situation that continued for over a year.

In 1973 the team members again gave most votes to the original majority-lineage team leader, in open defiance of the new secretary's wishes. By this time, however, the dissension within the brigade had reached the commune's attention, and a work team composed of five commune cadres was sent to investigate. Its imminent arrival may have encouraged the secretary to change his mind. In any case, he was transferred back to the commune administration, the former party branch secretary was returned to office, and the fish ponds and bamboo groves were returned to the production teams.

Elections by themselves may not have been a determining factor in the personnel and policy changes that occurred in the team and brigade. But their results were a signal of peasant support for a particular leader and of longstanding conflicts over the team members' income. The brigade's ability to impose a solution on the team under these circumstances was significantly weakened by the dissension within the brigade's own leadership.

Work Teams

Policy implementation in China has been aided by the dispatch of work teams (gongzuo dui) from higher levels to local units to investigate local conditions, collect data for future policy-making, and discover and solve problems in the process of carrying out current policy. Work teams also function as a channel through which peasants can participate in politics.

Work teams receive peasant demands and often either act on them to make changes on the spot, or report them back to higher levels. They are most likely to act on peasant demands when the policy being carried out by the work team coincides with peasants' perceived interests.[25]

In addition to implementing campaigns, work teams also are sent out on an *ad hoc* basis to make leadership changes at local levels, or on a more regular, even routine, basis to enforce production plans and to correct production deviations. Both campaign and non-campaign work teams have served as institutions through which peasants can participate in politics in rural China.

An example is provided by the work team which came to investigate the disunity of the suburban Guangdong brigade reported above. The work team was dispatched from the commune in 1974 as a result of concern about disunity in the brigade leadership group. It consisted of five commune-level cadres, three of whom lived at the brigade headquarters for one year, the duration of the investigation. They went frequently to the production teams, investigating their relationship to the brigade. After getting an initial briefing from the brigade secretary, the work team spent little time with him or other brigade cadres.

Production team members were willing to talk to the work team from the outset. Although peasants did not take the initiative to seek out work team members, they did not require a conclusive demonstration of work team power before they would speak out. This was probably because the work team members were not outsiders, as they usually are during national campaigns, but came from the commune to which they would return when the investigation was completed.

In addition, the scope of the work team's investigation was narrowly circumscribed, which was reflected in its procedures. Mass struggle meetings were not held, although the work team chaired brigade party branch meetings which were called to criticize the new secretary. One participant later observed: "He [the new secretary] was frightened, and had no power. The work team had the power to manage production. The work team also chaired brigade meetings, not him. . . . If a production team in the brigade had a problem it went to the work team."[26] The work team investigated brigade sideline production accounts and discovered several problems. Brigade records were badly kept and the accountant was taken briefly to the commune for questioning. "Still no mass meetings were held, and no explanations given. Everyone knew there was disorder in the accounts and the peasants were dissatisfied about it. They told the work team how they felt."[27] After the year-long investigation, the commune decided that the new secretary should be transferred out of the brigade. As noted above, the old secretary resumed his post and the team sidelines were restored.

In this example there was a close connection between the interests of one group of peasants and the goal of the work team. Peasants of the dominant lineages in the production team who had opposed the new secretary demanded that action be taken to restore the original situation. The work team agreed that such action would coincide with its interest in restoring unity to the brigade. The work team was therefore receptive to the influence of dominant-lineage production team members.

The work team here served as a channel for peasants to influence local policy-making. A relaxed non-campaign atmosphere, and more intense interest in the outcome of this purely local dispute than in issues raised by work teams during national campaigns, may have contributed to peasant willingness to speak out. Where peasants' perceived interests coincide with the policy goals of work teams there is a greater likelihood of peasants being able to use work teams to participate in politics.

Campaign work teams can also serve as channels for peasant participation. When, for example, peasants were dissatisfied with corruption among local cadres, they found sympathetic listeners among the Four Clean-Ups Campaign work teams in 1963-65. Peasants and work team members cooperated in a purge of local leaders during this period.

Mass Organizations

Peasants have attempted to influence government policy-making at local levels through a variety of rural mass organizations, including poor and lower-middle peasant associations (*pinxia zhongnong xiehui*) and the brigade-level women's federation (*funu lianhe hui*). Although these organizations function primarily to mobilize support for the regime, individual association and federation representatives have successfully exerted pressure on brigade and commune authorities to change unpopular policies.

Poor and lower-middle peasant associations, set up in the mid-1960s by Four Clean-Ups Campaign work teams,[28] had a structure similar to the earlier Land Reform peasant associations, although they never possessed the power of the earlier associations and served chiefly to legitimize work team decisions. Each production team appointed a representative to the brigade-wide poor and lower-middle peasant association, which was charged with supervising local cadres,[29] particularly in the areas of financial management and the prevention of corruption. The fact that association representatives could not simultaneously hold cadre positions was one indication of the government's resolve to make the associations into powerful supervisory bodies at local levels. Still, the Draft Association Rules explicitly put the associations under party supervision, opening the way for role conflict. What the associations were supposed to do if their role as the supervisor of local cadres, mandated by the Party, clashed with their duty to comply with party directives, as articulated at local levels by the same local party officials, was never made clear.

Whether in practice poor and lower-middle peasant associations ever afforded peasants an opportunity to influence decision making about personnel matters is unclear. Official sources from 1963-67 indicate that the powers of the associations were real and effective, while interview data for the same period indicate that they had no real power by themselves, but were in fact used to legitimize directives of the Four Clean-Ups Campaign work teams and quickly became inactive when the work teams were withdrawn. Interview data indicate that where individual poor and lower-middle peasant representatives carried out their supervisory tasks after that time, it was only because they were concurrently either local cadres (as happened in a few places, contravening the 1964 Draft Rules), former cadres, party members, or "old experienced peasants," that is, when they could speak with authority for reasons other than their role as poor and lower-middle peasant representatives.

Informants reported that poor and lower-middle peasant representatives disagreed with team management committees on some production issues (e.g., what crops to plant)[30] and, in one production team in Zengcheng county, attempted to dismiss a team leader for his "bad" work style. In the latter case, the representative reported the situation to the brigade leadership, which then criticized the unpopular team leader but took no other action.[31] These representatives were, however, either cadres or party members.

The women's federation, organized at the brigade level, has also acted as an institution through which peasants can influence brigade and commune officials. In one model brigade in Hubei, for example, during the 1973-74 campaign to criticize Lin Biao women complained to a women's federation official in the brigade that they were not receiving equal pay for the same work done by male workers during the wheat harvest. The official, who was also a party member, discussed this with brigade officials at a party branch meeting and women's work points were raised for wheat harvesting tasks.[32] Representatives of mass organizations have, then, sometimes served as a channel through which peasants can participate in politics.

The Media

By the early 1970s the government had established local reporting groups among educated peasants and sent-down youths to write for local brigade and commune broadcast stations. By 1975 more than 93 percent of the production teams in China and 70 percent of its rural households were linked to wired broadcasting, with 106 million loudspeakers in rural areas, or one for every seven persons.[33] This made the broadcast stations an important medium, and peasants have been able to use these local reporting groups to influence government decisions. The reporting groups had some discretion about what they reported. They were assigned by the head of the station at each level to attend cadre meetings at commune and brigade headquarters and to travel to neighboring teams and brigades. In this capacity they served as an additional investigation unit of the commune and the brigade ("We were their eyes and ears!"). The reporting group members reported progress when they saw it, but also reported deviations from state plans. In this sense they were part of the commune and brigade compliance apparatus.[34]

They also served as a channel for peasants to influence the decisions of higher levels, as the following example illustrates. One former commune reporting group member, on a visit to a production team in Taishan county in 1973, was told by production team cadres that they faced a serious insect problem. However, the supply and marketing cooperative (headquartered in the commune) had ignored their special requirements and distributed the same quantity of insecticide as it did every year. Therefore some teams had insecticide surpluses, while others (this one among them) could not get enough. The reporter transmitted this to the commune: "When I discussed this problem with the commune's cadres, they arranged for more supply. They immediately distributed insecticide to the team. And afterward, they sent me back to the team to write an article about the struggle of this team with insect pests."[35] When this issue was raised by the reporting group member with commune cadres it brought an immediate response.

Reporting groups also wrote articles for commune and county work newsletters (*gongzuo tongxun*), issued as monthly publications in the 1970s. These articles were occasionally reprinted in provincial or regional publications, such as *Southern Daily*. Peasants attempted to influence policy through this written media, expressing grievances to reporters that were intended to influence government policy or personnel choices.

In one 1970s case, a Taishan county brigade secretary suggested to a member of his brigade's reporting group that he write a story criticizing the commune supply and marketing cooperative head for corruption. Peasants in the brigade had been indignant when the co-op head's activities were first revealed locally a few weeks before.

What was needed for the story, according to my informant (the former reporting group member), was a convincing theme: "I saw that 'poor and lower-middle peasants managing schools' was being advocated in the press at the time, so I could report this case as 'poor and lower-middle peasants managing commerce,' because brigade members were so dissatisfied with the co-op head."[36] The story was written and sent by the reporter to the commune, county, and province. The commune printed it, the county ignored it, and the province sent it on to a regional newspaper, *Southern Daily*, which dispatched a reporter from Guangzhou to the county to investigate it. The county, which had ignored the story ("because they weren't concentrating on commercial problems at that time," according to my informant), then dispatched three people to the brigade on two different occasions in 1972 to make inquiries. They talked to the brigade secretary and held a meeting of all commune members with grievances against the co-op head, who by this time had been dismissed. "What they wanted to hear was how to have the peasants manage commerce. How could they supervise it? And what was the relationship between peasants working in the co-op and peasants in the brigade? They were very interested in whether letting poor and lower-middle peasants manage commerce was common or rational."[37] *Southern Daily* then published a 9,000 character story about "a commune's poor and lower-middle peasants managing commerce" based on the experience of the brigade.

The example illustrates how a local grievance could be taken
through the media and communicated to higher levels. It also high-
lights the crucial role of the brigade secretary, for it was he who first
suggested to the reporting group that the story be written.

Informal Channels

Peasants have attempted to influence policy-making through
informal channels or networks as well as formal institutions and
organizations. In rural China the ties of lineage and village have
been particularly strong.[38] In Guangdong and Fujian the countryside
is composed of many single surname villages, which compounds the
influence of the "five kinds of personal relationships" (*wutong guanxi:*
same surname, same lineage, same village, same school, and same
work place).[39] Peasants from the same village may also be from the
same lineage and have the same surname. Because primary schools
and production units are organized geographically in the countryside,
peasants often, at least in single-surname villages, find that they are
bound to their neighbors not just by kinship, but through school ties
and as coworkers, that is, by all "five kinds of personal
relationships."[40] Even in multi-surname villages the ties of school,
work unit, and village are strong. At the level of the production
team, it is therefore difficult, if not impossible, to sort out which of
these personal relationships is instrumental to peasant behavior.
They may all contribute to any particular action.

Peasants may use personal relationships to gain access to
decision makers and thus to influence governmental decisions. For
example, during the grain-short years of 1960-62, production team
members in Sichuan used personal ties to the People's Liberation
Army (PLA) to bring to the government's attention the extent of food
shortages among them.[41] In letters written in 1961, which were
eventually turned over to PLA authorities, and through visits by
relatives, the peasant-soldiers learned of serious food shortages in
their native districts. PLA authorities found that the information
affected the soldiers' performance and "ideological work" (18 percent
of those receiving letters in one group "became restive"). As a result
of peasant complaints, soldiers were permitted to take food to their
families and a number of groups from the PLA were sent to the food
shortage areas.

Interview data indicate that the use of personal ties to influence
policy-making has persisted in the countryside throughout the 1960s

and 1970s. Brigade cadres in many areas acted to protect the production teams in which they and their families lived. Some brigade cadres, for example, ignored planning deviations, or false reporting by cadres in their teams,[42] favored individual and team loan applications from their teams,[43] granted permission for special sideline industries in their teams,[44] gave better opportunities to work outside the brigade to their relatives but not to others,[45] or protected their team from land confiscations needed for improvements like new roads.[46]

Within the production team, same surname relationships were sometimes helpful in getting easier or more remunerative work assignments.[47] In some places relatives also tended to speak up for one another at work point assessment meetings.[48] Loan applications were sometimes treated more favorably by team management committees if the applicant had close personal ties to influential committee members.[49]

These scattered examples, mostly from the early 1970s, indicate that personal relationships have been an informal structure through which peasants have sought to influence decisions. These may appear to be of little consequence, but nonetheless affected their incomes and their lives. The team and brigade in each case was the final decision-making authority.

Modes of Political Participation

In using the available channels, peasants chose among a wide array of modes of participation. Voting, speaking out, grumbling, contacting officials, and lobbying – all modes of peasant participation – are implied in the above discussion of various institutions. But peasants also have engaged in other activities, such as writing letters, petitions, and big character posters (*dazi bao*); corruption; slow-downs and strikes; withholding goods and services; withdrawing from collectives; demonstrations; and false reporting, all activities designed to influence government policies.[50]

Written Modes

Peasants have tried to influence the implementation of government policy through letters to the editors of newspapers, party and government offices, and radio stations. Letters exposing cadre corruption, for example, were common from 1963-65. In one case, a peasant wrote to the editor of *Southern Daily* complaining that three cadres in his team had misappropriated 1,900 work points and demanding that peasant supervision of cadres be carried out more closely.[51]

One of the most extraordinary cases of letter-writing came from model Shengshi brigade in Guangdong during the Four Clean-Ups Campaign in 1964. Two old peasants wrote twice, once to the Guangdong Provincial Party Committee and a second time to the General Office of the Party Central Committee in Beijing, exposing the brigade party branch secretary's corruption, with the startling result that Wang Guangmei, wife of party leader Liu Shaoqi, came from Beijing to lead an investigation into the charges. They were later substantiated and the offending cadre arrested.[52]

Peasants also sometimes petitioned the government to change unpopular policies. In one 1973 case, a production team leader drafted a petition asking that his team be allowed to divide up into two smaller units. The petition was signed by the entire team management committee and then sent to the brigade, which forwarded it to the commune. The commune reacted by sending down an investigation team with the final result that the production team was permitted to split up.[53]

Writing big character posters was an officially approved means of airing grievances in China from the early days of the People's Republic until recently, although posters only appeared in great profusion during the Cultural Revolution.[54] In practice, however, they have sometimes been suppressed.[55] These posters were attractive vehicles for influencing policy-making because their authors could remain anonymous and yet effectively make and publicize grievances without having to rely on officially controlled channels. There is evidence, however, that they were not widely used by individual peasants in the countryside, but were usually posted by outsiders or officially inspired.[56]

When peasants did post them, it was generally in cooperation with local cadres. Posters were usually posted in the name of production units, not individuals. In the 1970s, for example, a land dispute between two production teams in Guangdong was aired in big character posters with team cadre approval.[57] And a team in Jiangjun village posted a big character poster in August 1974 protesting the brigade's decision to sell the sand on its beach next to the river, rather than to develop the land for agricultural use.[58] What these examples have in common is that local cadres either inspired or cooperated with the posting of the *dazi bao*.

The nature of village society helps to explain why big character posters were used so infrequently by peasants: anonymously written *dazi bao* are unknown in the countryside. Unlike those in urban areas, peasants who chose this mode of expression were immediately recognized by their neighbors and by local cadres and ran the risk of becoming targets of criticism, ostracism, or revenge. In one Cultural Revolution case, for example, a peasant who put up a poster attacking a commune cadre was immediately identified by the cadre concerned and scolded.[59] In another case, a team cashier who criticized a brigade cadre using a *dazi bao* was for several subsequent years the subject of the brigade cadre's revenge.[60] From a peasant's perspective, then, big character posters are not worth the risks of exposure and criticism.[61]

In my data, local cadre initiative or active cooperation was always present in cases of successful petitioning or posting of *dazi bao* in the countryside. Although the initiative for letter-writing lay in peasant hands, the cadres chose the letters to be publicized or used as a guide for policy. Thus, effective use of these written modes of peasant participation depended on winning over local cadre support. Lacking this, only letter-writing offered individuals or small groups of peasants a reliable and sometimes effective channel to higher levels.

If these legitimate modes of participation by peasants have been used, so too have less legitimate, quasi-legal, and illegal modes, ranging from slowdowns and strikes to withholding, corruption, false reporting, and demonstrations. I turn now to a discussion of these activities.

Withholding

Peasants partially withheld their labor (or slowed down) to express their displeasure with work point distribution systems in the countryside. The system of work point distribution directly affected household income. A piece rate system was used in much of rural China, especially during the busy season, in the early 1960s and after 1971. This meant that labor-rich households earned more than if a time-rate or "democratic assessment" system was used.[62] Many informants reported that strong workers simply "slowed down" when time-rates were applied, a kind of protest against the work point distribution system itself.[63] Under time-rates, strong workers would rest longer than at other times and operate machinery more slowly.

"They produced less than before [under piece-rates], but still more than the average peasant, so cadres and peasants were embarrassed to criticize them."[64] Scattered documentary evidence supports these findings. In Bao'an county, for example, peasants "slowed down" in 1962 because "work points didn't reward harder working groups."[65]

If peasants sometimes "slowed down" to protest low incomes, they also sometimes withheld goods and services in an attempt to force policy changes. We saw that they withheld goods from a brigade in Taishan county until three teams were compensated for land needed for a new road building project. Similarly, peasants refused to heed a commune's call for laborers to build a reservoir in Zengcheng county soon after the Cultural Revolution. They would derive no direct benefit from the project, peasants reasoned, and while not seeking to have the project scrapped, they sought informally to shift the burden of its construction to those teams that would benefit more directly. "We discussed this at a team management committee meeting and decided to send only twelve workers (the commune had asked for twenty)," the former team leader explained.[66] When the twelve workers arrived at the work site, the commune realized that labor was being withheld and for two days "ordered" the production team to comply by sending the remaining eight workers. It did not, and the matter was eventually dropped.

Peasants also withdrew from collective agricultural production to express their dissatisfaction with production team and brigade organization or with the incentive system as it was being implemented at local levels. Reports in early 1979, for example, indicated that in some areas peasants "divided up the land to go it alone," or organized "teams of brothers" and "father and son teams." In the latter cases, villagers withdrew from the larger collective and replaced them with much smaller groupings of extended or nuclear families. The effect, however, was to withdraw from the collective and to rely on the efforts of households.[67]

Corruption

Corruption was sometimes used by peasants as a means of political participation through bribing officials to influence policy decisions. The press has reported banquets being given for cadres in exchange for "special favors,"[68] and peasants of the national model Dazhai brigade were alleged to have presented their cadres with cartons of cigarettes "in the hope of speeding things up."[69] Women were also reported to have exchanged sexual favors for quicker approval of their exit or travel permits.[70] Although the issues in these cases were local, peasants were attempting to influence the implementation of public policy.

False Reporting

Peasants falsely reported grain and cash crop output figures to reduce their liabilities to the state. By underreporting these figures, peasants and production teams sought to have their surplus grain (*yu liang*) and cash crop sales quotas reduced, or at least not increased as real output rose. Underreporting (or *manchan:* hiding production) was thus a method of influencing the implementation of state purchasing policy. One former Guangdong production team leader explained: "After lowering the total output figure, we reported this lower figure to higher levels, leaving more for us to consume. . . . If we didn't do this, the amount of grain left for us would be insufficient after deducting tax and the 'surplus grain.'"[71]

Underreporting of cash crops usually meant submitting false figures either for output or for sown area, and often for both, sometimes calling for elaborate and deceptive strategies to fool higher authorities. In one Taishan county production team, for example, the brigade had permitted five *mou* of collective vegetable land to be planted, but the team actually planted eight *mou*. To conceal this: (1) the vegetable plots were scattered throughout the production team; (2) per *mou* yield figures were altered (each *mou* produced 2,000 *jin,* but was reported as producing 3,000 *jin);* and (3) the recorded sales price was three *fen* per *jin* higher than the real price.[72] The result, then, was that the team was able to alter the implementation of the state's cash crop purchasing policy. Such action, if it was widespread, could influence state purchasing policy, either driving up prices of cash crops, or lowering the quotas for compulsory sales to the state.

Peasants, and particularly local team and brigade leaders, sometimes overreported output in order to win for their production unit designation as a "model," because increased state investment in the unit always followed, in the form of such increased agricultural inputs as fertilizer, cement, seed, tractors, or loans.[73] Deliberate overreporting to increase collective income, then, was usually associated with model or would-be model units. Once model status was achieved, continued exaggerated reporting was sometimes necessary to maintain it.[74]

Overreporting was alleged to have occurred in Taoyuan brigade and was exposed during the Four Clean-Ups Campaign in 1964. The brigade party secretary "falsely claimed" output of more than 5,000 *jin* of grain which his unit had not produced.[75] More recently, the former national model Dazhai brigade has been accused of overreporting.[76]

Demonstrations

The first large-scale spontaneous mass demonstrations since 1949 to be reported in China's urban areas occurred in April 1976 in Beijing's Tian'anmen. But such demonstrations have been used by peasants to influence the implementation of state policy in rural China long before that time.

In one 1972 example, a production team in Taishan county reported to the brigade that its work point value for that year was only .07 *yuan* and that current grain supplies were very low. As a result, the team members cut grass to sell in the market in order to buy grain. The entire team went out to cut grass, leaving no one to plow the team's fields. The commune learned of this situation and dispatched a work team to the area. Mass meetings were held to criticize those peasants who had earned the most from grass cutting, meetings that simply made the villagers indignant. They felt that the work team's harsh treatment was unjustified and, moreover, that the work team was not trying to solve their problem.

Most households had a grain reserve of one month's supply which had to least for five months. Even in the presence of the work team, peasants continued to cut grass in order to buy rice. They received no state aid. The work team charged that peasants were "spontaneously developing capitalism," but peasants saw their activity as production self-help.

Several days later some peasants (those with more young children) were still spending the day cutting grass. When they returned to the village, the work team detained them for a mass struggle meeting. The villagers were furious: "Of course the work team can call on us only to do collective work, but then the commune must feed us!" Because it had falsified its own accounts, however, the commune had no real reserves (*jidong liang:* flexible grain) to send to the team. The commune's misallocation of reserves would have been discovered (as indeed it was) had it asked the county for help in this situation.

The more the peasants discussed the situation, the angrier they became at the demands being made on them by the work team, and especially at the refusal to allow them "self-help" in place of aid from the commune. The villagers demanded either a loan of grain, grants of aid, permission to cut and sell grass, or permission to further "discuss the food situation" with commune cadres at their headquarters. The implication of the last alternative was that peasants would turn up en masse to confront commune officials, and perhaps eat their meals at the commune-run mess hall for an indefinite period.

In the end, according to my informant, twenty to thirty team members took grass to the commune mess hall several miles away and dumped it. They demanded that commune cadres come to their houses to investigate the food situation. Because the commune head-quarters was in a market town, where news of the incident could easily spread, the commune leadership acted quickly, sending a group of cadres hurrying after the villagers. Several peasants were arrested, but the commune did help the production team out of its difficulties.[77]

Peasants in this example objected to the way the sideline pro-duction policy was being implemented by the commune and its agent, the work team. They sought first to ignore the demands of the commune and then to change them through a public demonstration.

More recently, peasant demonstrations were reported in Beijing in 1979. The demonstrators, pressing claims for "jobs, housing, and food,"[78] were removed to "reception centers" on Beijing's periphery, and in October the Party announced that it was sending teams of officials to the provinces to investigate the peasants' complaints.[79]

Scope and Frequency of Peasant Political Participation

The Issues

The range of issues on which peasants have attempted to influ-ence policy formulation and implementation is quite broad. Perhaps of most concern have been issues relating to the incentive system. Some peasants have sought from time to time to have work point systems more closely tied to physical skill and work done than to po-litical or oratorical ability, to increase the size of private plots, to en-sure the existence of free markets, to reduce quotas for grain and cash crops, and to increase the range of permitted sideline production.

The state, through its representatives at local levels, has from time to time opposed or sought to restrict these tendencies, particularly from 1969-72. Some peasants have also sought to make the team or even smaller work groups the basic accounting unit, and to distribute more grain for immediate household consumption, again tendencies resisted by the state and its representatives. Further, peasants have sought to plant more remunerative cash crops, resisting calls to concentrate on grain, and to conserve labor, resisting calls to mobilize labor for commune or county construction projects not of direct benefit to them.

Recent changes in agricultural policy indicate that many of these incentive system-based issues have now been resolved in favor of more private production in the countryside.[80] The regime is now openly encouraging private and individual enterprise to provide employment for the underemployed in poorer areas and to supplement the collective economy. The rights to private plots, free markets, and to engage in sideline production have been publicly reaffirmed, and their contributions to the socialist economy of China's hinterland acknowledged. We can expect that the issues on which peasants engage the state will change as this new policy is implemented.

There have been other issues as well. Peasants have usually preferred political leaders who represented the interests of their team at brigade and higher level forums, and the interests of their lineage where this was important in the team, sometimes to the detriment of state or other group interests. They have also sought to extend their private housing, have more children to enrich the family fortunes, and marry at an earlier age, all moves at times opposed by the state.

While this is not an exhaustive list, it does indicate the substance of many of the issues in local rural politics in China during the past several decades. Conflict on these issues was of two general kinds. Peasants' collective interests (organized in teams or brigades) were sometimes opposed to those of the state, when, for example, quotas were at issue; and the interests of some individual peasant households (usually those with more labor power) conflicted with those of other peasant households (with less labor power), when, for example, different work point systems were at issue. Thus conflict arises both between collective units and within them.

The Participants

If these are the issues in rural politics, who are the participants? Which sectors among the peasantry participate in politics depends on the forum of participation, for each has its own formal and informal requirements for participation. Until 1970 only poor and lower-middle peasants could participate in most formal political institutions like team mass meetings, mass organizations, and elections.[81] The "five bad elements" (landlords, rich peasants, rightists, counterrevolutionaries, and criminals or "bad" elements) were legally denied political rights, and therefore have been unable to take part in such institutions. This group, numbering no more than 1 to 3 percent of the total population,[82] was composed of those peasants judged during Land Reform to have owned land and hired labor for the three years prior to 1949, and those who subsequently have been found by administrative means to be "rightists," "counterrevolutionaries," or "bad elements," labels given by the public security organs to those with unacceptable political attitudes or behavior. Recently steps have been taken to reduce the size of this group. In 1978-79, authorities removed the labels of thousands of landlords, rich peasants, rightists, and counterrevolutionaries. Since then, officials have no longer discriminated against them in the exercise of their formal political rights of participation.[83] As "commune members," they will be treated just as poor and lower-middle peasants without bad political records have been since 1949.

Poor and lower-middle peasants, those with good class background, have also been the predominate users of informal, quasi-legal, or illegal modes of political participation since 1962. Peasants with bad class background (e.g., landlords and rich peasants) have not dared to engage in these activities. Indeed, one brigade leader was reported in *Southern Daily* to have lamented that: "The masses often turn a deaf ear to us. They are all poor and lower-middle peasants. We just cannot do anything with them. Were they 'four wicked elements,' we would have cracked down on them long ago. Yet they ['four wicked elements'] listen to us tamely."[84]

Further, most of the informal modes, such as withholding, false reporting, corruption, and demonstrations depended on the initiative or active cooperation of production team or brigade cadres, the same leaders charged with carrying out the policies of higher levels. These cadres operate at the focal point, mediating between the demands of their friends, relatives, and neighbors, on the one hand, and those of the state, on the other. The range of informal modes of participation is so extensive that it serves as one measure of the resourcefulness of local leaders in rural China as they attempt to accommodate village interests to those of the state.

The issues and participants have changed over time. First, the basic policy of collectivization, itself an issue in the 1950s, has been of less concern since 1962 than the appropriate level of ownership, and where precisely the boundary between collective and private production should be drawn. Certain features of the incentive system in the 1950s, such as the level of taxation, have also ceased to be issues.

Second, the users of informal quasi-legal or illegal modes of participation have shifted from "bad class elements," like landlords and rich peasants, to the poor and lower-middle peasantry. The resources for opposition used by landlords and rich peasants were taken from them when land was collectivized and hired labor prohibited. They came to see that using informal methods of opposition, such as bribery or withdrawal, met with unacceptably harsh state action. Poor and lower-middle peasants, on the other hand, have begun to use these modes, particularly when redress from formal institutional channels was not forthcoming.

Frequency

Although systematic and comprehensive data on the frequency of political participation in rural China is nonexistent, it is possible to offer some speculative and preliminary conclusions on this topic. First, it is clear that some groups of peasants participate more frequently than others. In general, the most frequent participants are male, those at the peak of their labor power (that is, between the ages of twenty-five and fifty), and skilled laborers of good class background without a bad "political history," and with more education than most peasants, perhaps even middle school graduates. Party members are more often drawn from the ranks of this group of activists.

The least frequent participants tend to be female; either younger or older than the most frequent participants, less skilled, physically weaker and less educated, of bad class background, or with a problematic "political history." Some of these characteristics are more important than others in determining whether a peasant is likely to participate in politics. For most of the period, class label, for example, has been of overriding importance. Those with bad class labels, whether male or female, skilled or unskilled, and regardless of age, tended to participate less than average.

Some issues also tended to be raised more frequently than others by peasants. Those relating to the implementation of agricultural plans and to the incentive system, particularly the distribution of work points and team surpluses, were frequently discussed at team meetings. Whether decisions on these issues were made by peasants, however, depended on other factors, particularly the policy cycle. When campaigns were being carried out at local levels issues were less often presented to peasants for their decision. Also, issues were more often put to peasants at the team level, and only rarely at brigade level forums.

Peasants and Rural Policy:
The Effectiveness of Political Participation

After seizing political power in 1949, the CCP sought first to gain control of and then to stabilize the economy before embarking on an ambitious modernization program. The Party's policy in these years stressed the development of urban industrial centers in China. The need to mobilize resources from the countryside for this program led, from the 1950s, to the imposition of new organizational structures on rural society and to strict limitations on peasant autonomy in consumption, production, and investment. The need to impose these limits set the basis for constraints on peasant participation which were both organizational and ideological.

Perhaps the strongest and most obvious constraint was the Party itself, which controlled all of the formal institutions discussed in the preceding sections. The party branch at the brigade-level had members attending or presiding over mass organizations, meetings and elections, and work teams. Party control of the mass media, if it varied over time, was always present in some form. The Party could and did suppress some demands, ignore others, and chose those to which it would respond. As we saw above, peasants resorted to illegitimate channels when they found that the formal institutions of participation were unresponsive.

The Party has valued participation not so much for itself, as for contributing to a "correct" outcome. The CCP has treated very gingerly attempts by peasants to influence policy in which it has a stake. In a case reported by Radio Hubei, for example, a commune secretary sent down to a production team intervened to change the decision of a production team mass meeting. At issue was whether the team should reclaim wasteland as part of the drive for modernization in agriculture. The issue split the team management committee, four to three, against the reclamation work. The visiting commune secretary suggested that the issue be put to a team mass meeting and the team management committee agreed.

> At the meeting, Tian [the commune secretary] did not say a word. The production team leader, after speaking for a while, said: "Those who do not agree, please raise their hands." He saw that most of the participants slowly raised their hands. Turning to Tian, he said: "Look, that is a majority, isn't it?" Tian glanced at the peasants' faces and said: "Probably not, if you look into their hearts."
>
> After the meeting, Tian said to the cadres who remained behind: "It was our intention to ask the masses to discuss the matter and make a decision. Not a few of our cadres spoke at great length. By the time they had finished, some peasants had had a sound sleep. They were not a true majority."
>
> The next morning, Tian invited eleven poor and lower-middle peasants to a discussion and after repeated comparison and summing up, all agreed to reclaim the waste land. After this affair, Tian has often said: "When seeking the views of the masses, we should not rigidly mouth 'majority' and 'minority.' We must listen to and analyze the views of both sides. All correct views should be supported."[85]

This example has been presented at length because rarely does one find in the official media such a forthright discussion of the status of mass meeting decisions. The example is instructive because it indicates that there is nothing absolute about decisions arrived at by mass meetings. Coming to the correct decision on issues like work point assessments and the size and distribution of private plots that are not purely local, is more important than coming to the decision through a majority vote at a mass meeting. Legitimacy comes from its correctness, not from the meeting process itself, although in the case cited the commune secretary did put the issue to a forum to obtain its agreement.

This case is not an isolated example. When the household contract system was being considered in Fujian in 1961-62, production team cadres were commended for having been resolute and not giving in to pressure for household contracting, "even though commune members raised disturbances (i.e., voiced approval for the system at each meeting that was held)."[86] The report does not say *some* commune members, at *some* meetings, but rather indicates that support for household contracting was widespread. Thus, although the issue was raised in an approved forum, it was illegitimate because it ran counter to a policy in which the Party had a stake.

The party and elites in China also supervise the educational system and thus, to varying degrees, its ideological content. Peasants, like other Chinese citizens, are taught to obey the Party, put state and collective interests above individual ones, and eschew localism. In party ideology, although the CCP recognizes the existence of individual interests, these interests have always been subordinated to those of the state and collective. When conflict between individual and collective interests arises, those of the collective are always to be given priority: "We permit no one to impair the interests and freedom of the majority, the public interests of the country and society, for the sake of the interests and freedom of any individual or individuals."[87] Conflicts between individual and collective interests are likely, according to the CCP, when individuals ignore their long-term permanent interests. Authorities, therefore, often justify their policies in terms of the peasants' long-term interests. The 1953 rural tax collection policy, for example, was said to be in the "greatest long-term interests of the greatest number of the people."[88] An appeal to long-term interests was the official justification for strengthening collective sideline production in the face of demands to turn it over to private producers in some parts of Henan in 1970 as well.[89] Peasants, authorities have said, "Must extend their view from their immediate interests to their permanent interests and to realize the necessity of subordinating their immediate interests to permanent interests."[90]

Conflicts of interest between collectives have also been recognized by Chinese authorities. Taking the interest of one's production unit as the most important, while ignoring the interests of the whole, has been a serious problem in rural China. In 1963 authorities denounced cadres in Henan, for example, for their localism: "A few cadres *only care about their own particular locality*, and not about the overall situation."[91] Local production units, then, are mandated not "just to look after their own interests,"[92] but to take into account the needs and interests of the whole.

While the effectiveness of peasant political participation has been limited by organizational and ideological constraints, it has also varied over time and by issue area, hierarchical level, and whether local cadres have lent it their support. This is especially true in the case of illegitimate modes of participation.

The data suggest that peasant influence is least felt during campaigns when local cadres are concentrating on responding quickly and efficiently to directives from above. Campaign mobilization crowds local issues off team and brigade agendas. Peasants realize this and know that political participation is more likely to be effective during non-campaign periods.

The particular issue at stake also helps to determine the effectiveness of peasant participation. Peasant influence is most effective on issues where decisions can be taken locally. It is less likely to affect issues decided at higher levels, and least effective where peasant influence threatens party policy.

Some institutions are more effective forums for raising particular issues than others. Work point assessments and other distributive issues are most often raised at mass meetings, while team investment issues are raised during elections. Work teams usually listen to and act on complaints about cadres or other local personnel issues. Other issues, such as quotas, cannot effectively be raised in any legitimate forum. In general, those issues which can be resolved by team or brigade cadres are raised at least initially in local formal institutions. Peasants only voice objections using less legitimate modes of participation when this appears fruitless.

Finally, as the above discussion suggests, cadre initiation or active cooperation is necessary for the success of the more illegitimate modes of participation—such as withholding, demonstrations, false reporting, and corruption. If team cadres refuse their cooperation, these strategies are much less likely to succeed, or in the case of false reporting and corruption, are impossible.

While this study has concentrated on political participation at local levels, we should not ignore the fact that since 1949 peasants have had a long-term cumulative impact on higher-level policy-making. This is the message of the policy cycles or oscillations that have characterized rural China.[93] What mechanisms do peasants use to influence higher level policy formulation and implementation? I can only speculate, but it seems likely that local interests are sometimes brokered into the political system through the extensive reporting/work and investigation team network, on the one hand, and through elite representation at party policy-making meetings, on the other. There is some evidence to support this speculation.

Parts of the reporting system have been examined in interviews with former cadres[94] and in collections of internal party and state documents.[95] These channels transmit peasant views to higher levels, as occurred when some peasants sought to reduce the speed of collectivization in the 1950s, as reflected in the comments of Deng Zihui, for example, and to express dissatisfaction with the incentive system in the early 1960s and 1970s.

It is likely that party meetings such as the Lushan Plenum of the Central Committee in 1959 involved some representation of peasant views, reflected either by party members who were themselves peasants or by higher level elites (e.g., Peng Dehuai). Especially by withholding cooperation and using other passive resistance strategies, peasants can bring their views to the attention of national and provincial elites. After all, the careers of these elites depend at least in part on the smooth implementation of party policy. Had peasants refused to cooperate in Sichuan, for example, it is unlikely that Zhao Ziyang would have been appointed premier in 1980.

Because national and provincial bureaucracies have their own interests based on their partial views of China's requirements and reflected in their struggle to maintain and increase both human and material resources, the articulated views of peasants from below becomes ammunition in the struggle for power and policy. It may well be that peasant dissatisfaction, particularly in more remote and poorer areas (as expressed through the reporting system and a series of demonstrations in Beijing in 1978 and 1979) was responsible, at least in part, for the recent changes of agricultural policy. Once again authorities have permitted poorer areas to "fix output to the household" and have given wider autonomy for private and individual production, all popular policies in many areas during 1961-62. Leaders are interested in increasing productivity in the countryside. Peasants have demonstrated that they want the new policy and there is considerable evidence that has resulted in higher rural incomes. All of these factors undoubtedly influenced the decision to permit the changes.

Problems and Prospects

Since 1978, in an effort to raise rural productivity and living standards, China's leaders have adopted a series of measures to both decollectivize agricultural production and institutionalize local government. While these policies have not significantly altered the effectiveness of peasant political participation in China (the system remains highly mobilizational), they have reshaped the organizational context of participation to a certain extent.

The introduction of the responsibility system in agriculture has had certain consequences for rural leadership and for the distribution of political resources in the countryside. First, implementation of the new policies has shifted responsibility to households for many duties previously performed by village and team leaders. The reduced functions performed by local leaders and the new emphasis on the legitimacy of "becoming rich through labor," has undermined the authority of village leadership and contributed to relatively high rates of local leadership instability.[96] The new policies have made assuming local leadership duties even more unattractive to peasants.

The decollectivization of agriculture has put more disposable income in the hands of rural villagers.[97] This has increased their resources, which they can turn to political purposes. Although there is no direct evidence, newly rich peasants would be in a better position to influence local cadres through illicit means such as bribery and to build up networks of poorer kin by providing them with the needed, but expensive, agricultural inputs now increasingly distributed in the market.

Because the new policies rely more heavily on market forces, political and administrative controls on economic activities have been relaxed. Authorities have expanded the realm of legitimate income earning activity and as a result have removed many of the more contentious issues in village politics. Conflict over the distribution of work points, private plots, and time for free marketing have all virtually disappeared as issues in village politics. Peasants continue to test the limits of the new reforms, and are trying to find new ways of investing their increased incomes.

In addition to implementing new agricultural policies, since 1979 authorities in China have attempted to institutionalize local government by strengthening and regularizing the local people's congress system and stripping the political and administrative functions from communes and brigades. Although some trends can be identified, it is too early to provide a definite assessment of these changes.

Although peasants throughout the country participated in the 1980 and 1984 elections of delegates to people's congresses at county (and presumably commune) levels, available data indicate that village participation in these elections was highly mobilized by elites.[98] In those areas where elections are seldom held, election propaganda, nomination of candidates, and election meetings undoubtedly provided villagers with some education in civic responsibility. Still, institutionalization of these procedures requires officials to call elections regularly, a practice not adopted in most places in the past.

By setting up separate township and village governments, Chinese authorities have begun to force communes and brigades to be more sensitive to market forces. Insofar as peasants can express themselves in the market, they will be able to influence the policies of these largely economic units. Still the Party can be expected to remain firmly in control of the new local governments and to dominate the recruitment of local administrative personnel. The general unwillingness of peasants to serve in these positions will make recruitment difficult, however.

It is unlikely that the reforms have opened up effective new formal channels for peasants to influence government decision making. Attempts to influence political authority will continue to remain largely local, confined to village and production team levels. Elites will continue to represent peasant interests at elite discretion and the reporting system will continue to transmit fragments of peasant views to senior leaders in Beijing. Opportunities to influence authorities informally, however, may increase as villagers accumulate more resources and local governments relax controls and increase their reliance on market forces.

CHAPTER 5

Riding the Tiger:
The Political Life of China's Scientists

Richard P. Suttmeier

It was not too long ago that a study of scientists pursuing interests politically in nondemocratic systems such as the People's Republic of China would have needed some explanation.[1] After all, scientists by their own values are not principally political actors, and it is generally assumed that collective group politicking within communist regimes is impossible. However, the phenomenal growth of science-government relations since World War II in virtually all modernizing systems has directed explicit attention to scientists in political roles. Such pioneering studies as *Interest Groups in Soviet Politics* by Gordon Skilling and Franklyn Griffiths have established the possibility of focusing on participation and group activity in communist countries.

When considering the political participation of scientists in societies such as China, we are confronted with two major methodological problems. First, there are significant problems with the availability and quality of data. We are never sure when participation is in fact occurring. In addition, it is often difficult to determine what the outcome or significance of participation will be, even when we know it is occurring, in large part because of our ignorance of the details of Chinese policy processes.

The second problem is that of satisfying ourselves about our underlying assumptions concerning motivations for participatory behavior. This is because the group that concerns us is composed of scientists (who seem to be less frequent political participants, and certainly are less frequently studied than other groups), and because we are dealing with a society that in crucial ways is different from those that are the usual objects of participation studies.

The discussion in this chapter anticipates these problems and attempts to deal with them as follows. To deal with the data problems, a detailed analysis of the most empirically rich case of participation, that surrounding the events of 1956-57, is made. It is argued that current patterns of participation cannot be understood without reference to this earlier case and what it tells us about the importance of motivations and organizational settings for participation. To deal with the problem of our underlying model of the participant, an effort is made at the outset to define methodologically sound, universally applicable assumptions about participation.

Collective Action and Political Participation

An initial methodological issue that must be addressed in any study of scientists in policy roles concerns the appropriate unit of analysis. Given the cultural and social setting of Chinese interest politics, much previous attention has centered on the role of informal groups.[2] These have ranged from horizontally-defined *guanxi* networks (relationships based on "connections"), to vertically-defined factional ties,[3] or more personalized patron-client groupings.[4] While these are plausible units of analysis, they are difficult to study. Moreover, the importance of formal organizational entities in a state-centered science community suggests a subordinate role for such informal networks. Substantive and empirical objections aside, such sociologically defined units of analysis tend to skirt a crucial issue in any study of interest politics: the importance of individual interest strategies in relation to collective entities.[5] All of these considerations suggest that the approach adopted in this chapter, which addresses the relationship between individuals and complex organizations, might be useful.

One of the classic statements of the "composition principles" by which individual behavior is related to that of the group is offered by Chester Barnard,[6] who suggested that individuals engage in cooperative action in order to achieve things which could not be accomplished by individuals acting by themselves. Once cooperative action begins, there exists a new collective reality, the persistence of which depends on the continuing participation of the members, dependent in turn on the benefits received from participation. Bernard, in short, postulates an exchange relationship of contributions by individuals and inducements offered by the group.

Mancer Olson likewise approaches principles of composition from the point of view of a contributions-inducements exchange.[7] Olson is particularly interested in the collective benefits of cooperative action, those collective goods which if available to one are available to all. It is the production of collective goods by groups or organizations which, in fact, leads Olson to question the conditions under which collective action, individuals pursuing common interests jointly, is possible at all. If the product of collective action is a collective good, and if the good by definition is available to all regardless of contribution, what then is the incentive for the individual to participate? Olson's well-known answer is that in large groups individuals will not contribute to collective action unless they are coerced or offered selective incentives to do so. Such groups can therefore be thought of as "latent" until mobilized either by coercion or selective incentives.

In smaller groups, the situation is somewhat different. In some small groups where there is a presumption that the collective good will be provided, each has an incentive to see that it is provided, even if the burden of providing it falls on one member. Olson calls these "privileged groups."[8]

According to the logic of the argument so far, if the value of inducements does not match the individual's sense of the value of his contribution, it is reasonable for him to withdraw from the group or organization. But is this the only choice? Is the calculus so clear? What if the individual has substantial sunk costs from past participation, or if there are other reasons why withdrawal would be very costly or impossible, as when faced with "collective bads" such as pollution, or coerced participation? What if the individual has a strong affective commitment to participate, as evidenced for instance in the patriotic commitment of Chinese scientists to the betterment of the nation?

These theoretically interesting questions have been treated in an elegantly simple way by Albert Hirschman.[9] Hirschman is interested in the conditions under which individuals leave groups or organizations, and the effects withdrawal has on organizational performance. In Hirschman's view withdrawal ("exit") is not the only choice for individuals who find that their interests are not being met by the organization. They may also either remain "loyal," or actively seek to change the organization through expression of "voice." The task Hirshman sets for himself is to explain when it is rational to choose one over the others.

The ability to exit is clearly associated with traditions of political and economic freedom, and seemingly therefore, the use of Hirschman's perspective in analyzing China is strained. It need not be so, however. Hirschman is concerned with mechanisms for arresting organizational decline and, by extension, with organizational effectiveness. A crucial element in arresting organizational decline is to get leaders to change what they are doing. Exit and voice both provide information to, and impose costs on leaders if they persist in their current behavior. By explicitly recognizing the potential for organizational members to impose costs on leaders, and thereby affect their behavior, Hirschman is implicitly making a statement about authority relations in organizations that is consistent with Bernard's rejection of conceptions of authority as a simple one-way flow of commands from superiors to subordinates.

In the past, China's scientists could not "exit." Although Hirschman recognizes that there are circumstances when it is rational and socially desirable for organization leaders and authorities to limit exit, the widespread restrictions on exit in China, including those affecting scientists, generally have not met Hirschman's criteria. As a result, limitations on exit have led to the result Hirschman would predict—Chinese organizations have not been notably flexible, innovative, and capable of arresting decline. The organizational reforms since the early 1980s are clearly intended to make exit more widely available in Chinese society.

In the past the absence of exit reduced the number of ways in which an individual could pursue his interest, and it deprived organizations of a useful feedback mechanism. It also made voice and loyalty all the more important to both individuals and organizational leaders. It is not surprising therefore that PRC leaders have encouraged input from Chinese scientists at times when they wished to arrest organizational decline, as in the early 1960s and the post-Mao era, or reorganize for greater organizational effectiveness as they did in the mid-1950s. During all three of these periods, encouragement to express ideas and opinions was accompanied by policies intended to engender loyalty.

Unfortunately, there have also been periods when such expression was discouraged or suppressed, as it was in the late 1950s, the Cultural Revolution, and most of the early 1970s. During these periods the loyalty of scientists as a group was called into question, and thus contributed to the dissipation of that loyalty. In Hirschman's terms, the discouragement of voice and the dissipation of loyalty, combined with the unavailability of exit could only be considered irrational. If however, authorities were dissatisfied with the outcomes of organizational processes, then of course radical intervention into those processes could be considered rational from the point of view of such authorities.[10]

While Hirschman's work expands our understanding of the choices available to the organizational member who is dissatisfied with the prevailing economy of incentives, there are theoretically interesting repertories of response, particularly for individuals in societies like China, that need more attention. First, when voice is suppressed or denied and exit is impossible, organizations run the risk of encouraging "surrogate exits." A number of these can be imagined, ranging from psychological exit or alienation to forms of organizational deviance. An example of the latter that has occurred among Chinese scientists has been the use of officially approved projects as "covers" for research work of importance to the individual. Discussions in the Chinese press in the post-Mao period of accomplishing objectives "through the back door" would be another example.

Second, although Hirschman recognizes the importance of clearly defined structures and procedures for the expression of voice, he leaves largely unexamined the possibilities of voice if these structures and procedures are unavailable. It has been noted by organization theorists that arbitrary or ineffective formal organization often prompts individuals to seek to protect their interests through informal group activity.[11] Students of patron-client ties likewise have identified flaws in formal structures of authority as a key factor promoting clientelist relations.[12] The formation of informal groups and patron-client relations may keep alive opportunities for the expression of interests when formal structures and procedures cannot be used. However, informal mechanisms usually involve the activation of particularistic loyalties which are often inconsistent with official organizational goals. Informal groups may, in fact, threaten authorities instead of making them more responsive to criticism.[13] Their existence can therefore push authorities toward greater organizational pathology. The case of the China Democratic League discussed below may be considered an instance of this tendency.

In spite of the theoretical importance of small informal groups, the data available on the group life of China's scientists biases attention toward formal organization. But the introduction of issues of informal groups, including the relationship between formal and informal organization, will be of use in interpreting the empirical record that is available. Thus while that record forces us to consider at the outset the highly structured setting for scientific activism in China, it should also be read with a sensitivity to the likely informal behaviors chosen by rational individuals unable to "exit." It is to the formal structures, however, that we now turn.

The Organization of Chinese Science

The formal organization of science that has emerged in post-Mao China (until the reforms of the early 1980s) resembled in most respects that which resulted from a decade of institution building during the 1950s, and characterized scientific affairs in the early 1960s. The two main structures of organization are those of the state and of professional societies.

Chinese professional societies have many of the attributes of professional societies in the West; they are committed to the propagation of knowledge, convene scientific conferences, and publish scientific journals. However, they also have been penetrated by political authorities and thus do not enjoy the authentic autonomy that the concept of professionalism normally conveys.

Many of these societies predate the establishment of the People's Republic and have a strong tradition of voluntary association. Many new societies were organized during the 1950s and early 1960s.[14] During the 1950s, the Party sponsored the establishment of a peak organization of societies, the All-China Federation of Scientific Societies. In 1958, the Federation was merged with the Association for the Dissemination of Scientific and Technical Knowledge to form the Chinese Association for Science and Technology (CAST). Throughout the pre-Cultural Revolution period, society meetings often served as forums for the discussion of policy as it pertained to planning for the development of particular disciplines.[15]

The activities of CAST and its member societies effectively ceased during the Cultural Revolution years. In the early 1970s CAST began to function again on a limited scale, playing an important role in the development of U.S.-PRC relations prior to normalization. It was not until 1978, after the major changes in policy following the downfall of the Gang of Four, that professional societies began to function again as they had before the Cultural Revolution. In the post-Mao period CAST has come to play a more important role in China's scientific development that at any time in its previous history. It has become an active spokesperson for the interests of scientists, assumed the responsibility for providing scientific advice for policy-makers, and has begun to promote the establishment of a network of technical consulting services throughout the country.

The second type of formal organizational structure is composed of the science-related state agencies in which most of China's scientists are employed. These include institutions of higher education, the research institutes under the jurisdictions of government ministries and local governments, and the institutes of the Chinese Academy of Sciences (CAS). While the Academy is not officially part of the state structure, the bulk of its resources comes from the state.

Until the recent reforms in science, state agencies in the post-Mao period, like professional societies, came to adopt organizational structures which resembled those existing before the Cultural Revolution. Those arrangements were the product of a decade of administrative experimentation and reorganization during the 1950s that were strongly influenced by the introduction of formal planning for science and by the Soviet presence in China during that period.

Until 1957, CAS had the central role in planning and national scientific coordination. Accordingly, it organized itself into five departments (physical sciences, earth sciences, biological sciences, technical sciences, and social sciences), each having its own governing council or "department committee" composed of leading scientists from relevant disciplines. These board members came from throughout the country, included individuals not exployed in CAS, numbered approximately 200 (excluding social sciences), and had a status comparable to academicians in the Soviet system.

At the level of the research institute, organization consisted of an administrative structure headed by an institute director, one or more deputy directors, and an academic structure centered around an institute academic committee. As with the department committees, the academic committees consisted of leading scientists in the field both from within the institute and from units (especially universities) outside the institute. Institute directors and most deputy directors were usually scientists, but non-expert political authority was also present in the form of the party organization, and frequently the party secretary served as one of the deputy directors. Reports of conflict and tension between scientists and unlettered party cadres were not unusual in the pre-Cultural Revolution period, although gradually, and with the support of the central authorities, accommodations between "reds" and "experts" were often reached.

The growth of scientific activities during the 1950s in the ministries, and to some extent in the universities, overloaded the capacity of the CAS mechanism for national planning and coordination. This led to the establishment of the Science Planning Committee (SPC) in 1956, which was reorganized into the State Science and Technology Commission (SSTC) in 1958.

The Cultural Revolution led to changes in these administrative arrangements. The SSTC was abolished; department committees ceased functioning, and existing institute-level organization was replaced by revolutionary committees. Since 1978, there has been a return to arrangements closely resembling the earlier *status quo*. However, certain aspects of the arrangements after 1978, discussed below, do differ in important ways from the pre-Cultural Revolution era.

By the early 1960s the patterns of formal organization described above provided the framework within which scientists pursued their interests. As such, they can be regarded as constitutional arrangements for political participation. The establishment of that framework, however, was not without controversy. An examination of the process of establishment reveals some of the parameters of formal organizational and group life, and the opportunities for and constraints on participation.

Participation and the Creation of
Constitutional Arrangements

The introduction of formal science planning and the establishment of the SPC represented active, visible, and very real new forces that would be shaping policy directly affecting the professional life of the Chinese scientist. Initially, the SPC was perceived as not representing the values and views of science of the scientists, but instead, as an instrument of the state designed to insure the dominance of the Party's views of science. Formal planning significantly narrowed options for research support, and thus made science more dependent on the state. The introduction of planning, like the establishment of the SPC, thus reduced the autonomy of the scientific community, and with decreased autonomy came a decrease in the scientific community's ability to establish a sense of collective identity.

By 1957 conditions existed for an extensive debate on Chinese science policy and the role of CAS. In the spring of 1957, the liberalism of the Hundred Flowers period was reaching its peak and

Mao's February 27 speech on contradictions among the people had encouraged meetings in all sectors of Chinese life to discuss these contradictions. In science, special meetings were convened by CAS and by the All-China Federation of Scientific Societies, and from May 22 to 30 the meeting of the Second Plenum of CAS's Department Committee was conducted according to the spirit of rectifying "bureaucratism" and "secretarianism."

In these discussions among scientists two categories of issues arose. The first involved selected individuals or groups of scientists, and many of the issues in this category were probably related to the adverse effects that the introduction of planning had on certain fields. A microbiologist, for instance, complained that he was suddenly ordered to terminate a long-standing research project and that he was not consulted about the sections of the twelve-year plan that affected his field.[16] Others complained that their suggestions were ignored. The geneticists had special complaints about "doctrinairism," which for a while restricted the publication of anything that was critical of Lysenko.[17] Similarly, certain geologists had complaints about the quality of geological surveying conducted by the Ministry of Geology.[18] Other complaints in this first category pertained to the neglect of social science, and to unfair practices in the publication of articles. The recently established system of academic awards was criticized as premature and as an unwise use of funds.[19] These issues in short were distributive ones involving divisible goods.

The second category included those issues that faced most, if not all, scientists. These included complaints that there was insufficient time for research due to political meetings and administrative responsibilities, that excessive secrecy frustrated scientific communication, that various aspects of the scientific information services (libraries, publications, distribution of foreign journals) were not working properly, and that the recently established systems for research probationers and post-graduates were full of problems. Post-graduates and probationers were so inadequately trained when they came to CAS that the Academy was forced to become an educational rather than a research organization. Also aired were criticisms of the blind application of things Soviet, and dissatisfaction with relations with party cadres.

This category of issues also included discussions of the role of CAS in the Chinese system of research. Some scientists thought that "in fame for bureaucratism, the Academy of Sciences ranked second, if not first, among all the academic establishments."[20] They cited the extremely poor relations that had been allowed to develop between CAS and the Ministry of Education, a problem related to bureaucratism in personnel management in both organizations and probably also to the uncertain involvement of universities in research at that time. A criticism of CAS from its own ranks blamed intersectional conflicts on the exclusiveness of CAS.

> Those outside the Academy of Sciences think that the entrance to the Academy is very small, there being closed-door or monopolistic ideas in the Academy. On the other hand there is inequitable division of labor and pay between those within the Academy and those outside it. This deserves some careful examination by our comrades within the Academy. The walls separating the Academy from the outside world must be demolished, and so must be the internal partition walls that seem to exist between the various departments.[21]

At the heart of the issue, however, were the goals and purposes of CAS activity, including such questions as the Academy's responsibility for basic as opposed to applied research, the extent of its administrative and planning responsibilities, and the much debated and apparently misunderstood question of "leadership in science."

It is not surprising that confusion over these matters existed in China early in 1957. Since 1949, the Academy had been the center of Chinese science, and had multiple responsibilities. To better discharge these, the various internal divisions discussed above were encouraged. In January 1956, however, Zhou Enlai in his report "On the Question of Intellectuals," concluded with new policy directives for Chinese research and development intended to stimulate research in the non-CAS sectors. He reaffirmed the importance of the Academy, but did so in sufficiently vague terms to cause much of the confusion of 1957. Zhou stated that CAS should be made "the locomotive for leading the work in the whole country in the raising of scientific level and fostering new scientific forces."[22] What was not initially clear was whether "leading the work" meant leading in an administration and planning sense, simply supplying new knowledge through basic research, or having a special status that was denied to other research centers.

The ambiguity was also due to the fact that Zhou instructed universities to "develop scientific research energetically under the guidance of the plan"[23] as well as to continue with the training of new science students and stated that

> government departments, in particular those in the fields of geology, industry, agriculture, water conservancy, transportation, national defense and health, should initiate and strengthen necessary research bodies with dispatch. Responsibility should be taken to introduce the most modern achievements in the world of sciences, in a planned manner and systematically to practical application, so that as rapidly as possible the world's most modern techniques will be installed in the different departments of our country.[24]

The new encouragement Zhou was giving to non-CAS research sectors continued with the establishment of the SPC. Both raised questions about the CAS as "locomotive."

This second category of issues, then, concerned the organization, rules and procedures under which all scientists worked, and can be thought of as constitutional issues. Unlike issues in the first category, those in the second involved collective rather than divisible goods. But as is sometimes the case with the allocation of collective goods, there were troubling distributive implications, and these exacerbated divisions among scientists.

The inability of scientists to reach consensus on consitutional issues invited intervention and authoritative solution by political authorities. In this sense, the politics of Chinese science is similar to that of other countries.[25]

The question of CAS's role was a lively topic of debate throughout 1956 and into 1957 until it was finally settled by the SPC acting on the direct order of Mao.[26] Nie Rongzhen, by then the chairman of the SPC, convened a special meeting on May 19 to discuss the issue, and it was an important topic at the Second Plenum of the department committees from May 22 to 30.

CAS president Guo Moro raised the issue at the Second Plenum in his opening address, but in vague terms.

> The Academy of Sciences is the center of academic leadership [*xueshu lingdao*] for the country and it is engaged in important scientific research at the same time. So far as its academic tasks are concerned, it

[CAS] must adopt the policy of "development of key sciences and adequate care of the rest," and it must also take care of nationwide needs and international interests. It must concentrate a definite amount of effort on basic theories, on absorption of the newest technical sciences of the world, and on comparatively long-range comprehensive scientific tasks.[27]

In concluding his speech, Guo described the basic tasks of the Academy as follows:

1. to take care of national needs and strengthen academic leadership;
2. to promote democracy and "let diverse schools of thought contend";
3. to strengthen harmony and unite the forces of science; and
4. to learn from the advanced nations and strengthen international cooperation.[28]

In the discussion that followed Guo's speech, there was considerable disagreement about the Academy's position. Some scientists attacked the speech and called for a clear-cut statement that CAS should be concerned with "the study of major basic theories, as well as comprehensive scientific research." These same scientists said that the four tasks making up Guo's conclusion sounded like they were the tasks of the All-China Federation of Scientific Societies.[29] While some scientists thought that CAS should be the center of academic leadership, others thought that present conditions would not allow CAS to play such a role, however desirable that role might be. Still others objected to CAS becoming the leader in research.

It is not difficult to understand why there was serious disagreement among the scientists about CAS' role. CAS board members served under a system of "concurrent positions." As we have seen, this meant that both those who were employed in CAS and outstanding scientists who worked at universities and various research departments of government ministries were included as board members. Thus, some university scientists were reluctant to see CAS become the center of basic research because they feared that this meant that basic research would be excluded from the universities. Physicist Qian Weichang, for example, had a vision for Chinese science in which the polytechnical universities, particularly Qinghua of which he was vice president, would model themselves on the California Institute of Technology to become centers of basic and applied research as well as teaching.[30] Much was at stake for the board members, since the settlement of the CAS question would affect the organization of science, and hence influence their own research.

The Academy was also seen as administratively incapable of leading science on a national scale. Its administrative structure was geared to its own operation, and the department committees and the institute-level academic committees reached out beyond the Academy for membership in keeping with the system of concurrent positions. These structures were at their best when rendering scientific judgments, providing scientific advice, or in setting the broad outlines for research plans. When the Academy was asked to address major issues of policy that would set the rules of scientists' professional lives for years to come, consensus built on common interests was weakened by divisions based on perceptions of the changes in distribution of goods that would be caused by the settlement of the constitutional issues. The outcome of the Second Plenum gave some sense of the possibilities and limitations of the department committee mechanism as a forum for pursuing interests.

The reports of the conclusion of the Second Plenum indicate that a minimal consensus seems to have been reached on the role of the Academy. It was given three clearly stated research tasks: research on major and basic theoretical problems; development of new areas of research; and responsibility for comprehensive research (a term used for interdisciplinary resource surveys).[31] In addition, the organs under CAS doing applied research and development, which was considered vital to national construction and could not be taken over in the near future by other organizations, were to continue in their work under CAS. While these conclusions indicated some success in reaching consensus, the important issue of CAS' leadership role in relation to universities and ministries could not be resolved and was referred to the SPC for final settlement. This outcome was neither surprising nor in itself a pernicious contribution to the growth of political control. It was nevertheless a step away from the self-governing professionalism that many scientists still hoped to realize at that time.

Questions relating to the supply of books, equipment, reagents, and secrecy problems were also forwarded to SPC with recommendations for action. Only four other matters were directly disposed of by the Second Plenum. These included agreements that the Department Committee should meet once rather than twice a year; awards should be made once every four years, not biannually; students going abroad to study should pass an examination given by the Ministry of Higher Education; and prospective research fellows for CAS must also be given entrance examinations.

It is clear that these four matters were not of great import. The more significant issues were left as "suggestions," with decisions to be made by higher authorities. These included: the democratic election of CAS leaders (the president, vice presidents, and the heads of departments and institutes); further definition and clarification of the roles of the departments and department committees; the delegation of more functions and powers to lower levels, especially to the institutes; and the establishment of administrative organs for simplifying routine.

In addition, suggestions were made to improve the planning system, although no decisions were reached. A basic budgetary figure for each research unit was recommended as a dependable constant in making yearly plans so that only the yearly incremental growth of expenditures needed debate. Second, the monitoring of research programs should be done within the Academy by the department or institutes, depending on the circumstances, not by groups outside CAS such as SPC. Finally, scientists should be able to conduct research on topics of their own choosing in addition to the work specified in the plans.[32]

Thus, the Second Annual Plenum of the Department Committee was a forum where much of substance was discussed but where few substantial decisions were made. The more important questions were referred to the SPC or to other authoritative groups such as the Party. The history of the Second Plenum indicates the salience of what I have called "constitutional issues" at that time: the real opportunities for voice enjoyed by high status scientists; the inability of scientists to reach consensus on important matters, and hence the limitations of the department system for conflict resolution; and the consequent growth in importance of the SPC. To gain further insight into the pursuit of political interests in the spring of 1957 it will be helpful to examine in detail one of the most intriguing series of events in the scientific development of the PRC.

The China Democratic League Affairs

The China Democratic League (CDL), perhaps the most active of China's "democratic parties" was deeply involved with the final blossoming of the Hundred Flowers and the subsequent Anti-Rightist

Movement, when leaders of the CDL became central targets. At the center of the storm were Zhang Bojun, Minister of Communications, and Luo Longji, Minister of the Timber Industry, both leading members of the CDL. They were instrumental in organizing an informal group of intellectuals and other "democratic personages" which became known as the "Zhang-Luo clique." At closed meetings this group set out to take advantage of the Hundred Flowers atmosphere and win reforms relating to more power for the small parties; freedom for science; the authority of those democratic personages in high governmental positions with titles but no power; and the elimination of party committees from the schools of higher learning or at least some limitation of their power.[33] The "Zhang-Luo clique" established four working groups to discuss these problems, but only one – the science-planning group, which is of interest to us here – actually met.[34] The work of the science planning group culminated in the publication of its proposals on June 9, and shortly thereafter the denunciation as rightists of two of the scientists involved. The chronology of events leading up to publication of the program is itself revealing.

Some members of the CDL who were interested in science apparently began discussions of the organization of science as early as March, 1957. On the fourteenth of that month Mao had instructed Nie Rongzhen to settle the questions of the organization of science by the meeting of the National People's Congress (May 26). In April, the CDL (science) group began to solicit the views of its members from all over the country, and on May 13 held a meeting to draft its own proposals for a national science policy. By this time the Second Plenum of the CAS department committees was a little over a week away, and the CDL members apparently wanted to define their position privately prior to the meeting. Accordingly, they convened a special meeting on May 14 for CDL members who were also board members. Nie Rongzhen also convened a special meeting on May 19 to discuss the science set-up, and apparently to achieve some consensus of opinion before the Second Plenum was to open on the twenty-second. The leaders of the CDL science group, physicist Qian Weichang (Sc.D., University of Toronto), and chemist Cong Jiaolun (Ph.D., MIT) were privy to all these meetings, as board members, as members of the SPC, and as members of the CDL. Qian was later accused of betraying his membership in the SPC, by disclosing what was said at those meetings to the CDL, providing its members with a realistic idea of what kinds of concessions it could expect. Both were later accused of being rightists.

On June 5, what became known as the "plagiarized" SPC solution to the problems of the organization of science was revised with the "reactionary ideas of the CDL." It would appear that the SPC did indeed have a program that was known to Qian but which was not satisfactory to the CDL group. On June 6, the group held an emergency meeting with Zhang Bojun to plan strategy. On the seventh, the CDL's program ("plagiarized" from SPC and revised) was sent to SPC. On the ninth it appeared in *Guangming ribao* (GMRB).[35] A special meeting was to be held by SPC to discuss the proposal. The scheduled fourth enlarged meeting of the SPC began on the thirteenth.

The criticisms of the CDL programs made at the special CAS Anti-Rightist meetings in July intimated that the program entailed more than what appeared in the June 9th GMRB. This would support the view that the GMRB version may have been a revision (possibly milder) of an earlier version or even, as was charged, of the SPC proposal. Nevertheless, the implications of the GMRB version would certainly fit these later criticisms, and it seems safe to assume that the GMRB version conveyed the meaning and main intentions of the CDL group.

The CDL program, known more completely as "Several Opinions Concerning the Question of the Science System of Our Country" was drafted by Qian, Cong, and mathematician Hua Luogong (Sc.D., Cambridge), biologist Tong Dizhou (Sc.D., University of Brussels), and economist Qian Jiaju. The proposal had five main sections.[36]

The first was concerned with the material and psychological conditions for research, with special mention given to experienced researchers and elderly scientists. The CDL program proposed that there be better use of scientists' time by freeing capable researchers of administrative responsibilities, and allowing old people to make their contributions while they were still able. Scientists should be allowed a period of time every year to do uninterrupted research. They should also be given vacations and opportunities for advanced training. Responsibilities to participate in such political activities as the National People's Congress should be minimized. There should be a greater availability of research assistants, particularly for experienced researchers, and facilities should be improved and their distribution rationalized. The CDL proposal was critical of the excessive attention devoted to secrecy, which restricted information. National expenditures for research should be increased and rationalized. There should be a research fund for universities, an unrestricted fund for scientists in need of support, and institution of new budget procedures. Finally a plea was made to allow scientists to work where their training is relevant and for easing transfers when necessary.[37]

The second section dealt with the relations among research sectors. The program was very critical of the "departmentalism" that manifested itself in the tendency of those in the various sectors to think only of their own personnel and in resistance to personnel transfers from one sector to another.[38] The CDL paper charged that even talk of inter-sector cooperation raised suspicions and prevented the sectors from acting in the way needed to achieve goals.

To deal with this situation the CDL program proposed that unnecessary concentration of research in one organization should be avoided, because "where scientists are, that is where the work should be done." In addition, the needs of the various sectors should be adjusted equitably through mutual consultation. The mechanism for improving intersectoral cooperation should continue to be the "academic committee" system of concurrent (professional) positions.

As for the nature of the research done by the three sectors, the CDL proposed that industry and other ministerial research be concerned with the "pressing problems" of those departments. CAS should limit itself to problems of fundamental and comprehensive research of national significance. Research in institutions of higher education was left flexible (reflecting the variety of such institutions) and could range from questions of basic science, to questions of pedagogy, or problems of production. And, while CDL recognized that new installations for research are often needed, it cautioned against indiscriminate proliferation of facilities without consultation.[39]

A third section on social science is not of direct interest here except insofar as it tainted the rest of the program. Social science, unlike natural science, was seen by the CCP as having a clear class character. The CDL program asserted that not all social science from capitalist countries was inherently bad. It went one step further and maintained that it was incorrect for the policies set and measures taken by the government to be regarded as objective laws and hence unsuitable for study and debate. The CDL scholars thought that a more independent social science would rationalize and improve government policy.

The fourth section dealt with the important question of leadership in science, but a firm position on this issue was not taken. The program affirmed the necessity of good leadership in research, approved of the work of the SPC, and urged that it be strengthened. It also suggested that SPC-type groups should be established in selected provinces and cities to deal with regional scientific affairs. The proposal gave explicit mention to scientific societies and suggested that these be strengthened to improve communications among scientists. On the question of the "locomotive" of academic leadership, the CDL program said that this should be allowed to emerge in the course of work. Once research was underway, it would become apparent which would be the leading organ. The question should not be subjectively predetermined.[40]

The final section of the CDL proposal dealt with the cultivation of new labor. The CDL scholars felt that in the selection and promotion of students and young researchers, professional criteria should be at least as important as political criteria, which the scholars felt had been overemphasized in the past. The proposal acknowledged the seriousness of the training problem and said that scientists should feel a personal responsibility for this work. However, it maintained that political authorities should respect the privilege of scientists to judge the qualifications of the young people.[41]

The publication of the CDL proposal on the science system coincided almost to the day with the Anti-Rightist Movement begun by the CCP in response to the Hundred Flowers criticisms it had received in May and early June. A *People's Daily* editorial of June 8 launched the counterattack and on June 18 a considerably revised version of Mao's statement on contradictions among the people appeared. By the middle of July, CAS was holding special Anti-Rightist forums which continued on and off into September. It was at these forums that Qian and Cong (but not the others), and the CDL program came under attack. Qian and Cong were denounced by their colleagues, branded as rightists, and criticized for their past involvements in science policy matters. The CDL program was repudiated as an anti-socialist document.

Two questions must be asked about the CDL program and its aftermath. First, was it made an object for attack because of the substance of its criticisms and recommendations? Second, in spite of its being drawn up by only a handful of scientists, can it be taken as representative of the views of the great number of Chinese scientists, including those who denounced it? These questions can be approached by making a point by point review of the program.

On the question of working conditions, all scientists would approve of improved conditions and, indeed, most of the suggestions made in the first section had been made before by others. However, it is not clear that all scientists would have stated the position as forthrightly and as critically as did the CDL group. At the Anti-

Rightist meetings which followed it was argued that the Party was moving to improve at least the material conditions for work through the SPC, as indicated by the increases in the science budgets for 1956 and 1957. By not telling the whole story of the SPC's efforts to improve conditions, and not using language that was sufficiently appreciative, the CDL group allegedly was creating the impression that the government was against the scientists.[42]

In the second section, on the relations among research sectors, the CDL seemed to have identified problems recognized by all parties. Even such politically reliable scientists as Qian Sanjiang were critical of departmentalism, and of the poor relations that existed among the research sectors, particularly between CAS and the Ministry of Higher Education.[43] While no proposal would be likely to meet with the approval of all scientists, the prescriptions of the CDL group did seem to follow the emerging policy of the SPC. The SPC's approach was to coordinate the work of the different sectors and cut through departmentalism. Similarly the allocation of research goals—basic science to CAS, applied research to government research units—followed the SPC and certainly anticipated what later happened. The SPC's precise research policy for institutions of higher education was not clear, but it probably stressed the distribution of applied research to all institutions to a greater extent than the CDL group would have wanted. However, in general there do not seem to be major differences between the CDL program for this area and that of the SPC.

The question of social science had far more serious political and ideological implications than the other four points. The fact that the CDL group came down on the wrong side on this issue may have contributed strongly to the vigor with which it was later attacked.

The CDL position on leadership in science was similar to that of the SPC. The CDL recognized the need for the kind of leadership SPC was to provide, and urged the strengthening of professional societies, but it demurred on the issue of "locomotive." This was attacked as a serious mistake. The CDL statement which was critical of premature attempts to identify the locomotive was tantamount to accusing Zhou Enlai of subjectivism, since Zhou originally cast the CAS in the locomotive role.

Qian was also attacked for wanting to turn Qinghua into a Chinese California Institute of Technology. The charge, which was probably true, is not surprising. The foreign experiences of Qian, Cong, and many others who had been trained abroad undoubtedly shaped their views about how science should be organized. It is likely that many scientists were skeptical of the Soviet academy system. Qian and Cong had both been politically reliable and sympathized with many CCP goals. However, they had experienced institutions that had successfully combined broad preparation in the basic sciences, advanced training, and basic and applied research in such a way that the different activities reinforced one another. The California Tech or MIT model was contrary to the Soviet approach, but was not entirely incompatible with Chinese goals for research or Chinese conditions. The experience of these two men in the West, plus the fact that both had vested interests in improving university research, seemed to be the bases for the CDL group's hesitation about arbitrarily designating a "locomotive" for Chinese research.

The extent to which most of China's scientists would have endorsed the SPC as fully on this question as did the CDL group is unclear. The SPC and the planning system imposed a new and unpalatable mode of organization that many found objectionable. People like Qian and Cong were rather deeply involved with this new approach; they were part of the "establishment" and probably were benefitting from it.

Finally, most scientists interested in maintaining professional standards would have been supportive of the CDL group's state-ments on training new people. It will be recalled that some scientists had been critical of the low standards of new research probationers or students scheduled to go abroad. The official reply to this section of the CDL program, made by Guo Moro, was that the stress on pro-fessional standards was a subterfuge for maintaining the numerical superiority of scholars from bourgeois backgrounds in the academic ranks. Guo offered statistics that were intended to show that in fact the CCP had not ignored professional criteria in recruitment as charged.[44]

The substantive faults of the CDL program from the point of view of the political authorities were as much with what was not said as with what was. SPC leadership was acknowledged, but planning as an integral part of the science system was barely mentioned. There was no mention of the importance of party leadership in science, a concept that was fundamental to the CCP's views of science and which, as a result of the spring of 1957, was to become more fully articulated. Finally there was no mention of science serving socialist construction. This concept also was basic to the Party's understanding of the scientific enterprise. Indeed, one of the justifications of the 1956-57 liberalization period was that it would produce an atmosphere more conducive to the kind of fruitful research needed for national development.

While much of what was said was not inherently "rightist" and in fact contained proposals that were later implemented, the tone of the CDL document and its omissions could, in the right political atmosphere, be construed as the reemergence of the bourgeois ideology of science. This ideology, at least as it was interpreted by the CCP, stressed "science for science's sake" and the primacy of professional values, minimized responsibility to the society that sustains research, and stressed the importance of expert leadership in technical affairs.

The above reflects the substantive difficulties of the CDL program. These would not have warranted singling out the CDL program and Qian and Cong for the intensive attacks they received, however, had other considerations not been present. The CDL working group on science was identified as part of the larger and more politically significant "Zhang-Luo clique," which became a prime target for the Anti-Rightist Movement, especially in Beijing and Shanghai.[45] Thus the association with Zhang and Luo made the CDL scientists far more susceptible to attack than they otherwise would have been.

The political significance of the CDL proposal was also amplified by its timing. Coming when it did, at a time when tighter political controls were being applied, the proposal represented too much of an intrusion into a domain of policy that was reserved for the state and party, and suggested methods that in themselves were unsatisfactory to the authorities. To have approved the CDL proposal would have been to legitimize a decentralized and potentially pluralistic process of policy initiatives. Thus, even though the substance of the CDL's policy proposals did not differ greatly from the emerging, but poorly articulated policy of the SPC, the partisan mode of interest expression represented in the CDL episode represented a structural challenge to the CCP's legitimacy and ability to lead.

Finally, the methods used by the CDL were unacceptable. It proceeded privately and went outside the officially sanctioned channels of action, for instance by holding a special meeting of those CDL members who were also CAS board members just prior to the Second Plenary meeting. In addition it relied on the presence of Qian and Cong on the SPC to sound out opinions of the SPC.[46] It was felt that the affairs of the SPC should have remained privileged and not reported back to the CDL.

The Lessons of the 1950s

The cases above illustrate a number of points about the pursuit of political interests by scientists, but leave a number of questions unanswered. They make it difficult to sustain the view that scientists pursuing their political interests act as an associational interest group. By the mid-1950s, the scientific community was already too penetrated by the political system to be able to define its collective interests. Hence, the associational basis for the organization of science was too weak to sustain resistance to the further interventions of the regime. As a result, expressions of *voice* tended to reflect organizational interests rather than professional interests, except on those issues that involved collective goals (i.e., constitutional standing). But even on these, the inability to reach agreement on certain issues of the organization of science resulted in the preemption of the issue by state authorities. These cases also illustrate that participation and the expression of voice depended to a great extent on the pleasure of the authorities.

The voices heard during the debates of 1956-57 were mainly those of the elite, and it is important to attempt an assessment of how representative these were. While it is likely that the elite scientists thought of themselves as representative, there were many points of cleavage among scientists, including those based on age and place of training. In spite of the invective against western-trained "bourgeois" scientists voiced by authorities, there is no doubt that these individuals occupied high-ranking positions and enjoyed prestige, salaries, and perquisites not available to the rank and file.

There were indications that younger scientists were concerned about having their career advancement blocked by elders[47] and did not always feel that the elite status enjoyed by older scientists was deserved.[48] Many members of the elite were made institute directors or deputy directors, or were given other types of administrative positions. In some cases these administrative assignments came shortly after returning from study in the West. Some members of the elite therefore had relatively little experience as "bench scientists" in China under Chinese research conditions and facing Chinese problems. It is quite possible therefore that many of the elite scientists were more cut off than we have commonly assumed from those administratively below them.[49] If so, they may neither have represented the interests of, nor enjoyed the support from subordinates, a situation which could only have gotten worse over time as the elite's active involvement in research faded further into the past.

How was the role of the elite scientist perceived by the political elite? The answer to this question turns in part on how the interests of scientists were perceived. One can discern a certain ambivalence on the part of the regime on this question. At times the political authorities have acted as though the interests of scientists and the relation of science to the public interest could be objectively determined through an analysis of the laws of history. At other times, which have coincided with the active encouragement of voice, the regime has acted as though these matters could only be determined after considering the subjective expressions of interests from the scientists themselves. In the latter case, elite scientists have been treated as representatives of scientists as an occupational category. In the former, however, they were regarded more as fiduciaries, or "trustees." The result was an additional element of ambiguity in the elite scientist's role during periods when voice was encouraged. As representatives, elite scientists could legitimately act as special pleaders; as trustees they were to be disinterested specialized servants of the working class.

The theoretical considerations introduced at the outset suggest a slightly different interpretation of the role of the elite scientists. The case above illustrates that the main collective good sought was a beneficial constitutional standing. However, it was not possible to achieve this through collective action since only political authorities could grant it. Instead, scientists sought to provide a proposal for constitutional status. As we have seen, this was not the product of the collective action of rank and file scientists. It was rather the creation of elite scientists acting in a way that was reminiscent of Olson's "privileged group" providing a collective good. As such, the elite scientist is not the selfless champion of the rank and file, or the fiduciary of the public interest. Instead, he is the self-interested beneficiary of a collective good, the cost of which he is willing to bear individually or with a select group of others without full contributions from all beneficiaries. As with any situation where collective goods are provided by privileged groups (e.g., collective security arrangements where one or a few powerful states bear most of the costs), the rank and file may not be entirely satisfied with the good supplied, but it is usually better than nothing.

In the case examined, the organizational setting affecting the expression of voice was certainly not limited to formal structures, role perceptions, and role relations. Unfortunately, however, we know considerably less about informal organization, although scattered evidence suggests that it was exceedingly important. The existence of the Chang-Luo "clique," for instance, illustrates informal organization in action. Furthermore, it is not unreasonable to postulate that clientelist relations and *guanxi* networks were quite important for linking rank and file scientists, elite scientists, and political decision makers, thus serving as an important channel for voice. But while *guanxi* networks could at times serve a useful function in integrating what had become formally a highly differentiated system, they could also run counter to the collective interests of all scientists and efforts to devise, on universalistic grounds, a science policy serving China's national interest. The frequent criticisms of "departmentalism" during this period suggest that this danger was more than hypothetical.

The introduction of questions about informal groups opens up yet another possibility for interpreting the role of elite scientists, one congenial with a patron-client perspective. In this view, the elite scientist acts as a patron for junior scientists or is himself subject to the patronage of those with political authority. Patron-client ties are, of course, mutual exchange, *quid pro quo* relations, and thus are theoretically distinct from the privileged group-rank and file relationship discussed above. It is quite conceivable that both roles may be descriptive of elite scientists at different times, however. When issues of collective goods were at hand, elite scientists could be expected to play the privileged group role. Faced with distributive issues and divisible goods, particularly in the face of considerable organizational uncertainty, elite scientists in their informal organization behavior could be thought of as participants in clientelist relations.

A final complication in interpreting the events of 1957 is the question of what party membership meant for the behavior of scientists. In the mid-1950s, the Party made an active effort to recruit scientists, and had some success among the elite. While it is likely that most scientists joined the Party in the belief that their own individual interests would be furthered, it is also true that party membership provided opportunities to represent the collective interests (as defined by the elite) more directly to the political decision makers. On the other hand, party membership carried with it the obligation to observe party discipline. In this sense, the recruitment of scientists into the Party may have introduced an additional, very significant cleavage into the scientific community (between party and non-party members), and actually led to a reduction of voice among party scientists subject to party discipline.

Toward Cultural Revolution

By the middle of 1957 the organizational environment for the pursuit of interests was complex. There was the formal state organization with its three main sectors for research and its central science policy agency. And, there were professional societies, with their legacy of voluntary association. These had been penetrated by the regime and converted into mass organizations for purposes of mobilization and control, and had been brought under a new regime-sponsored umbrella organization.

This diversified organizational environment provided a variety of forums and channels for participation and the expression of voice, but it also widened cleavages among scientists. As the case analysis above shows, these cleavages did not stop scientists from pursuing common interests associated with collective goods (although they may have weakened the efforts), but they were activated when scientists pursued interests related to a divisible good such as research support allocated via the plan.

The authoritative resolution of the debates of 1956-57 had the effect of establishing rules of participation, or what could be called a constitutional framework. The most important changes brought by this framework were the undermining of voluntary professional associations and the establishment of an ultimate arbiter for determining the interests of scientists in the form of the reorganized SPC. It is significant that under these new rules, the new SPC (and the State Science and Technology Commission after 1958) did not include scientists as members, whereas the original SPC did.

The constitutional framework would prove to be durable as long as the status of scientists and their patrons in the central bureaucracy was maintained. Except for perturbations during the Great Leap years, this was the case until 1966. There was a gradual routinization of voice through the planning system, and through the STC-encouraged activities of the professional societies. The importance of the latter for policy-making was recognized by the SSTC, and the organization of new societies was promoted.[50]

During the Great Leap Forward science was subject to a campaign-style leadership which called into question the constitutional status of scientists, subjected them to numerous political meetings, and disrupted bureaucratic routines. Active efforts by the Party were made to accelerate ideological remolding of scientists and to bring a closer match between research and the needs of production. All of this made the exercise of voice costly to scientists, and in some cases attempts at surrogate exit were made by using politically determined but scientifically uninteresting research projects as covers for the work scientists took more seriously.[51]

By 1961 political authorities recognized the need for "recuperative" mechanisms and therefore again actively encouraged voice. In contrast to the Great Leap, when the Party thought it knew the proper ways to rationalize research and link research with production, in the early 1960s the views of scientists were solicited, not only through formal organizational channels, but also through debates conducted in the media.[52] Individual scientists were quite forthcoming with suggestions, but in the process were able to press claims for better working conditions, material support, and greater autonomy. Two types of participatory roles—advisor and advocate—came to be legitimized during the 1960s within the constitutional system that was reaffirmed in 1961.[53] While these roles generally were played by elite scientists, the encouragement of individual voice also opened participatory opportunities for the rank and file.

The Cultural Revolution was a serious blow to the status of science and that of central science administrators. As a result, the rule-induced patterns of voice and interest pursuit from the preceding eight to ten years were eliminated, and indeed the rules themselves were the subject of political struggle. At the outset of the Cultural Revolution, there was a clear central directive that scientific research should not be disrupted. But as the movement gained in intensity, high-level patrons of science—such as the leadership of the STC—came under attack and were removed from office. As this occurred, disruptions inevitably came to research institutes, although it is generally assumed that military related research fared somewhat better than civilian science. Indeed the privileged access to equipment and personal that military R&D units are thought to enjoy now is a reflection in part of the protection they received during the Cultural Revolution.

The Cultural Revolution did, however, also reveal social cleavages within the scientific community based upon age, educational background, and technical competence. And while Red Guards were responsible for some of the disruption, it should be recalled that struggles within research institutes were often between competing groups of intellectuals. Thus, the Cultural Revolution was perceived by the participants as benefitting some as it hurt others. The Cultural Revolution continued to be an issue in the politics of science throughout the 1970s, as it did in the PLA (discussed by Professor Harding in this volume).

By the end of the Cultural Revolution, the science policy system that had characterized the early 1960s had been severely disrupted. The SSTC had been abolished, most professional societies were inactive, universities had undergone major transformations, and CAS had been radically decentralized. As a result, the structure and political conditions for the patterns of interest articulation which had characterized the early 1960s were gone. The Cultural Revolution of course was an occasion for an enormous surge of political participation. But in the absence of stable political structure as an aid to individual calculations of interest, the intense politicization of society resulted in a more highly personalized politics, including the politics of science.

The Slow Return to the Old Constitutional Order

In 1977, major new directions in science policy were initiated which were designed to terminate the influence of the Cultural Revolution on science. These changes, however, have their origins in events going back at least to 1972. As we currently understand them, they were not brought about mainly through the effectiveness of scientists pursuing their interests in an attempt to overcome the ill-effects of the Cultural Revolution. More important was the intervention of high political leaders in consulation with elite scientists to upgrade the status of scientists and of central bureaucratic agencies (and bureaucrats) supporting science. These political initiatives were prompted in part by the opinions of foreign scientists who began visiting China in the early 1970s.

In short, initiatives from the highest political authorities were required to reestablish a constitutional framework that would allow the voices of scientists to be heard. It seems to have been largely the top leadership—Mao Zedong, Zhou Enlai, and the rehabilitated "bureaucratic leaders," especially Deng Xiaoping—who were responsible for reconsidering science and the status of scientists following anti-professional Cultural Revolution reforms.[54] As noted above, foreign scientists visiting China in the early 1970s did have an influence, one of the most important instances of which was an audience granted by Mao to Nobel Laureate C. N. Yang of the State University of New York at Stony Brook in 1972.[55]

Once the top leadership became committed to reform, the role of elite scientists expanded. Zhou Peiyuan, for instance, played an important role in implementing instructions from Zhou Enlai on reforms in research and university life. It is also likely that elite scientists were active in preparing the "Outline Summary Report of the Work of the Academy of Sciences" (generally regarded as the blueprint for the reforms of 1977), even though the main responsibility for this document belongs to non-scientist Hu Yaobang.[56] In addition, there have been reports that certain senior scientists have over the years enjoyed special informal access to senior political leaders, and it is at least possible that they had an influence on Mao and Zhou in the early 1970s that contributed to a reconsideration of the Cultural Revolution legacy.

But in spite of these initiatives for reform, struggles within science were intense until Mao's death. The personalized politics which was the legacy of the Cultural Revolution manifested itself in the entrenched resistance from followers of the Gang of Four in scientific organizations to the reestablishment of the pre-Cultural Revolution order.[57] It was only after the Gang of Four was arrested and its followers gradually weeded out that the reforms envisioned in such documents as the "Outline Report" could be implemented.

The Post-Mao Era

The policy of the "four modernizations," first advanced in 1975, has been vigorously reaffirmed since Mao's death and the elimination of the Gang of Four. With this reaffirmation has come the corollary assertion that science and technology are the keys to the realization of the four modernizations. This new policy environment, not surprisingly, has opened up new opportunities for scientists as political participants able to pursue their interests.

The policies of the post-Mao era have affected the political lives of Chinese scientists in a number of ways. In some respects those policies have returned scientists to a political life reminiscent of the pre-Cultural Revolution period. In other ways the current situation is characterized by participatory opportunities that are new in the history of the PRC. Finally, while there are many echoes of the pre-Cultural Revolution period, the leftist view continues to influence the ways scientists pursue their interests.

In the discussion above, I stressed the importance of understanding the formal organizational setting for science and technology for understanding political participation. This is also true for the post-Mao era. The notable features of the current organizational setting include the reestablishment of the SSTC, the redesign of CAS to resemble the Academy of the pre-Cultural Revolution era (including the reestablishment of the departments and department committees, and of academic committees at the institute level), and the reinvigoration of CAST. An important innovation, which gives science access to the highest level of government decision making, is the establishment of the Science and Technology Leading Group directly under the State Council and the naming of Premier Zhao as the titular head of this body.

In CAS, other changes also strengthen the voice of scientists. Theoretically, the Academy is to be a self-governing body in which the highest authority is invested in the reestablished Academy Council, election to which is supposedly based on scientific merit. The Council, in turn, elects the officers of the Academy, including the president who is now an accomplished scientist.[58]

Before the Cultural Revolution, the effectiveness of the voice of the scientific community was in large part a function of the relationships between the scientific community and the science administrators within the government bureaucracy. In recent years, many of the pre-Cultural Revolution science administrators have reemerged and begun to play an enhanced role in national policy-making. This, in conjunction with two related developments discussed below, is perhaps the most significant indication that opportunities for effective expression of voice by scientists are more assured than at any other time since the establishment of the PRC.

To appreciate this, let us first consider the two related developments. The first is simply the new commitment the regime is showing to the recruitment of technically trained individuals to serve in science and technology related government agencies. Not only are the old bureaucratic patrons of science again in office, but their numbers are being expanded. This is not to say that the interests of such personnel are identical to those of the scientists. However, as long as China has the type of highly bureaucratic political and economic systems it does, having bureaucrats sympathetic to the scientific enterprise is an essential component of interest representation for the scientific community.

The second new development is the growth of science policy analysis, both inside and outside the government. Officials at the State Council level have clearly become interested in technical advice, and have set up research centers (*zhongxin*) to provide it. These have responsibilities that pertain to the interests of the R&D community, and members of that community contribute to their work.

But in addition to such high level bodies, it is also important to note the development of a national network of science policy analysis that was formalized by the establishment in 1982 of the national Association of Science and Science Technology Policy Studies (ASSTPS). The association includes scientists and engineers around the country who are concerned with a spectrum of issues that pertain to the interests of the technical community, ranging from research priorities to the living and working conditions for technical intellectuals.

What is of particular interest is the fact that among the officers of the association are key science policy officials from the SSTC and CAS. When one considers that the SSTC is linked to the S&T Leading Group through a few leading officials who hold concurrent positions in both, and that the SSTC in turn is linked to the network of science policy analysis represented by the ASSTPS, it is possible to postulate with some confidence that the scientific community is able to make its views known on matters of importance to it, with a guarantee of access and sympathetic reception.

Underlying the currently favorable environment for participation by scientists is the commitment by the current leadership to upgrade the political standing of technical intellectuals, and to acknowledge the past wrongs done to intellectuals in the name of proletarian revolution. It was noted above that the termination of the Hundred Flowers interlude was followed by the Anti-Rightist Campaign of 1957, during which a large number of intellectuals were branded as rightists. In many cases, technical intellectuals were removed from positions requiring their technical skills, and sent to do manual labor. Just as the policies of the Anti-Rightist period had a chilling effect on the expression of voice from scientists for over twenty years, so the policy of acknowledging the mistakes of the Anti-Rightist Movement in the early 1980s has encouraged scientists to speak out on issues of importance to them as a group, and on issues of importance to the nation's progress, such as the direction of scientific development, environmental protection, and the design and planning for large technical projects.

The reinstatement of political rights for technical intellectuals has also meant that intellectuals who are not Communist Party members could again seek political association with non-Communist political groups, including the China Democratic League. In conjunction with the reactivation of the Chinese People's Political Consultative Conference, this possibility has reopened opportunities for forms of participation that had been denied since 1957.[59]

However, the new political status accorded intellectuals has been made in a society that at least since 1966 (and more realistically, since 1957), had institutionalized hostility and suspicion towards intellectuals. In this sense, it has been impossible to recreate fully the conditions of the 1950s. The terrible legacy of anti-intellectualism is most evident (and most problematic) in the profound resistance of cadres at lower levels to fully implement the new central policies intended to improve the status of intellectuals. The fact that the Chinese press in 1985 is still reporting on discrimination against intellectuals some seven years after the new policies were announced, indicates just how deep is the resistance to the idea that intellectuals too can be part of the working class. Thus, however many gains scientists have made with the central leaders to improve their political standing, their ability to pursue their interests in their own work units is all too often still severely constrained.

In ways that have not been seen since before the Cultural Revolution, the Party has organized itself to direct science affairs, and has placed individuals with long science administration experience in key positions in the state's science bureaucracy. Under current policy, again reminiscent of the 1950s, the Party is making an active effort to recruit scientists and engineers into its ranks. Indicative of the new relationship between the party and the intellectual community is the fact that the president of CAS (Lu Jiaxi), while an accomplished scholar, is also the secretary of the Party "leading group" in the organization. Whether an individual scientist is in a better position to pursue his interests as a member of the Party is still impossible to determine, but the fact that more scientists are becoming party members seems to be a move that provides the scientific community with more of a voice in political councils.

When one looks at the policy issues which engage the participatory energies of scientists in the 1980s, there are again echoes of the 1950s. The role of CAS is still debated, as are issues pertaining to the political standing of scientists, their living and working conditions, and the proper levels of support for basic versus applied research. Indicative of the new influence scientists carry in some quarters is the strengthening of university research, long an objective of China's senior, western-trained scientists.

Some issues are new, however. Among the most interesting are those pertaining to changes in research policy and organization that have resulted from economic reforms. One consequence of these reforms is that a number of industrial research institutes previously under the jurisdictions of industrial ministries, and thus assured of research support via annual budgetary appropriations, are now being cut loose from such support and are being asked to generate revenues by engaging in competitive contract research. Researchers in such institutes, alarmed at the thought of losing their "iron rice bowls," have taken to the pages of the new policy analysis journals to defend the "generic research" work of the ministerial institutes.

A legacy of the PRC's tortuous history which alters the way scientists pursue their interests in the 1980s, in contrast to the mid-1950s, is a complex pattern of center-locality (the latter including province and sub-province units) relations. These are a product of various efforts at decentralization which first began in the late 1950s and continue along new directions today. They have resulted in the dispersal of authority over a range of issues, from expenditures for science to personnel management, which influences the participatory choices faced by scientists.

For example, lower-level cadres have resisted the full implementation of policies to upgrade the political standing of intellectuals. In this situation, one can surmise that scientists' interests would be better served by less dispersion of authority and more centralization. On the other hand, in the area of funding, dispersal of authority through decentralization has increased the number of potential funders of research, in effect creating a pluralism of funding sources which works to the benefit of scientists as individuals and to the collective benefit of the scientific community.

Scientists now have opportunities to secure funding from a variety of central and local sources. As more industrial research is shifted out of the institutes of government ministries, and left instead to the discretion of enterprises, the opportunities for a more free-wheeling system of contract research will increase. The implications of this increased pluralism for greater scientific autonomy should not go unnoticed. It is precisely pluralism in funding sources that many observers believe is the key to the autonomy and intellectual vibrancy of American science, and the lack of it which limits Soviet science.

Two other features of contemporary China also distinguish the current pursuit of interests by scientists from that of the 1950s. The first is the greatly expanded ties with the international scientific community. These ties offer international standards of reference in policy discussions relating to levels of research expenditures, organizational arrangements, working conditions, and a variety of other issues in which scientists have interests. Expanded international ties also create opportunities for Chinese scientists to enlist foreign scientists as allies in the pursuit of domestic interests. Perhaps the best example of this is the international support which the Chinese high energy physics community was able to enlist to buttress its claims on resources for a world-class particle accelerator.

Second, the major organizational and managerial reforms now being tested promise to widen opportunities for efficacy of participation in fundamental ways. The most significant of these reforms is the expanded use of markets which, if successful, should introduce new performance criteria for evaluating both organizations and individuals. Indeed, following the logic of Hirschman, the existence of viable market mechanisms is necessary (although not sufficient) if the potential of both exit and voice as recuperative mechanisms is to be realized. Should the reforms be fully implemented, markets can be expected to influence the political participation of scientists in two ways.

Proposals for a relatively free labor market for technical personnel are now being considered. Such a market would have a direct effect on the individual's ability to participate, especially because it would open the possibility of not doing so. In the short run, it may be costly to exit but its presence as a choice would make the exercise of voice more effective.

More indirectly, managers and cadres faced with mechanisms that generate a more accurate accounting of their performance are likely to become more dependent on those who can enhance performance. In a society that will increasingly require scientific knowledge and sound technical judgments as bases for decision-making, improvement of performance is dependent in part on those who can supply that expertise. This is not to say that scientists will emerge as a new political elite. However, if current reforms continue to go forward, technical values will quickly become far more important within administrative structures. This change should make it easier for scientists to pursue their interests than it was in the old structures based upon political values enforced by technically ignorant cadres.

Conclusion

The patterns of political participation by Chinese scientists over the history of the PRC reveal some features that are consonant with our understanding of participation by scientists elsewhere. Others are of significance mainly in the context of Chinese experience;

among these the perennial uncertainty of the political standing of scientists stands out. Scientists have not been able to influence this fundamental feature of their condition in any significant way, although there are some indications of successes in the early 1970s among elite scientists working with the political elite.

When the regime has sought to reaffirm the political rights of scientists, it has done so in part to solicit the contributions of the scientific community to national development efforts. That is, it has intended to encourage what Hirshman has referred to as "voice." At such times, scientists have had concerns about both collective and divisible goods. The former category has included the organizational arrangements for Chinese science and living and working conditions, conditions which in part are a function of how the underlying issue of political standing is resolved. We saw that in the 1950s collective goods could not be pursued without introducing distributive issues involving divisible goods. Once these issues appeared, cleavages within the scientific community were revealed which suggested that Chinese scientists lacked the cohesion of interests which would justify our regarding them as an identifiable interest group. The ability of the scientific community to achieve a workable sense of collective identity has been limited by uncertainties about political rights and the penetration of science by state and party organizations which turns issues of common concern to scientists into "special interest" issues of distribution.

On the other hand, in the post-Mao period the concern for improved working and living conditions has been articulated effectively by CAST. Under current policies, CAST has been able to act more like an associational interest group on issues of common concern than had previously been the case. The common interests of the technical community also find expression in the network of policy analysis that has arisen in recent years, and in providing the scientific advice that is now actively sought. Those setting the agenda for policy in technical areas have also become more sympathetic to science and technology.

However, the interests scientists deem worth pursuing are by no means limited to common concerns for the provision of collective goods. One suspects that as the new political standing of scientists comes to be accepted, the collective lot of the technical community will improve, and therefore will become less of an issue. Indeed, one would expect that the pursuit of interests will increasingly involve divisible goods and their distribution.

As in the pre-Cultural Revolution period, the pursuit of special interests may be through professional structures or through state agencies. The type of science, and particularly its artifactual requirements, is important in determining the type of strategy followed. The pursuit of interests through the state structure is illustrated by the case of a CAS physics institute which sought to procure an expensive piece of equipment and new facilities. The formal course of action followed was to press the demand through CAS internal planning procedures. But because of the size and expense of the project, a number of other agencies, including industrial ministries, were brought into the decision-making. And, high-level political cadres from the province in which the institute is located, with interests in the role of local industry in supplying the institute's needs, attempted to promote it as well.[60]

An example of the use of professional organizations to promote disciplinary interests across state structures is the activity of the Chinese Nuclear Society in promoting nuclear power. Active advocacy of nuclear power began at the society's first meeting in February 1980.[61] It is characteristic of the new opportunities for participation that by November the SSTC had responded by establishing a new advisory committee on nuclear power with a cross-ministerial membership drawn from what were then the first and second ministries of machine building; the Ministries of Power, Metallurgical Industry, Chemical Industry, and Education; the CAS; and the Office for Environmental Protection under the State Council.[62] Thus, the role of advocate has clearly been relegitimated, and depending on the kind of science, the best strategy may be creating alliances with a variety of bureaucratic actors.

While there is much about the pursuit of special interests in the current situation that is reminiscent of the past, there is also much that differs. The complexity of center-locality relations, the new organizational diversity brought about by various reform measures, and the expanded international contracts enjoyed by the scientific community have all changed the context in which this pursuit occurs.

It is not too difficult to imagine the new diversity working for the good of many individual scientists, or for that matter, for the good of groups or even whole disciplines. What is of greater interest, however, is whether it will gradually produce greater collective autonomy for scientists by making them less dependent on particular bureaucratic patrons. Such autonomy would seem to be a precondition for the scientific community to develop what it has lacked since the introduction of Soviet-styled institutions in the mid-1950s — a sense of collective interest. Such a development would mark the beginning of new constitutional conditions for science and, indeed, would be indicative of a new relationship between state and society in China. Ironically, were it to come about, it would be less a result of scientists pursuing their interests than an epiphenomenal outcome of other policies; in a real sense, more the result of "exit" than of "voice."

CHAPTER 6

Dissident Intellectuals in the People's Republic of China

Merle Goldman

Since the establishment of the People's Republic of China (PRC) in 1949, the overwhelming majority of intellectuals have followed the directions of the leadership, but a small number of well-placed intellectuals have periodically questioned the Chinese Communist Party's policies. They are a critical, politically-active group, in the tradition of the principled Confucian literati and the nineteenth-century Russian intelligentsia. Although they are generally trained in history, literature, or philosophy, and have been active in academia, journalism, the theater, and literature,[1] they are defined more accurately by a set of ideas than by a profession or discipline. They are distinguished by a sense of responsibility for addressing issues of policy in public forums. Even those whose purpose is also to enhance their own political positions regard themselves as the conscience of society.

Though these intellectuals are usually on the periphery of power in the universities, research institutes, media, and cultural organs, major political leaders have often enlisted them as allies in factional and ideological conflicts. Their alliances with political leaders give the intellectuals opportunities to express their views. However, there is always inherent tension within these alliances. For example, while political factions like those of Liu Shaoqi in the 1960s or Deng Xiaoping in the post-Mao era may be moderate in a pragmatic economic sense, the intellectual groups attached to them tend to be moderate in a western political sense and are more immersed in China's cultural traditions. The intellectual group attached to Mao in the Cultural Revolution could be called radical; it was unswervingly committed to class struggle, voluntarism, and ideology. Yet, during the same period Mao himself was sometimes willing to compromise with these commitments. When such groups seek to shape policy in ways the leadership does not intend, their ability to express their views is abruptly stopped either by their own political faction or by the opposing faction.

The Historical Prototype

The methods, style, and procedures used by modern dissident intellectuals to influence policy have precedents in Chinese tradition.[2] While the number is proportionately smaller than in the West, there were always a small number of intellectuals who were both participants in and critics of their own government. Older intellectuals in the PRC may consciously follow these models, while younger intellectuals who have less knowledge of their own tradition may use them in an unconscious or preconscious way.

Confucian tradition obligates any literatus to speak out when the government deviates from Confucian ideas. The literatus was to espouse his principles regardless of the personal consequences. His approach was based on the Confucian belief that moral and ideological principles transcend the will of the rulers and their officials, and that rectification of ideas will lead to rectification of policy. The belief that cultural and ideological transformation are prerequisites to political change was also an article of faith for Mao and the radical intellectuals associated with him. Even reformist intellectuals who put more stress on economic change believed that views expressed in the intellectual realm would lead to change in the political realm.

The literatus, however, was to act as an individual, not as part of a group. The formation of groups to fight for certain views was regarded as disruptive; the principle of group rights was never institutionalized. Intellectuals lacked both a corporate entity and autonomous organizations with sufficient power to exert their influence. Yet, in periods of economic and political crisis groups of intellectuals did gather together informally to express dissident views. By the Song dynasty, there were some Confucians who favored the association of literati on the basis of common principles. Ouyang Xiu, in his essay "Pengdang lun" [On factions], demonstrated through historical examples that rulers who listened to criticisms from groups of literati prospered, whereas those who suppressed them were destroyed.[3] The early Qing dynasty scholar Huang Zongxi defended centers of learning that expounded differing views, not because he desired a diversity of ideas but because "ultimately right and wrong are to be determined by scholar-philosophers in the schools, for they are the custodians of the Truth."[4]

Although these groups may have acquired an ideological justification, they never had institutionalized rights. They were unable to make themselves heard except through patrons in positions of authority, which was most likely to happen when political rivals sought to use the literati's talents and moral stature to gain adherents. In the process of articulating a patron's position, they could sometimes express their own ideas. Their PRC descendants similarly use such opportunities to express values and views that differ from the prevailing orthodoxy, and sometimes even from those of their patrons.

In their efforts to shape public opinion as a means of influencing the leadership, the literati used the tools of their trade: essays, philosophical debates, discussions of history, literary criticism, poetry, the theater, conferences, and pamphlets. By the late nineteenth century, the definition of public opinion was expanded to include students, academics, writers, professionals, managers, and skilled workers, in addition to scholar officials.[5] The literati presented their views in the newly-established newspapers and journals to reach both this enlarged group and the emperor and officials. This broader definition of public opinion, which sometimes also included some stratum of the peasantry, would apply to the post-1949 period, as would the methods used to disseminate information and opinions.

Even the type of vocabulary used today resembles that of the literati, with political criticism veiled in pedantic language and moralistic rhetoric.[6] Intellectuals in the PRC speak less about specific policies than about broad ideological issues because they have little access to specific information. More important, subtle, indirect writings are less likely to be censored than direct criticism.[7] They write in a style more abstract than concrete, more general than detailed; their ideas are shrouded in discussions of ideology, philosophy, literature, and history. The PRC intellectuals use a variety of Marxist sources to support their positions, as the literati once used the Chinese classics.

The traditional prototype for literati involvement in factional disputes is the Donglin movement at the end of the Ming. The Donglin was a group of literati which formed at a time of crisis, when scholars at the Donglin Academy met to revitalize philosophical ideas on public morality that they believed the regime had corrupted. Its activities were originally philosophically dissident, and only became politically dissident when a factional struggle broke out at court. A political faction with ties to the Donglin drew them into the struggle as a base of support, and the movement was suppressed when they and their backers were ousted from government. They had not put together a coherent political program or broadly-based organization, concentrating only on an ideological and philosophical approach. Consequently, like their descendants, they failed.[8]

The May Fourth Tradition in the PRC

Intellectuals in the PRC are also heirs to the May Fourth Movement, which sought to create a westernized culture as a solution to China's social, political, and economic problems in the early decades of the twentieth century. May Fourth intellectuals created the vocabulary, symbols, and models that helped prepare the way for change; their goal was regeneration, unity, and revolution for China. For the first time, intellectuals who did not hold official positions formed their own organizations and communities. However, all of them, including those who, like the prominent writer Lu Xun, were committed to the Communist movement, believed in intellectual autonomy. They continued to regard their activities as free and independent.

This emergence of independent intellectuals can be attributed both to the breakdown of political authority and the influence of western liberalism. But unlike the intellectuals who formed similar movements in the West, particularly in nineteenth-century Russia, they were not alienated from their country.[9] Though in despair over China's situation in the modern world, they did not cut themselves off because of rootlessness or *weltschmerz*. On the contrary, they sought to tie themselves to their society and its people; they believed their autonomy would enrich and revitalize China. This May Fourth tradition of the intellectually independent yet politically committed intellectual has served as a model for a small number of post-1949 intellectuals.

This model is reflected in a 1955 letter to the Central Committee from the writer Hu Feng, a close follower of Lu Xun, in which he protests against the stifling of intellectual life and pleads for individual and intellectual autonomy. In response, the Party denounced Hu Feng and his associates and launched its first major campaign to compel intellectuals to accept party authority. Hu Feng was imprisoned and the Hu Feng Campaign of 1955 turned into a massive movement that went beyond the intellectuals to the nation as a whole.

However, the May Fourth spirit was to revive shortly afterwards in the Hundred Flowers Campaign from mid-1956 through the first half of 1957. To prevent Polish- and Hungarian-style uprisings, which he regarded as movements of repressed discontent, Mao encouraged intellectuals to criticize the bureaucratism of party officials and granted them some intellectual freedom. He believed that the intellectuals had been sufficiently indoctrinated to stay within the limits he set. However, an initially cautious response turned into a grass roots movement in the large cities, particularly in the universities by the spring of 1957. Intellectuals and students not only spoke out in the established journals and newspapers, but also in wall posters, unauthorized pamphlets, and large-scale meetings and demonstrations. Though they had been isolated from the West by China's alliance with the Soviet Union, they continued to express May Fourth values. They criticized the domination of Soviet-style scholarship and sought a return to a western orientation. They demanded that intellectual and creative activity be removed from political direction, and that they be given the right to choose the style and content of their work.

Even writers who had been long-time supporters of the Party pointed out how difficult it was to function under the control of the regime they had helped bring to power. Lao She wrote that "a writer who is always scared stiff of overstepping set principles or doing damage to the revolution is certain to find himself bound hand and foot and incapable of writing boldly."[10] The demand for nonpoliticized intellectual activity was not only a protest against party direction, it was also an effort to allow literature to fulfill the function it had in traditional times and in the May Fourth era: expressing criticism on political issues.

The most controversial literary works were not by the older left-wing writers, but by two young writers, Wang Meng and Liu Binyan, published in *People's Literature* in 1956. They had been brought up in the communist system and had a strong commitment to its principles. They were not only influenced by the May Fourth spirit, but also by the intellectual thaw that occurred in the Soviet Union in the wake of Stalin's death. Using the prototype of Soviet stories in which characters who lived up to communist ideals came into conflict with bureaucrats who did not, they depicted courageous, resourceful, idealistic young men and women struggling with apathetic, inefficient, cautious bureaucrats to improve the well-being of the people.

Some intellectuals went beyond the limits Mao had set and criticized Party domination as the root of China's problems. The editor-in-chief of the intellectuals' newspaper *Guangming ribao*, Chu Anping, wrote: "I think a party leading a nation is not the same as a party owning a nation."[11] Student demonstrations against one-party rule and demands for an open trial for Hu Feng went beyond the limits Mao had set for criticism. Disillusioned with intellectuals and students, and under pressure from the bureaucracy, Mao abruptly ended the Hundred Flowers Campaign in June 1957. A campaign against the critics of the Party, who were labeled "rightists," was launched, during which an estimated 400,000 to 700,000 intellectuals were dismissed from their jobs and forced to undergo varying degrees of labor reform. The network of May Fourth writers and western-educated intellectuals which had continued to function as distinct communities with shared values after 1949, was finally smashed by the Anti-Rightist Campaign of 1957-59.

The Tradition of Dissident Literati in the PRC

The factionalization of the leadership and the coalescence of informal groups of intellectuals around political factions after the Great Leap Forward resembled the traditional relationship between dissident literati and the political leadership. Disagreements over methods, values, and even visions of how China should develop became polarized in the aftermath of the Great Leap Forward. Mao and a group of radical intellectuals associated with him in the early 1960s still saw the Party as a revolutionary ideological force dedicated to the utopian goal of developing a classless society through unending class struggle. They believed that the Great Leap Forward values were still appropriate and sought to indoctrinate the population in them more intensively. On the other hand, the party bureaucracy, headed by Liu Shaoqi in alliance with a group of highly-placed intellectuals saw the Party as a rational organizing tool dedicated to gradual, systematic economic development. They rejected the Great Leap Forward use of ideologically mobilized movements and sought more conventional economic methods.

Because the disagreements within the top leadership could not be resolved behind closed doors, the conflict moved into the public arena, where the divided leadership used groups of intellectuals to publicize their views and differences. In the process of articulating their patrons' views, these intellectuals took advantage of the opportunity to articulate their own special interests. They were not autonomous groups and could not express themselves too distinctly from their political sponsors, but their transmissions could not be completely controlled; they were not mere objects of manipulation.

Although the intellectuals involved with various political factions differed ideologically, they shared an ability to formulate arguments that could win support. They also had access to influential newspapers and journals which gave them public forums for debate. Some denounced tradition, yet they all expressed their criticism and ideas traditionally, in the guise of historical, philosophical, or literary discussions. Though some of their writings had value in themselves, their main purpose was to express views on current questions.

In the period between the Great Leap Forward and the Cultural Revolution, the intellectual participants divided into two major camps. Those espousing the views of Liu Shaoqi and the party bureaucracy were a group of older intellectuals associated with the Beijing Party Committee headed by Peng Zhen, and the Party Propaganda Department led by director and deputy director Lu Dingyi and Zhou Yang. The radicals, representing the Maoist faction, were a group of younger intellectuals associated with the Shanghai literary and journalistic community under Mao's close associate Ke Qingshi, head of the Shanghai Party Committee and the Social Science and Philosophy Department of the Chinese Academy of Sciences. In some ways they had as many similarities as differences. Most of them, even the radical intellectuals, came out of the cosmopolitan, westernized, urban culture of the May Fourth Movement. They were well read in western culture as well as in their own traditional culture and took on the obligation to speak out against wrongs in the manner of their predecessors among the traditional literati and in the May Fourth Movement.

Though they were members of professional associations, research institutes, party municipal committees, and the Propaganda Department, the intellectuals did not express their views through formal organizations or structures. Their associations, such as the All-China Federation of Literature and Art and the Chinese History Association, were large, unwieldy bureaucracies with chapters in all provinces and many affiliated societies. More important, these organizations were divided into groups attached to different political factions. Consequently these formal structures could not act as cohesive organizations that pursued common interests. Though most were in the humanities and were members of the same professional organizations, they were held together less by their professional interests than by similar positions on such issues as the Great Leap Forward, and by their personal connections.

The two groups differed not only on ideological issues, but in geographical origins, generation, and rank. Most of the reformist intellectuals associated with the Beijing Party Committee and the Propaganda Department were born around the first decade of the twentieth century. While they were too young to have participated in the May Fourth Movement, they lived in Shanghai in the 1920s and 1930s, where they were exposed to the influx of western ideas. By 1949, this group had already achieved prominence, and its members moved into important positions in the cultural, academic, and journalistic hierarchy in Beijing.

Though several of the radical intellectuals had been brought up in Shanghai, they were children at the time of China's opening to the West. Most were educated before 1949 but achieved prominence only in the late 1950s. While the older reform-oriented intellectuals occupied relatively high positions in Beijing, the radicals were lower-level officials in Shanghai cultural circles and in the academic hierarchy. The struggle between these two groups of intellectuals, therefore, was not just a conflict over policy in the aftermath of the Great Leap Forward, but was intertwined with personal and generational rivalry.

The reformist intellectuals' public, albeit subtle, criticism of Mao and the Great Leap Forward could not have been published if it had not been tolerated and, most likely, encouraged by Liu and the party bureaucracy. As head of the Beijing Party Committee, Peng Zhen's connection with the reformist intellectuals was more direct. Early in 1961 he brought together a number of them in the Beijing Party Committee to inspect the documents issued from 1958-61 and analyze the reasons for the failure of the Great Leap Forward. He was quoted as saying, "Let us trace the responsibility for the hunger we have suffered for these few years."[12] Mao and his wife Jiang Qing directly encouraged and assisted the radical intellectuals. But though these intellectual groups were tools of their respective political mentors, for the most part their frames of reference and styles of presentation were of their own making.

At the center of the reformist intellectuals was Deng Tou, journalist, historian, poet, and classicist. Born in Fuzhou in 1912, at an early age he joined a youth movement organized by Peng Zhen. Though trained in Chinese and western history, he was known as a journalist active in the Border Areas. In 1953-58, he was editor-in-chief of *Renmin ribao* [RMRB (People's daily)] and in 1954-60 he was president of the All-China Journalists' Association. For reasons that are not entirely clear, he was dismissed from RMRB in 1958.[13] His old associate Peng Zhen then appointed him to the Beijing Party Committee, where he established a theoretical journal *Qianxian* [Frontline]. He worked closely with a vice mayor of Beijing, Wu Han, a prominent historian of Ming history born in 1909 who was at one time associated with Hu Shi. Wu Han was also on the standing committee of the China Democratic League and head of its Beijing branch. Another collaborator was the May Fourth writer Liao Mosha, director of the United Front Work Department of the Beijing Party Committee and also in the Propaganda Department. Although these three intellectuals came from different backgrounds, they had a long personal association and agreed that the Great Leap Forward had been a disastrous policy.

Overlapping and closely associated with the Beijing Party Committee intellectuals were the writers, playwrights, and film writers who filled the top positions in the Propaganda Department, among them Zhou Yang, Xia Yan, Tian Han, and Shao Quanlin. Other intellectuals expressed similar views, but were less closely connected, such as the traditional Marxist ideologues Yang Xianzhen and his students at the Higher Party School in Beijing; and westernized academics such as Zhou Gucheng, an official of the Chinese History Association. Each group used its own discipline in the aftermath of the disruptive Great Leap Forward to advocate reconciliation and unity and denounce the Maoist approach of class struggle and mass mobilization. Wu Han and Tian Han, for example, used historical operas to express their support for Peng Dehuai, who had been purged by Mao for criticizing the Great Leap Forward. Wu Han depicted the dismissal of the upright Ming official Hai Rui; Tian Han described the bravery of Xie Yaohuan, a lady of the Tang court who pleaded with Empress Wu for better treatment of the peasants. Zhou Gucheng presented a view of Chinese history as the coexistence of different ideologies; Yang Xianzhen coined the phrase "two into one" in an effort to lessen conflict; and Shao Quanlin urged writers to depict "the middle man," the ordinary peasant who had been oppressed in the Great Leap Forward and was not yet ready to embrace the revolution.[14]

The sharpest weapon wielded by the reformist intellectuals was the *zawen*, the short, subtle satirical essay form that Lu Xun had used so effectively against the Guomindang and other ideological enemies. Deng Tuo and his two major collaborators, Wu Han and Liao Mosha, were masters of this art. They published sixty-seven

zawen, "Notes from a Three Families Village" [Sanjia cun zhaji] in
Qianxian from September, 1961 to July, 1964. The title "Three
Families Village" comes from a poem written in 1196 by the Song
poet Lu Yu about a high official who lost his post and was spending
his last years in a three families village, an image that is reminiscent
of Peng Dehuai's plight. Under the pen name Ma Nancun, Deng Tuo
published another series, "Evening Chats at Yanshan," [Yanshan
yehua heji] for which he wrote 152 zawen from March, 1961 to
September, 1962 in Beijing wanbao [Beijing evening news]. From
May 4 to December 8, 1962, Liao Mosha, Wu Han, Xia Yan, Meng
Chao, and Tang Tao did another collective series, "The Long and
Short" [Changduan lu] in RMRB, showing that they had access not
only to the Beijing newspapers, but also to the party's major
newspaper.[15]

In their zawen in the popular press and in their scholarly
articles, these intellectuals went beyond their patrons' desire for
criticism of the Great Leap Forward to demand a degree of
autonomy for scholars and a voice for scholars in political decision
making, as their colleagues had in the Hundred Flowers. They
eulogized Song, Ming, and Qing scholars, poets, artists, and advisers
who were courageous and honest in speaking out against harsh
rulers, no matter what the cost. Deng Tou advised the government
to "welcome miscellaneous scholars" by whom he meant intellectuals
who would not only enrich Chinese intellectual life, but, because of
their wide-ranging knowledge and diverse viewpoints, also enrich the
government. They could be used "for all kinds of leadership as well
as for scientific research."[16] He quoted the Song councilor San Yaofu
who advised Sima Guang, "I trust that my Sovereign will allow the
affairs of state to be discussed by many people. One should not plan
everything by one's self."[17] Deng observed that, "Human intelligence
is limited. Only a fool can imagine in his fantasies that he knows
everything. . . . No one can be intelligent about all things."[18] Deng's
advice was not only directed at the ruler. In another zawen, "The
Cases of Chen Zhang and Wang Geng," he charged not just one or a
few people, but the government itself with becoming increasingly
corrupt. He criticized the reign of the incompetent Empress
Dowager, Ming Su of the Song, in which the prime minister as well
as high officials were also incompetent. This description could be
interpreted as a criticism of both Mao and the top party leaders.

Liu Shaoqi, Peng Zhen, and the party bureaucracy encouraged
criticism of the Great Leap Forward, mass mobilization, and economic inefficiencies, and supported greater intellectual and cultural

freedom and diversity. They hoped that a loosening up of ideological restraints on scholarship and creative work would help resolve some of the problems brought on by the Great Leap Forward. But, there was no evidence that they were willing to give up political and ideological control over scholarship in the humanities or the sciences as Deng Tuo and his associates were asking. Neither Liu and the party bureaucracy nor Mao were willing to allow intellectuals a voice in policy-making or the right to criticize their government publicly. Because the leadership encouraged specific criticism and a relative relaxation of control did not mean that it would tolerate pluralism or the diffusion of power.

As uncontrollable as the content of the *zawen* columns was their proliferation. As the columns were reprinted around the country, newspapers from Yunnan and Guangdong to Shandong started similar features in which even the titles, such as "Rambling Talks at Lixiao," indicated that they had been modeled on the ones in Beijing.[19]

The attacks of the reformist intellectuals petered out toward the end of 1962, though some of their columns continued to appear until 1964. Their end was due not only to Mao's call for a renewed ideological class struggle at the Tenth Party Plenum in September, 1962, but also to the counterattack of a newly emerging rival group, the radical intellectuals, under the patronage of Mao and Jiang Qing. Battles were fought on the cultural front through Jiang Qing's reform of the Beijing operas, an effort to take control of the theatrical format that had implicitly criticized Mao. Others were fought in the pages of the party newspapers and academic journals. Although both the radicals and reformers were academically trained, the radicals had a more Marxist-oriented education, and less experience in organization and administration.

The leaders of the radical intellectuals were Zhang Chunqiao and Yao Wenyuan. Zhang was the elder of the group, born in 1910 into an intellectual family. Like his rivals, he was active in left-wing literary circles in Shanghai in the 1930s and did propaganda work in the border regions in the 1940s. But it was not until after 1949 that he began to achieve important positions. In 1955 he became a vice chairman of the All China Federation of Journalists of which Deng Tuo was chairman, and acting secretary of the Literature and Art Work Committee of the Shanghai Party Committee. During the Great Leap Forward he published an article calling for restrictions on material incentives similar to those used in war communism and the Paris Commune. It caught Mao's attention,[20] and shortly afterward he became a member of the Shanghai Party Committee and of its standing committee. His contact with Mao's inner circles came in 1963-64, when Ke Qingshi gave Jiang Qing the opportunity in Shanghai that officials in Beijing had denied her—to reform the Beijing opera. The Shanghai Propaganda Department, particularly Zhang and his close associate Yao Wenyuan, were selected to help her.

Yao, born of a father active in left-wing literary circles in the 1930s, first made a name for himself by allying with the literary bureaucrats around Zhou Yang in the Propaganda Department in opposition to the writers once associated with Lu Xun. He was active in the campaign against Hu Feng and in the Anti-Rightist Campaign attacks on Ai Qing, Ding Ling, Feng Xuefeng, and Wang Rouwang. But in the spring of 1962 he, in turn, was criticized by Zhou Yang for having attacked the famous writer Ba Jin. Some of Yao's articles were then blocked from publication. Thus Yao and Zhang joined with Jiang Qing as natural allies against the Propaganda Department, which gave them the opportunity to rise in the hierarchy. Their opposition to the cultural establishment had as much to do with personal vendettas, ambitions, and rivalries as with ideological disagreements.

Zhang and Yao joined with a group of young scholars associated with the Philosophy and Social Science Department of the Chinese Academy of Sciences who were later to become the nucleus of the Cultural Revolution Group. Zhang had been associated with a few of them at least as early as the Great Leap Forward, when several wrote articles similar to his in support of Mao's position.[21] The leading intellectual of this group was the philosopher Guan Feng, a scholar of ancient Chinese thought who became known in the late 1950s for his attacks on established scholars, particularly the prominent philosopher Feng Youlan. He criticized Feng's view that the relationship between materialism and idealism could be one of mutual influence, insisting that these philosophies could only be in sharp and constant struggle: "They cannot . . . coexist in peace."[22] Guan's work in 1961-62 reflected the retreat of those years. But, in 1963-64, after Mao's Tenth Plenum speech calling for renewed ideological struggle, he and other radicals took up Mao's call and returned to the denunciation of senior scholars with alacrity and persistence.

In contrast with the reformist intellectuals' stress on gradual change because of economic limitations, Guan and his associates reiterated the voluntarist approach of the Great Leap Forward, but now in the political instead of the economic context. At the end of 1963 Guan and his colleague Lin Yushi prophesied the Cultural Revolution: "The historical facts show that the relations between the economic foundation and the super-structure are not mechanical. Under given conditions the status of the two can be transformed. The state power is the primary thing in the super-structure and the struggle for the change of the economic system must be expressed in a concentrated manner as the struggle for capture of state power."[23] Guan also insisted that it is not the intellectual and political elite, but the masses who in the past and present create new worlds. He predicted that "new characters, new deeds, new morals, new values, and new experiences [will] spring up everywhere like dandelions in a spring lawn. The broad cadres and masses are in high spirits, doing things unprecedented in history and creating new things not found in books."[24]

Mao's patronage allowed radical intellectuals to publish their views in the major newspapers and journals, though still shrouded in historical and philosophical language. But, they were unable at this time to criticize members of the Beijing establishment directly. As we have seen, they attacked prominent intellectuals like Feng You-lan, but only those not closely connected with the Beijing Party Committee or Propaganda Department. Some of Wu Han's ideas on classless morality were criticized, but not his *zawen* or his use of the Hai Rui figure. In 1964 Guan Feng, Lin Jie, and other associates wrote direct criticisms of Wu Han's play *Hai Rui's Dismissal*, but their articles were blocked from publication by the Beijing Party Committee and the Propaganda Department. The Party deliberately kept these debates within an historical and philosophical context in order to prevent an attack on specific individuals and specific policies. Consequently these debates had the appearance of intellectual discussions rather than the political and ideological struggles they were.

It was only during the Cultural Revolution that radical intellectuals were able to expound their ideas and attack their rivals directly, as Mao, with the support of Jiang Qing and the army under Lin Biao, moved the debate into the open as a political factional struggle. When the Beijing intellectuals and their political backers were purged in the spring of 1966, the radicals finally published their attacks on specific individuals and policies. As they became activists in the Cultural Revolution, they ceased to be an intellectual group and became part of a political faction. It was their contention with reformist intellectuals in the period prior to the Cultural Revolution that gave them the opportunity to move from the periphery to the center of power when the Cultural Revolution was launched. More important, whether they merely articulated the views of the Maoist faction or acted as a stimulus in launching the Cultural Revolution, or both, there is no question that their arguments, models, and intellectual frame of reference provided the ideological underpinnings of the Cultural Revolution. However, in 1967-68, when Mao retreated from his own radicalism due to military pressure and his unwillingness to accept the anarchy of the Cultural Revolution, all but the Shanghai group led by Zhang Chunqiao and Yao Wenyuan were purged as ultra-leftists.

The Gang of Four as a Political-Intellectual Group

With the conclusion of the more violent stage of the Cultural Revolution in 1969 the leaders of the Shanghai group and their political patroness Jiang Qing became members of the Politburo. They formed a political faction at the highest level of government. Yet, with the subsequent fall of Lin Biao in 1971, the management of the government by Zhou Enlai, and the return of Deng Xiaoping in 1973, the distribution of power once again became favorable to the bureaucratic leadership. Their purged colleagues were brought back in increasingly large numbers to fill the state ministries and the army. The Shanghai group, with a later addition of the young "worker" Wang Hongwen, became known as the Gang of Four, and was increasingly on the defensive as it was isolated more and more from the centers of political and economic power. It took on a dual role. Though still a political faction, it assumed again some of the characteristics of an intellectual group. The ability of its members to express themselves publicly and, in fact, its very existence was dependent on Mao. Its members' bases of power were primarily the universities, the arts, newspapers, and journals—the areas from which they had ousted the reformist intellectuals. Despite their weakened position, they were still able to persecute other intellectuals, who continued to be purged and sent away for labor reform in the first half of the 1970s. But because they were no longer politically dominant, they were forced once again to use the camouflage of historical and philosophical analogy, ideological debate, and literary criticism in order to perpetuate Cultural Revolution policies and attack the bureaucratic faction.

In the summer and fall of 1972, as Zhou Enlai and his associates gave priority to economic development and tried to modify Cultural Revolution policies, they sought to return to more conventional academic practices and upgrade theoretical work in the sciences. Along with the reintroduction of formal entrance exams at some universities, a spate of articles appeared in the leading newspapers on the need to teach theoretical sciences in the universities in order to correct the damage caused by the anti-intellectualism of the Cultural Revolution. Some were written by scientists, others by education groups at various universities, including Fudan University in Shanghai, an indication that the radicals' control over education, even in Shanghai, was not as complete as they or their opponents claimed. These articles argued that without research in theoretical science and work in laboratories China would be unable to achieve the modernization it sought. "If we do not subject practical experience to a process of systematization and theorization, then we can only fall behind others and have to start from the very beginning in solving production and technological problems."[25] They denounced what they called "the short-sighted view which holds that fundamental theoretical subjects are useless and one may not study such things or needs to study only a little."[26]

Zhou Peiyuan, a physicist and then a vice chairman of the Scientific and Technology Commission, was the most authoritative voice to be heard in the early 1970s on the need to study the theoretical sciences and to separate the theoretical from the practical. Engineering could satisfy current needs, but the function of science was not immediately apparent. "Sometimes there is no obvious connection between abstract math and production," he said, "but we must treat with care specialties that are abstract and for which no application can be found at present."[27] Zhou also stressed that scientific study should take place in universities rather than in factories, as the Shanghai group sought, because the university "assembles together a large number of scientists and technical personnel and is continuously supplied with reinforcements by admitting new students."[28] More important, it brings together specialists from many basic disciplines who can influence one another and work together on scientific experiments.

These demands for greater attention to theoretical science, laboratory experiments, and more conventional university education did not necessarily reflect the increasing importance of the scientific community. Though an effort had been made in the early stages of the Cultural Revolution to isolate scientists from the upheaval of the

Cultural Revolution, apart from such exceptions as defense research, most scientists were swept up in its wake. Zhou Peiyuan himself was harshly criticized. There is no evidence that in the early 1970s scientists gained a strong enough base in their own associations or in the government to assert their claims on the regime. They were concerned about China's scientific and economic development, but neither they nor any other group of intellectuals could have expressed these concerns without the initiative of China's top leaders — in this case Zhou Enlai.

After Mao's death, Zhou Peiyuan revealed that in 1972 Zhou Enlai had asked him to encourage the study of scientific theory in the universities and had asked Beijing and Qinghua universities to revise their curricula so more attention could be given to theoretical science. Nevertheless, the Shanghai group had stopped Zhou Peiyuan's article emphasizing theoretical science from appearing in the RMRB, though he was able to publish it in the intellectuals' newspaper, *Guangming ribao* [GMRB]. Zhang Chunqiao had also ordered his followers to criticize Zhou Peiyuan's article and his "behind-the-scenes boss."[29]

In addition to sabotaging the revival of conventional scientific and academic education, the Shanghai group also launched a series of ideological campaigns — on Confucianism, the Dictatorship of the Proletariat, higher education, and *Water Margin* — to undermine the bureaucratic leaders and block the retreat from Cultural Revolution policies. These campaigns were widespread and intensive, extending down to the villages and the factories, but did not lead to the emotional, uncontrolled struggles of the Cultural Revolution. Moreover the bureaucratic leaders fought back with similar ideological verbiage. In the mid 1970s both sides seemed to accept certain defined limits within which the ideological struggle would be waged. With the exceptions of some journals established by the Shanghai group, the major newspapers — RMRB, GMRB, and the party journal *Hongqi* — did not contend with one another as in the Cultural Revolution. Though the Shanghai group appeared to dominate the media, both views were represented throughout the campaigns.

In contrast to the early 1960s, the spokespersons for the two sides were not famous intellectuals with their own reputations and their own constituencies. With a few exceptions, they were virtually anonymous writing groups. Zhou Enlai and his associates used a variety of university groups. The Shanghai group used a more consistent body of writing groups in Beijing, Qinghua, Fudan, and

Liaoning universities. Some of these groups also wrote under different pseudonyms. The Shanghai group communicated with their collective spokespersons directly through liaison on the various campuses. Yao himself edited some of their writings. It was much easier to control anonymous collectives than prestigious intellectuals with their own styles and ideas.

With Zhou Enlai's death in January, 1976, the Gang of Four was finally able to launch a straightforward campaign against Deng Xiaoping's educational views and Deng himself. With Mao's support, they succeeded in purging the Minister of Education, Zhou Rongxin, and in denying the premiership to Deng. But Mao's support did not extend to a full-scale purge of Deng's other bureaucratic associates. When their patron Mao died in September, 1976, the Gang of Four was easily suppressed by the bureaucratic faction.

Dissident Intellectuals in the Post-Mao Era

In the post-Mao era the emerging pattern of the Party's policy toward intellectuals and their response in some respects resembles that found in the post-Stalinist Soviet Union. The indiscriminate terror and massive coercion of the Anti-Rightist and Cultural Revolution campaigns has given way to a mixture of cajolery, manipulation, and intimidation. A small number of intellectuals continue to express criticism through official channels, and in 1978-79 a small number of workers and students were able to express criticism through unofficial channels like those in the Soviet Union. But neither official nor unofficial dissent has been possible without some degree of official sanction.

The post-Mao leadership under Deng Xiaoping sought to win the intellectuals' cooperation in repairing the devastation of the previous campaigns. Deng used them to criticize Maoist holdovers in the Politburo, and in 1978-79 allowed the expression of spontaneous, grass-roots criticism of Maoist policies. Other protests had occurred in the PRC, including the large-scale demonstrations and unofficial pamphlets on university campuses in May, 1957 and the Tian'anmen demonstration against Mao's radical policies on April 5, 1976. However, these earlier protests were suppressed very quickly, while the series of protests in 1978-79 were more widespread and lasted much longer. The earlier protests took place primarily in urban centers, but in 1978-79 the protest was nationwide. At its height, from late 1978 to early 1979, it was allowed fairly free range because it was a substitute for official condemnation of Mao and a support for Deng in his battle with the remnant Maoists. Equally important, it expressed the wide and deep revulsion of both officials and non-officials against Mao's use of terror and chaos.

This movement had many of the same trappings as the Soviet underground movement in the post-Stalin era. It circulated hand-to-hand stories, poems, petitions, and documents, put up wall posters, and made contact with foreign journalists in order to publicize its cause. Like its Soviet counterparts, it attacked the supreme former leader and demanded laws that protected human rights. Although the demands for greater cultural and political freedoms were similar to those of the Hundred Flowers, the protesters of 1978-79 also called for regularized institutions and legal procedures to guarantee these freedoms and to prevent the lawlessness and chaos they had experienced in the Anti-Rightist and Cultural Revolution campaigns. Unlike the Hundred Flowers, the emphasis was not so much on moral appeals to the leaders as on laws to protect civil liberties and prevent mass suffering and arbitrary treatment.

When the remaining Maoist segment was finally purged from the Politburo in 1980-81 and some unofficial dissenters demanded democracy as a prerequisite for modernization and denounced the Chinese invasion of Vietnam, the protest movement was quickly and harshly suppressed. By April, 1981, its leaders were imprisoned and its sympathizers intimidated into silence. Despite the publicity given the unofficial protests, they are marginal movements. Though they may have many sympathizers, the number of active participants even in the 1978-79 movement was no more than a few hundred youth who could easily be suppressed.

The more traditional and semi-official dissent of established intellectuals that had occurred in the early 1960s and resumed after Mao's death was more difficult to suppress. Most of these intellectuals were associated with the reform group around Deng Xiaoping. They published in RMRB, GMRB, *Renmin wenxue* [People's literature], and other prestigious national newspapers and journals. All of them were determined to prevent a recurrence of another Cultural Revolution, but expressed a wide range of views as to how to do so. Some wanted traditional Marxism cleansed of Maoism. Others wanted freedom of speech combined with a socialist economy. Some stressed cultural pluralism; others stressed economic pragmatism. Despite their disillusionment with the system, few rejected it outright. Most expressed a different opinion or alternative view within a Marxist-Leninist context, both because they still believed in the doctrine and because it was the one with which they were most acquainted. Moreover, they had no other choice if they wanted to publish in the official media. Still in the tradition of the dissident intellectuals of the premodern, May Fourth, and Maoist periods, they were like a loyal opposition, addressing their messages to the political elite and influencing public opinion in order to change or negate certain policies.

In the immediate post-Mao era, literature, as in traditional times and in the Soviet Union, was the principal means for expressing dissent. It began with the "literature of the wounded": stories, plays, and poems denouncing the persecution by the Gang of Four during the Cultural Revolution. But by the fall of 1979 this genre had become outmoded as the mood of the nation turned more to the present and future than to the past. It was replaced by a more controversial genre, "exposure" literature, which, in the May Fourth mode, blamed the injustices, social ills, corruption, and official privileges not only on the Cultural Revolution activists and the Gang of Four, but also on those now in power and those in power before the Cultural Revolution. In the tradition of Lu Xun and the May Fourth writers, this literature exposed the abuses in society so that they might be corrected.

Among the the most daring exponents of the "exposure" genre were the writers who spoke out in the Hundred Flowers Campaign and were purged in the Anti-Rightist Campaign. They were closer to the May Fourth era than the younger writers and were more willing to take risks than the older May Fourth writers who had been so active before 1949. These Hundred Flowers writers had been silenced for virtually twenty years, not by the Gang of Four, but by the very people in power when they were rehabilitated in the late 1970s. They sought to expose the system that allowed the Anti-Rightist Campaign and Cultural Revolution to happen. The army writer, Bai Hua, in the Confucian and May Fourth tradition called on his fellow writers at the Fourth Writers and Artists Congress of 1979 to fulfill their "sacred duty" to courageously criticize the abuses of officialdom.[30] In his scenario "Bitter Love," he depicts an artist who returns home from abroad out of a feeling of patriotism. But he is persecuted and finally dies in the Cultural Revolution, a haunted criminal. In one scene, his daughter asks him: "You love your motherland, but does your motherland love you?"[31] This line and his scenario were interpreted as expressing the intellectuals' disillusionment not only with the Cultural Revolution but with the political system itself.

Another former rightist, Wang Meng, dissents artistically
rather than ideologically. He writes of political issues less than of
everyday emotions and relationships, and experiments with a
variety of styles. Leo Lee has pointed out that in the 1920s and
1930s, before the Party prescribed socialist realism, Lu Xun and
some experimental poets were the few writers who were not
dominated by the nineteenth-century western realist style with a
social message.[32] Wang Meng and a number of younger writers have
attempted to break the bounds of the realistic narrative and
experiment with intricate language and stream of consciousness that
evoke memories, inner feelings, and random associations. In the
post-Mao era, the Party has allowed greater leeway in style than in
content, as if this concession might placate the writers.
Nevertheless, Wang Meng explained at the 1979 Fourth Writers and
Artists Congress that his apolitical approach was based on his belief
that concern with political issues in literature stultifies the writer's
ability to express human emotions and create artistic works.
Although artistic dissent may be safer than ideological dissent, it is
still a challenge to the Party's politicization of culture.

Another former rightist, Liu Binyan, presented just the opposite
view at the Writers and Artists Congress. He upheld the May
Fourth tradition that literature must continue to expose the ills of
society. Describing his own experience of being sent down to the
countryside in the Anti-Rightist Campaign, he charged that writers
had falsified the realities of peasant life by not depicting its harsh-
ness and bitterness and ignoring the indifference of officials to peasant suffering. In the manner of his Confucian predecessors, he
exhorted his fellow writers to assume their "responsibility" by telling
the truth. He denounced those who would "break the mirror" rather
than correct the ugliness it reflected.[33]

His mirror in the post-Mao era, as in the Hundred Flowers,
reflected the ugliness of the new class of officials spawned by the
communist system. But while in the Hundred Flowers he wrote
stories of enthusiastic, idealistic youth who struggled against this
class of cynical, opportunistic officials, in his most controversial work
of the post-Mao era, "Between People or Monsters," published in
1979, he emphasized the corrupt bureaucrats. In the form of an
investigative report, he describes a female official who used her
connections (guanxi) and a widespread system of corruption to
embezzle huge sums of public money to build her own financial
empire. Hers was a powerful political and economic organization,
unrestrained by any laws, institutions, or moral code, in which party

officials were obedient to her rather than to the Party. Liu's description recalls Lu Xun's condemnation of traditional society as "man-eating": "Party and government officials slowly degenerated into parasitical insects that fed off people's productivity and the socialist system."[34] Unlike the "wounded literature," Liu did not treat this phenomenon as just the aberration of the Cultural Revolution, but as inherent in the system: "The Communist Party regulated everything, but would not regulate the Communist Party."[35] Unlike Liu's earlier works and ignoring the renewed call in the late 1970s for socialist heroes, no young hero came forth in this work to rectify the system.

A number of the Party's ideological theorists expressed criticisms similar to those of the unofficial dissidents and establishment writers. Also having suffered the violence of the Cultural Revolution, they used the works of the younger Marx to point out that Marxism advocates humanism and that alienation can exist under socialism as well as under capitalism. Chief among them was Zhou Yang, who returned in the late 1970s to a position of cultural leadership from which he had been purged. He and other ideological theorists, among them Wang Ruoshi, deputy-editor in charge of ideology at RMRB, explained that alienation occurred under socialism because of the cult of the personality, irrational economic programs, and political practices in which officials who were "the people's *servants* abused the power invested in them by the people to become the people's *masters*."[36]

These literary works and the discussion of alienation supposedly were in line with Deng Xiaoping's effort to reform the bureaucracy. However, as the aftereffects of the Cultural Revolution subsided and the Deng leadership consolidated its power in the early 1980s, the Party no longer wanted such critical works. The "crisis of the socialist spirit" which the Party initially attributed to the Cultural Revolution had intensified rather than diminished with Deng's reforms as the Party had anticipated. Therefore, in 1981 the Party charged that literary works were exaggerating the gloom, weariness, and sadness within the population and were spreading a feeling of utter hopelessness. As in the Maoist era, literary works were singled out as examples to be criticized and held responsible for the ills of society. Specifically, "Bitter Love" was blamed for inducing disillusionment with the system. As always, political factionalism was involved. The initial attack on "Bitter Love" was by the army newspaper *Liberation Army Daily* in April, 1981. It was not until August, 1981 that the party newspapers fully joined in the attack.

By late 1981, as the criticism of "Bitter Love" became more vociferous and the use of such epithets as "bourgeois liberalism" more frequent, it was evident that the Party was increasingly concerned with the continuing disrespect for authority and growing western influence.

This concern culminated in a campaign against western spiritual pollution in which Zhou Yang, Wang Ruoshi, and a number of party ideological theorists and writers were singled out for attack. The Party charged that these "engineers of the soul" had led the population, particularly the youth, to question and doubt socialism and the Party. It countered that the concepts of humanism and alienation represent Marx's early period when he was still influenced by idealism and were not at the core of Marxism. Rather than solving the problems of socialist society, the discussion of these concepts had caused great confusion. Zhou Yang made a self criticism in which he confessed to weakness in ideological leadership, and Wang Ruoshi was dismissed for focusing attention on socialist alienation.

The Deng Xiaoping leadership may have been pressured into carrying out this campaign by party conservatives and the army as it had been in the Bai Hua Campaign. It is true that when the Deng leadership assumed power after Mao's death, it renounced such practices as campaigns, purges, and suppression of criticism. However, after the Deng leadership had purged the Maoists and critics went beyond the Cultural Revolution to protest against Deng's actions and policies, it cracked down on the critics it had previously encouraged. Its repression and imprisonment of activist students and workers in 1979 was done without outside pressures. Whereas the 1981 suppression may have been prompted by the pressure from the army, the campaign against spiritual pollution was first mentioned by Deng himself at a party meeting in October 1983. The 1981 campaign affected a small circle in the intellectual community, but the nationwide scale of the 1983 campaign carried out in factories, unions, and youth groups, as well as among intellectuals, signified the full support of the top leadership. That the campaign may have been provoked by factional disputes within the leadership and that it was concluded within a month in the economic and scientific communities does not mean that Deng was reluctant to launch it. Moreover, it lingered on into 1984 specifically attacking such western thinkers as Freud, Kafka, Sartre, and Euro-Marxists, whose ideas, the Party charged, evoked ideological confusion and questioning of the Party and socialism.

However, as the Deng leadership accelerated its economic reforms in late 1984 and intellectuals were again urged to learn from the West, a number of writers and ideological theorists questioned why the economic-scientific sphere was given more leeway than the literary-ideological sphere. Their protest was reminiscent of the *ti-yong* [principle-utility] debate in the nineteenth century, when China sought to acquire western science and technology while excluding western humanistic and political ideas. They pointed out that the twentieth-century effort to acquire western science without changing the overall political culture would prove as unsuccessful as the nineteenth-century effort. They demanded a share in the relative freedom and the opening to the outside world permitted to scientists and economists.

Although the literary intellectuals may not contribute directly to modernization, they argued, the way they are treated affects the scientific intellectuals. To treat writers repressively and prevent them from access to the West also inhibits scientific experimentation and scientific contact with the West. As the ideological theorist Li Honglin explained, such a division not only harms literature and art, but the whole reform effort. He acknowledged that "decadent and degenerate ideology and culture will enter our culture along with science and technology and contaminate the air." But, such "dirty things" will "enter anyway from the outside, through cracks in the walls."[37] Thus he urged China to open its doors wider because once the door is open it is impossible to filter out unwanted ideas.

A move toward a change in the *ti*, principle, is seen in the famous "Commentator" article of December 7, 1984 in *People's Daily*, based on a talk by the Party's Secretary-General Hu Yaobang: "We cannot expect people to use what Marx, Engels, and Lenin wrote years ago to solve today's problems." Even though the next day "today's problems" was revised to read they cannot solve "all of today's problems,"[38] it was clear that Marxism-Leninism was no longer considered relevant in some areas.

Also unprecedented was the Fourth Congress of the Chinese Writers' Association in late December and early January, 1985, where leading reform official Hu Qili of the party secretariat called for "freedom of literature and art" to the thunderous applause of the eight-hundred participants. The congress used procedures that suggested the beginnings of a democratic process. A correspondent for the China News Agency reported that "at the congress, writers exercised their democratic rights on many occasions, something which seldom happened in the past."[39] For the first time at an intellectual gathering the delegates voted their own rather than the Party's preferences. The delegates refused to rubber-stamp the official party slate of officers, and voted by secret ballot to elect a different group of candidates. Liu Binyan, who in late 1984 had uncovered several notorious cases of bureaucratic corruption all over the country, was not on the official list for a vice chairmanship of the China Writers' Association. Yet, when the secret vote was taken, Liu, along with the poet Zhang Guangnian, ran second only to the famous writer Ba Jin in the number of votes received. At the same time, other famous older writers, such as Ouyang Shan, who had participated actively in the Spiritual Pollution Campaign, lost their positions as vice chairmen.

Those who had been active in the Spiritual Pollution Campaign fared badly and those who had been criticized fared well. Politburo member Hu Qiaomu and Director of Propaganda Deng Liqun, who had led the campaign, were conspicuous by their absence. When their telegrams of greetings to the congress were read aloud, there was deadly silence. When the telegram of the hospitalized former cultural czar Zhou Yang, was read, there was enthusiastic, sustained applause. Zhou Yang had been one of the chief targets of the Spiritual Pollution Campaign for his articulation of the sense of alienation at large in society.[40] The contrast between the positive treatment accorded Zhou Yang and the negative treatment accorded Hu and Deng was another means of expressing the preferences of the participants. Furthermore, public inquiries were made about writers who had been personally condemned by the reform leaders, the supposed patrons of the congress. One of these writers was Ye Wenfu, whose poem "General, You Cannot Do That" attacked the privileges and corruption of high army officials. His work was no longer published. In the past, no one had dared to mention a non-person at an open meeting, but at the congress, several delegates inquired as to what had happened to Ye. Subsequently, in the February, 1985 issue of *Shikan* [Poetry], his poems reappeared.

The congress also ratified a new constitution for the Chinese Writers' Association. Although its content did not deviate from the reform line since the December, 1978 Third Plenum, the constitution presented by the leadership, like the vote for the literary officials, was not merely rubber-stamped by the participants. Its provisions were debated and revised on the congress floor before it was finally adopted. Moreover, the Chinese Writers' Association was designated as the institution to protect the writers' freedom of creativity, rights, and economic interests, as well as conduct international exchanges.

However, the writers' constitution, like the national constitution, was superseded by the Party and did not have the force of law to limit the powers of the political leadership. Consequently, some of the delegates at the congress demanded legal protections for writers, an echo of the demands of the 1979 democratic activists. Most eloquent was the screenwriter Ke Ling, who pointed out that "fundamentally it is a matter of whether it is rule by law or rule by individual. In regard to the rights and obligations of writers and artists, there should be explicit and rational regulations to allow for individual achievements and shortcomings, rewards and penalties and the legality of their actions. . . . The aim is . . . to free them from bureaucratic restrictions." Ke Ling acknowledged, however, that laws alone could not protect writers if officials did not enforce them. "Of course, even if there are laws to follow, the problem of deviation in exercising the law may emerge."[41]

While the Writers' Congress was in session, a *People's Daily* editorial of January 3, 1985 talked of the need for democracy if economic modernization was to succeed, an argument the democratic activist Wei Jingsheng made in his "Fifth Modernization," for which he had been imprisoned. Now the Party's official newspaper expressed a similar view: "The four modernizations must be accompanied by political democracy." The editorial points out that centralization of political authority hurts economic development: "Forbidding people to speak out . . . practicing rule by the voice of one man alone . . . acting on the will of those higher up . . . this kind of centralization cannot in the least push forward modernization. On the contrary, it can only impede modernization." It also adversely affects stability and unity, the editorial argues, because "its bureaucratic, authoritarian style suppresses the people's reasonable political and economic demands." Consequently, "a very important principle is to develop democracy, thus allowing people to speak out, criticize and vent their anger if any." This should not mean, as some comrades believe, that "I give you democracy and allow you to speak out, but you must not say anything I don't like to hear." Rather, "a range of differing opinions from the people is not something dreadful but something good. What is dreadful is that the Party and government cannot hear any differing voices."

The editorial asserted that a strong, confident government allows people to speak; a weak, insecure government does not. "Let the people say what they wish and the heavens will not fall. If we do not allow people to say things that are incorrect, that is just the same as keeping everyone's mouth shut. If a person is to be punished for saying the wrong thing, no one will dare to say what he thinks. If this is the case, it is called 'giving up eating for fear of choking'. . . . Then, there will be neither people's democracy nor democracy within the Party nor a lively situation."[42]

A new journal, initiated by thirty famous scholars, writers, and journalists who were to guide its editorial activities, was established in early 1985 to push for greater democracy. Its very title, *Qunyan*, "everybody has a say," states its purpose. The ideological theorist Li Honglin, on the occasion of its first issue, wrote that to change the practice of "one person alone has a say," is not simply to change a "style, but a system."[43] Like the *People's Daily* editorial, he explained that this change is necessary for economic modernization. "One person has a say" is unsuitable for an economy that is moving from a closed, self-sufficiency to an open commodity-type economy. Similarly, he insisted that "everybody has a say" was necessary for a more stable government. He cited examples from Chinese history, such as Jing Li of the Zhou Dynasty who "suppressed public opinion and this ended in his fall." One of the reasons why the reign of the Emperor Tai Zong of the Tang was so successful was because of "his readiness to listen to the opinions of his ministers," such as Wei Zheng who confronted him with straightforward criticism. Only when everyone's views are "genuinely respected, welcomed, and urgently needed,"[44] will the government, Li concluded, be stable and strong.

The Writers' Congress, the establishment of *Qunyan*, and the *People's Daily* editorials unleashed a barrage of demands. In addition to freedom of literature and art, there were calls for freedom of academic research, publication, comment, and news that grew louder and louder in the early months of 1985. Other intellectual groups demanded the right to use the same procedures for electing their officials and protecting their members as the Chinese Writers' Association. Hu Jiwei, deposed as editor-in-chief of *People's Daily* in the Spiritual Pollution Campaign but subsequently made president of the Federation of Journalists, called for legislation to protect freedom of speech in the press. He had traveled to Hong Kong to inquire about the journalistic practices there and was encouraged by Hong Kong journalists to demand more rights at home, an indication of the liberalizing effect of the Hong Kong contact. He asked the regime to define exactly what it meant by "spreading rumors" and "divulging secrets" so as to prevent journalists from being accused of such practices. He pointed out that the vagueness of these terms hindered the journalists in gathering news freely.[45]

The demands unleashed by the Writers' Congress were out of control. As in the past, when the regime loosened its reins and encouraged the expression of diverse viewpoints, the views expressed went beyond the Party's limits and evoked a reaction even from the reform leadership. The first indication of this was Hu Yaobang's tough speech against freedom of the press at an inner-Party meeting of the secretariat in February, 1985. It is not clear whether the reformers' step back into the intellectual-ideological realm expressed their own concerns, was meant to co-opt opposition from the more conservative members of the leadership, or was forced upon them. However, Hu's speech, published in the party press in April, 1985, unequivocally stated that there could be no freedom of the press—the press must be "the mouthpiece of the Party."[46] This meant that the press should write about "the mainstream of Chinese society" which is "bright and hopeful." He acknowledged that China had "a seamy side," but it was "non-essential."[47] Thus, he ordered the press to give 80 percent of its space to good things and achievements and 20 percent to exposing the seamy side and shortcomings. By Chinese standards, that is not a bad percentage, but even the 20 percent is qualified because it should not evoke "gloomy feelings."[48] Moreover, before reporting important news, permission must be sought from higher authorities. Thus, only the Party's view of the shortcomings in Chinese society is to be presented in the media.

Given the freedom for literature and art granted at the Writers' Congress, Hu explained that writers and artists were different from journalists. They were indirect rather than direct mouthpieces of the Party. Thus they could write whatever they wanted in any style they wished, but, he warned, that does not mean that they will be published. "The editorial boards of publications, newspapers, and publishing houses can also make a choice and have the right whether or not to publish a work. . . . Writers can never use their freedom to deprive the editorial boards of their freedom."[49]

Perhaps even more threatening for intellectuals in general, Hu revived the spectre of another attack on spiritual pollution: "The central authorities . . . never abandoned the slogan of opposing and overcoming the erosion caused by decadent, moribund capitalist ideas." He cautioned against "bludgeoning" people as in the Cultural Revolution, "but that does not mean we should abstain from criticizing or punishing those" who do not abide by the Party's policy.[50] Such criticism, however, should be handled more judiciously and with milder language than in the Spiritual Pollution Campaign, Hu advised, so as not to frighten away China's friends abroad.

Even though the Deng leadership promised never again to attack intellectuals, launch campaigns, or carry out purges, it continues these Maoist practices. Despite its pragmatic approach, it is still Leninist. As western pluralistic ideas eroded the ideological unity on which the leadership's one-party state was based, the leaders resorted once again to the old practices in order to stop any challenge to their political order.

Nevertheless, these practices under Deng have been more restrained than those under Mao. This restraint does not signify a lessening of the Party's will to prevent any challenge to its authority. It does indicate an awareness that the sweeping, emotionally-charged campaigns of the past might incapacitate the intellectuals needed for modernization. The Party still represses dissent when it threatens political stability and challenges the Party's power, but it uses the more selective Soviet method of choosing a few intellectuals as examples to keep the whole intellectual community under control. While the limits of the permissible are still wider than at any time during the Maoist era, selective attacks on a few writers and ideological theorists since 1981 have made them narrower than those of the late 1970s through 1980. Prominent intellectuals can now publicly criticize specific policies with which they disagree, but the political system itself must be depicted as leading the nation toward a glorious socialist future.

The Future of Intellectuals

The relationship between dissident intellectuals and the regime in the PRC remains in the traditional pattern rather than moving toward a new one. Intellectuals can express themselves publicly only when the regime gives them the opportunity to do so. Because there are no laws or institutions to protect dissident intellectuals and no rules that define permissible criticism, the intellectuals speak at the regime's discretion. The years under the reformist leadership of Deng Xiaoping suggest that intellectual autonomy, while expanded, is still limited and intermittent. The Party still has the power to isolate, discredit, and elicit self-criticism from any intellectual as it did with Bai Hua in 1981 and Zhou Yang in 1983, because the intellectual critics have no real power or mass base.

Intermittent relaxations to gain the cooperation of intellectuals have kept alive the tradition of semi-official dissent. The intellectuals are not merely transmission belts between the leadership and public opinion, and the Party cannot simply crush them without alienating the educated elite needed for modernization. And, sometimes ideas expressed during periods of relative freedom are realized later. The views of the radical intellectuals in the early 1960s were implemented, though briefly, in the Cultural Revolution. Some of the ideas of the reformist intellectuals, rejected in the Cultural Revolution, were adopted in the post-Mao era.

Because intervals of relative relaxation have become more frequent and sustained in the Deng era, the small number of intellectuals who express the criticisms and aspirations of the intellectual elite and comment on political issues have more opportunities than in the Maoist era. Moreover, they speak out more directly and openly against policies with which they disagree. There has been an influx of western learning and scholars and an efflux of Chinese intellectuals to the West, making China more open to western influence than it has been since 1949. In addition, the skepticism engendered by the sharp, contradictory shifts of policy, and the expression of semi-official dissent of past decades makes it unlikely that the Party will be able to reimpose the kind of monolithic ideological control that existed in the early years of the regime.

Since the Party regards any criticism of itself as a challenge to its power, it would be incorrect to judge a group's influence by the Party's reaction to it. Nevertheless, the fact that the Party has deployed such enormous resources to discredit a small number of intellectuals demonstrates that they are seen as having important social roots. Moreover, their continued reemergence despite recurring campaigns against them reflects a resilient, vital movement of dissent beneath the surface of conformity and coercion.

Thus, a small number of intellectuals will continue to express loyal opposition, nonconformity, and even individuality as they have in the past. They do not represent the mainstream, but as long as the Party's goal remains modernization, they are likely to increase in numbers and become more outspoken because the Party cannot completely repress them without jeopardizing modernization. Yet, if it gives into their demands for more autonomy, it jeopardizes its own control. In its troubled relationship with dissident intellectuals, the Party thus continues a pattern established by earlier governments of China.

CHAPTER 7

Leadership and Participation: The Case of Shanghai's Managers

Lynn T. White III

Even among western theorists there is no agreement on how to evaluate participation. In liberal countries participation is widely thought to be a good thing, and many political philosophers believe that contributing to political community offers a basic kind of human self-fulfillment.[1] Others fear participation may overburden the political system and render it unstable.[2] If a study of Chinese managers faces obvious difficulties, it also offers opportunities. Insights gleaned from the study of different forms of participation may throw into relief dimensions of the problem not obvious in the more familiar western cases.

Conceptual Issues

Participation is *intended influence*. For heuristic purposes, we need a definition of influence, and Dahl's will serve surprisingly well: "*A* influences *B* to the extent that he gets *B* to do something that *B* would not otherwise do."[3] Any such influence, if it is effective, implies at least a temporary authority structure; but "participation" also includes influence that proves to be ineffective, so long as it was intended.

This definition is broad, including any attempt to shape policy or to influence the choice of those who make policy. Several traits of this definition should be noted. "Influence," as used in this definition, is hierarchical in a political rather than an administrative sense. "Lower" agents can certainly influence "higher" ones by participating; when they are effective, the real power hierarchy may invert the usual or nominal hierarchy.[4]

Second, participation need not be entirely spontaneous; it can be organized. In China it is often so, intended to support rather than to initiate policies. Participants in collective settings are often concerned with their day-to-day work. This aspect of the definition differs from the usage of some scholars,[5] but if "occupational" politicking in the workplace were not included then most actual participation by Chinese managers would be defined as irrelevant. Of course, managers have national and personal interests that are not simply parts of their economic roles, and they sometimes promote the policies of organizations other than their own.[6] It would be unrealistic, however, to exclude from an analysis of their participation all efforts to change their occupational settings.

Third, participation need not be sustained or effective. Often it is just sporadic and hopeful. It need not even be very active, because withdrawal from the performance of a normal function can "get B to do something" as surely as a more active approach. Albert Hirschman's concept of "exit" can greatly enrich the usual notion of participation, for cases in which withdrawals or threatened withdrawals affect the resources of organizations.[7] In liberal states participation has been mainly conceived in terms of "voice," but under conditions that Hirschman specifies "exit" is a form of political participation which democratic theory tends to ignore, and which a study of China cannot afford to ignore.

Finally, participation can be illegal. Most writers admit this much, even if they do not admit its corollaries. When laws and norms are ambiguous for the purpose of inspiring activity rather than coordinating it (as has often been the case in China), then the rules prevailing at a higher public level may be inconsistent with those at a lower level. In China, the Party's latest directives are often vague, and indicatives are as important as directives. Participants at one place have often quite legitimately concocted rules that are different from those in other administrative jurisdictions—even though both are nominally in the "public" realm. Instructions sent down from Beijing have been tempered by the principle that they should be "used in a lively way to suit local conditions" (*yin dizhi yiling huoyun yong*).[8] Also, there has been no emphasis in contemporary China on the distinction between public and non-public authority structures. From household to government, all "levels" have been seen as viable places for political participation (a situation some would call "totalist"). When the forums for rule making and the degrees of rules' specificity vary, participation does not just provide input to an authoritative black box high in the political system.

Instead, decisions of changing restrictiveness take place in communities of many sizes, none of which are either fully private or fully sovereign.

The problem of participation in western polyarchies has been to find the type and amount of public activity that makes for autonomous citizens without destabilizing the state. Some western theorists emphasize the need for extensive and concerned participation, while others emphasize its limits. In China, where ecological and historical conditions have for millennia fostered collectivist traditions, the basic problem is different. In this oldest of polities, the strength of authority itself is usually not in doubt. Particular governments have of course come and gone, and the fortunes of some sizes of collectivity have risen or fallen with respect to others—but Chinese have long been strongly socialized into their communities. The size and population of the country and the weak communication among its parts influence politics there; the main problem of participation is not how much there should be. Instead, it is how the possible forums for participation relate to each other. The western version of the problem is "stretched" so that the participants and forums are not just the individual and the state, but also many units in between.

Even with serviceable definitions, the difficulty of identifying the pattern of intended influence through China's limited documentary record is obvious. When a community conceals its disagreements, research on the directions of influence is difficult. In any complex society, groups of people with different interests come to exist, whether or not they enjoy the benefits of lobbyists and lawyers. Franklyn Griffiths suggests one way to study such unreported attempts at participation: major policy options on current issues can be studied, even when participatory groups cannot be identified. Griffiths calls these options "tendencies of articulation."[9]

The job in this essay is to identify policy issues on which managers may have opinions. Most of these are economic, since it ordinarily boots little for Chinese managers to become active political participants in other areas, and they have seldom done so. Rather, their participation centers on policies affecting changes in the allocations of three kinds of resources: finances, personnel, and access to markets. The strategies by which managers seek to realize their probable goals on those questions will be the object of analysis. The aim will be to find on the basis of data from these three areas what groups existed, what were their participatory values and styles, what administrative levels they occupied, and what resources proved crucial in deciding the policy issues they faced.

This analysis treats two major periods, 1950-57 and 1963-66, with some extrapolation into the post-1977 era. Most of the 1950s, up through the "liberal" period before the Great Leap Forward, saw a crucial management change in China. In many ways, the Leap and its subsequent economic depression simply represented an interruption between the mid-1950s and the 1963-66 era, the second era to be considered below. The Cultural Revolution (1966-76) may also have been an interruption, but to a surprising extent the post-1977 years continued trends from the mid-1950s and mid-1960s, which were the earlier formative and consolidating periods for Chinese management. All three of these periods were times of sustained industrial and commercial expansion in China. The two intervening eras will be neglected here, despite their inherent fascination, because of their real differences from the present. Our data will come from Shanghai, partly because so many managers work there, and partly because the data available from that city are so rich.

In general, the thesis emerging from these investigations is that changes in managers' possibilities of participation depended on institutional questions, especially on the degree to which they controlled the funds, staff, and markets relevant to their jobs. They are best conceived as an "attitude group." Managers are not an "organized group" in any formal sense—but their collective tendencies in decision-making make of their actions a cluster of important informal institutions. Concepts of participation that sharply distinguish public from other authority structures are inadequate to the cases of complex countries. Participation and leadership are seen here as two institutional aspects of the same phenomenon, because any effort to reflect the existence of an attitude among managers, and thus to assume some leadership there, is participation in a larger community.

The Socialization of Management in the 1950s

Managers in a capitalist city such as pre-1949 Shanghai might be expected to oppose the arrival of a Communist peasant army—and, indeed, many of them did so. After the Guomindang (GMD) suppression of Communist workers' organizations in the 1920s, many of the Chinese Communist Party's (CCP's) urban supporters were largely from families headed by enterprise managers. Conflict between GMD militarists and Shanghai capitalists increased sharply in the 1927-37 decade. After the war against Japan, in 1946

Shanghai's leftist journals sharply criticized the GMD for its police control of managers. In particular, they castigated a law that empowered officers "at any time to go into any private home or shop ... for regular or irregular visits."[10] This law gave GMD policemen pretexts to demand bribes from capitalist managers, and a CCP-oriented magazine claimed that "all the legal businesses of Shanghai are objects of their extortion."

In some large industries, such as textiles, the GMD authorities occasionally expropriated all the produce at low state-fixed prices to outfit troops. It was hardly surprising, therefore, that some of Shanghai's managers were willing actively to support the new regime after 1949, although others refused to do so and fled. The great majority, especially those who did not own large firms, took a wait-and-see attitude. They often complained that the Communist cadres who were sent to monitor them could be meddlesome, but they attempted to carry on business as usual.

This is not the place to offer a complete description of the Five-Antis Campaign of 1952,[11] in which the CCP mobilized enterprise employees to criticize managers and initiate the first major steps toward socialized planning. It was not until the end of 1952, however, that they made a really thorough attempt to register all Shanghai businesses.[12] These changes will be analyzed here in a somewhat unconventional manner: not from the viewpoint of the government and its campaigns, but instead from the viewpoint of managers and their resources.

Finances

Managers need monetary credit, as well as staff and access to markets, in order to make their enterprises run. One of the major issues of the early Communist period in Chinese cities was the CCP's attempt to gather information on the flow of funds between enterprises and then to enforce laws that redirected those flows in the official interest. An early measure toward this end was the reorganization of taxes. The GMD blockade and the loss of foreign markets caused a decline in business; pressure on the old managers at such a time was tempered by concern for production.

During the first five months of 1950 alone, 12 percent of Shanghai's factories were "suspended." About 6 percent of the commercial establishments which existed at the beginning of that year had to close within the next five months.[13] Despite these difficulties, "tax enforcement groups" were formed jointly by courts and tax bureaus "to deal with cases of deliberate delays of payment on the part of unscrupulous merchants."[14] The accounts of some firms were audited strenuously during this period and especially during the Five-Antis campaign. "Tax aides" were recruited among worker activists, and "plans of payment" were drawn up for firms that had taxes due. "Mutual help groups" set up "collective reporting and payment systems" under the tax bureaus of Shanghai's ten urban districts. These districts competed with each other to see which could be first in meeting their established quotas of imposts due. Even managers' wives were occasionally persuaded by lane committees to report their husbands as tax evaders.[15] The government's information about managers' financial resources during the early 1950s remained very incomplete, however. In 1953 a "random check" of nearly three thousand firms in Shanghai showed that 85 percent of them "employed methods to evade taxes."[16] In 1954, when another check was made, the authorities concluded that over 80 percent of a large sample of industrial and commercial firms still continued these practices.[17]

A major factor determining the rate at which high officials learned about resources was the willingness of low-level managers to further their own careers under the new regime by disclosing this information. Campaigns (especially the Five-Antis Movement) speeded this process; but although they are emphasized in the Chinese press, campaigns are inherently temporary and unrepresentative. Western analysts relying mainly on campaign literature may tend to overstate the speed with which campaign decisions could change China's very complex urban economies. Memories of these movements, at later times, may be just as important. The process of change was indeed quick in comparison with patterns in the cities of other developing countries; but it was not so quick as the Chinese press has sometimes suggested during campaigns.

Tax campaigns (and the confiscations of property of people who fled the revolution) increased the resources of government planners during the early 1950s. But many sources of funds still remained available to both bourgeois and socialist managers of small or medium-sized firms. Newspapers voiced occasional criticisms of overcentralization in the economy, and high-level authorities were sometimes required to answer local arguments that financial credit should be allowed for specific projects.[18]

The banking system was extensively reorganized during this period, but it was less important than political campaigns in efforts to prevent the kinds of autonomy among private managers that officials wished to repress. Government hopes for socialism often conflicted with government plans for production—and banks specialized in the latter area. For example, a 1952 ordinance declared bank overdraughts illegal, but it soon became evident that enforcement of this law was going to be selective and unsystematic.[19]

The government made clear that long-term credit would be available only to enterprises which became branches of socialist corporations, joined cooperatives, or otherwise became subject to state plans. For many managers, financing became contingent on having a socialist title. Even dispersed and non-strategic light industries (such as leatherware, toothbrush making, tailoring, bookbinding, and baking) were to be guided toward socialism by this means.[20] In many cases, the "joint enterprises" of this period were lightly controlled by occasional visits from representatives of commercial bureaus and bank auditors (especially from the Communications Bank, to which most such firms in Shanghai were first assigned).[21]

In 1956, when the "Transition to Socialism" regularized such controls for all legal firms, the government clearly overextended its capacities for effective auditing. Signs on managers' doors were changed. Officials made—and then often abandoned—promises of financial support for whole categories of firms during the Transition Movement. In lines of business enjoying high government priority, the Transition to Socialism made financing easier. In other industries, funds ran dry. Overall, a framework was created for state price-setting in many commodity exchanges. During the later period of stability after 1963, this framework more closely determined the financial resources available to firm-level managers.

The pricing system generally set the values of both inputs and outputs and, with production quotas, this basically determined the profits that managers could make for their socialized enterprises. By late 1956, even cigarette hawkers faced state wholesale and retail price regulations.[22] The managers of much larger companies, and of the great majority of legitimate firms,[23] faced similar laws. However, the local Commodity Price Committee in Shanghai had little time between the Transition to Socialism and the Great Leap Forward to consolidate the implementation of this system, so the financial resources available to many small-firm managers remained difficult to inventory in practice.

Personnel

The training of more accountants after 1949 changed the language and style of Chinese management more than it changed the decision-making or even the class backgrounds of Shanghai's executive staff. In the first half of 1950 the Shanghai Education Bureau set up nearly fifty "factory schools" in large and medium-sized enterprises, enrolling over 17,000 students. New trade unions taught almost as many more in one hundred smaller schools.[24] In these socialist business schools, many of the students were still from capitalist class backgrounds.[25] The project of creating a new cadre of social managers to look over the shoulders of the previous bourgeois enterpreneurs, and eventually replace them, involved the admission of many capitalist-background youths to education in accounting. The managerial personnel who emerged by the mid-1950s were of mixed social origins.

The government's approach to many managers during the early 1950s had been coercive, but controls could not be administered effectively for long and incentives could not be developed to supplement them until the CCP recruited loyal workers to supply information about the activities of pre-1949 managers. These workers— many of whom later joined the ranks of new socialist managers— began to participate in the decisions of some enterprises during the early and mid-1950s. The rate of socialization in any pre-1956 unit depended on the existence of such personnel, as well as on many additional factors: the firm's size, the ease with which officials could control the inputs or markets for its trade, the importance of the products to government, the strength of previous non-Communist labor organizations, and the firms' location in the city.

This situation was further complicated by the fact that production, not just socialization, was a major official aim for Shanghai. The CCP's generally cordial relationship with top "national capitalists" was propagated as a symbol of its need for the productive talents of the old managerial class. There was constant tension within party circles concerning how quickly to compel capitalist managers to heed state plans. There were also tensions among bourgeois managers concerning the extent to which the Communist government deserved patriotic trust. High CCP officials in the city took different approaches to these problems. Probably the most important reason for the purge of First Secretary Rao Shushi in 1954 was his relationship to capitalists. The arrest of United Front leader Pan Hannian the following year was apparently related to his laxness toward them. Among the bourgeoisie, even so compliant a figure as Guo Linshuang (head of the Wing On Co. and a relative of T. V. Soong and thus of Chiang Kai-shek) publicly praised the formation of socialist enterprises but was later criticized for supporting them only half-heartedly.[26] The patterns of participation that arose from widespread conflicting motives were thus complex.

In this situation, the Party established schools to educate the owners of large and medium-sized enterprises, involving them in temporary courses for "industrial and commercial circles." Magazines were printed for them. District and subdistrict "preparatory committees" were established to convert their guilds into respectable unions.[27]

Production was not the only important activity of managers. Decisions on hiring were key, and even in the new economy they often reflected less than fully public concerns and were affected by informal institutions. For example, in a Shanghai factory a trade union's health committee directed the party secretary to influence a capitalist owner to employ a certain female nurse. When she had an affair with a married local doctor, the local Youth League branch influenced the capitalist to fire her. But the next day, they all returned to accuse him of having been unreasonable — and it emerged that the nurse had a relative high in the Party who had ordered her reinstatement.[28]

At least until the Anti-Rightist Movement of 1957, the people who made crucial economic decisions at many levels were leaders who had maintained local political respectability and also had functional expertise. This situation survived the many rapid changes of this period. But the effects of the transition to socialization became more important after 1963, when it was consolidated. In other words, the education of specialized managers from various social backgrounds was a more important and immediate result of the early years of the PRC than were the big changes in formal economic organizations. Many enterprises were merged, renamed, created, or reorganized; but participatory patterns are most easily understandable in terms of the fact that some of the old managers survived to cooperate with new ones. The pell-mell legal changes did not have their full practical effects until several years later.

Markets

Managers not only need credit and staff to do their jobs, they
also need access to factor and product markets. After 1949 the
blockade of Shanghai's port was probably more important than some
managers' anti-Communism in causing businesses to close. Chinese
participation in the Korean War, however, brought a strong,
government-led demand; local authorities licensed many new firms to
produce more.[29] The trend began in early 1951 and it reached a
fever pitch during that summer.[30] As the war-induced demand
receded, government plans for socialization became more prominent.
In general, managers needed little influence to assure their product
markets, but their materials supplies became a great problem as
planning and pressure for development increased. During the First
Five Year Plan, the price of quick production progress was chronic
shortages on raw materials markets.

Excess demand with controlled prices became a widespread phenomenon even before socialist cadres became the most important
kind of managers. "Tense" (*jinzhang*) is the word Chinese managers
invariably use to describe such markets. In theory, high-level cadres
were supposed to obviate such problems by fixing prices and
scheduling production to meet the needs of managers facing output
quotas. But elegant econometric exercises bore little relationship to
reality. The main sorts of institution-changing participation, in
which socialist enterprises managers engaged by the mid-1950s,
reflected their concern to ensure input supplies.

"Wholesale relations" were established by managers with up-
stream suppliers, and many a career depended on the stability of
these flows.[31] In this long-term seller's market, the most crucial
political link for a manager is with his supplier of scarce materials.
Industries tend to develop vertically, and their political structures
have an even stronger tendency to take this form, especially when
their administrative structures do not. Managers gather to ensure
sources of supplies by forming large conglomerates, usually state
corporations attached to municipal bureaus or occasionally to central
ministries. These units seldom voice open criticisms of defaulting
suppliers, lest their future relations in the same direction be
impaired, but they must and do develop ways of meeting supply
problems that arise.

Sometimes the use of substitute inputs is possible. This can
result in a reduction of product quality, however, and consequently
official campaigns have been launched against it.[32] Another means

by which a local corporation can increase its input supplies is to station permanent purchasing agents throughout China. For example, the Shanghai Chemicals Corporation had agents in Shenyang, Canton, Chongqing, Tianjin, and Hangzhou to organize supplies in the mid-1950s. The local Metals and Wood Company had similarly far-flung representatives.[33] Even when specialized managements maintained their separate factory identities within larger companies — as Shanghai's Chinese medicine shops did — they banded together to obtain supplies. Herb shops with names like "Deer Horn Hall" and "Thunderous Improvement" willingly became part of the Shanghai Medical Materials Corporation, because otherwise they might have had no antlers to sell.[34]

The main difficulty was that agents from other places descended on Shanghai to procure materials in exactly the same way. During the periods not treated here (the Great Leap Forward and especially the Cultural Revolution), non-Shanghai purchasing agents were attacked in the city. Even in 1956, local newspapers were blaming shortages on "procuring agents from other places."[35] By the beginning of 1958, pressure from local managers in need of materials apparently led to a temporary Shanghai autarky: local materials-supplying firms, including iron and steel factories, "which formerly did not like to take local orders for odd jobs, will act differently this year."[36]

Summary of the Socialization Period

The early and mid-1950s were a time of pressure on Shanghai managers, who generally kept their jobs but had to be indirect in political participation. The first firms to be socialized were very large, and their managers on the whole were compliant with government demands, for both political and market reasons. As late as 1953, however, 67 percent of the output of Shanghai's industry and 77 percent of its retail value in commerce were still handled by private companies. Only 27 percent and 15 percent, respectively, were in state-owned firms (and the residuals in joint firms by 1953 were still small).[37] In the next year, however, the portion of industrial output from private firms decreased to 49 percent.[38] By this time government programs had made more than 19,000 private retailers into branch consignment agents (selling supplies from state-planned sources), or they became joint enterprises or closed business. Most managers assumed jobs in state or joint companies.[39] Retail rice traders became state consignees in 1954, for example. By the end of 1955, the government's attention included many small firms selling disparate products, and newspapers even spoke of the need for "readjustment work" among Shanghai's 200,000 stall merchants.[40]

Managers' most important resistance to these changes came quietly, in the form of reduced production. During the first quarter of 1955, the variety of products made in Shanghai decreased, and newspapers reported problems in light and machine industries.[41] Over 90 percent of the output of private industry in 1955 was "produced under direct manufacturing or processing contracts for the state" and this represented a sharp increase from previous years.[42] Capitalists were accused of causing slowdowns in that year,[43] so certain Shanghai firms were urged to "learn and penetrate" patriotism and law.[44]

In Shanghai, the Great Leap Forward really began in 1956. In May of that year, the city government announced major investments for heavy industry.[45] By January of the following year, offices began to move out of Shanghai's central business district, and the space they had commandeered reverted to use by commercial hotels.[46] Municipal bureaus that had been swamped with routine economic decisions after the Transition to Socialism now delegated many powers to enterprises, beginning a trend toward the decentralization of power (quanli xiafang). At the start of 1957 the city government abolished many of its organs, merged others, and reorganized (or reduced) municipal oversight of districts and enterprises. The main bureaus for planning and construction were merged, the two main light industrial bureaus were consolidated, the two largest rural purchasing units were joined together, and the Materials Supply Bureau was combined with the Materials Storage Bureau under a new name. More than a quarter of the personnel of all "Shanghai state organs" were slated at one point to be laid off (although there is no evidence this actually happened). Schools to educate against bureaucratic tendencies were established for officials.[47] The slogans of the time were liberal, and deputy mayors, including some very prominent capitalists, were given more public functions.[48]

Although a few Shanghai managers participated actively in the Hundred Flowers Movement of 1956-57, protesting excessive party control of their firms, the CCP's most severe critics were definitely not managers. Serious entrepreneurs did not endanger their firms and careers by indulging in open political criticisms, even if they might for the same cause have to violate state regulations. A private-sector businessman in a jointly owned rubber shoe factory, who had apparently been pressed to fill his quota of complaints in mid-1957, ventured to complain that his workers were no longer cutting pieces for the outer and inner layers of shoes to fit together well. Another manager in the same factory caviled that austerity movements had disallowed the use of wrappers around the shoes for marketing: "The shoes can be damaged very easily. When they are placed in shopwindows, they are exposed to the sun, and this affects the quality of the shoes."[49] These timid criticisms from managers were published as late as May 4 — a date when something bolder might have been more appropriate. The indirect, but patterned, forms of political participation used by managers at this time fitted their needs and established a defensive, bureaucratic style which served them fairly well even in the turbulent decade that followed.

The Consolidation of Management in the 1960s

As China's urban economy recovered from shortages after the post-Leap depression, management patterns became more predictable and regular. Many small firms had been put out of business by the shortage of raw materials from rural areas in the first three years of the decade. Many others had become parts of larger corporations for the sake of assuring their supplies.

Under these conditions, the centralization of responsibility for supplies became the main issue for managers. At the same time, their memories of the Anti-Rightist Movement and the increased importance of centralized official opinions made their expressions of opinion even more circumspect than before mid-1957. Strategies of participation and conflict became even more difficult for an outside observer to ascertain than they had been in the 1950s. The identities of opinion groups in the 1960s remained obscure until the Cultural Revolution provided more data to make the previous "tendencies of articulation" look like participation.

Finances

There were great differences in the amounts of financial autonomy enjoyed by various firms in the 1960s, and a major goal of managers was to increase such independence. Some enterprises had the right to negotiate loans autonomously, even for purposes outside of the state plans. In some cases, these loans could be large.[50] Even

more important, financial decisions in many complex industries were
increasingly made by only a few municipal authorities controlling
large numbers of firms. This administrative change, which centralized financial risk, increasingly separated the main money
managers from the main managers of production or sales.

This phenomenon is certainly not unique to developing economies, or to socialist ones. In China it increased the power of any
organization (the Party) that monitors recruitment to managerial
jobs in both factories and banks. Increasing separation between
heads of production and finance made for better political stability in
both groups—if only because it allowed the representatives of each to
blame the other whenever problems arose. The People's Bank of
China controlled credit, but the bank's original, earlier mandate to
inspect production and influence factory decisions was honored
mostly in the breach. By the same token, the foremen of production
could somewhat distance themselves from full responsibility for
financial quotas. They developed an engineer's antipathy to the
whole idea of profit, for which they were still nominally responsible.
This frustration surfaced in polemics during the Cultural Revolution.

In extreme cases, economic units might become administrative
organs (xingzheng danwei) that received appropriations of tax money
and were not responsible for profits. Other businesses (shiye) also
received grant money from government budgets, although they were
supposed to run on the basis of their own revenues. Finally, regular
enterprises (qiye) were responsible for remitting profit.[51] Managers
worked to assure that their firms would enjoy the most favorable
combination of a good accounting classification and administrative
independence. To some extent, these values could be traded for each
other. When responsibility for profit quotas was reduced, centralized
control was often increased with the managers' happy acquiescence
and support.

When managers improved their autonomy by specializing their
risks, they could often obtain monies from local non-plan sources.
Certain funds are normal for medical services to workers, for
innovation bonuses, education, welfare, and propaganda. But
interviewees report that these funds could sometimes be used by
enterprise managers for non-designated purposes. Also, if an
enterprise manager should require funds outside the financial plans,
the firm might apply to the People's Bank of China (with a copy to
the local economic planning committee). Such loans are normally
granted if a case can be made that the firm is subject to unforeseen
circumstances outside the state plan (for example, if an accident

occurs or the firm assumes a "special production responsibility"),[52] and if the manager has established a good working relationship with officials in the bank and the higher administrative organ. The on-site managers' opinions can be crucial in such decisions, because they have more information about conditions in their firms than do cadres at the bank or in the supervising companies.

Managers' participation may thus be directed at influencing inflows and outflows of credit. The regularization of planning has made socialist businessmen eager to minimize the profit quotas they must send to higher levels. Any improvements in productivity, for instance new techniques, are likely to result in over-quota output and thus in over-quota profit, a greater portion of which may be retained in the firm. This usually results in local glory and career stability for the relevant managers – at least until the profit quota is raised! For this reason, as an ex-cadre reported in a Hong Kong interview, "Factory administrators, such as party committee secretaries and factory directors, seldom underestimate their budgets. They usually raise the budget figures a little higher than the exact amount. When this occurs, it is never ever (*juewu jinyou*) just for the purpose of making profits."[53]

By the mid-1960s, Shanghai financial departments somewhat reduced low-level managers' financial resources by conducting random audits and surprise visits to enterprises. The tax bureaus of the urban districts were particularly charged with this work. In a campaign during the last quarter of 1963, for instance, audit teams would arrive at selected firms to look at the cashboxes, account books, capital stock, and inventories. Too much coal was found at the Nanshi Bathhouse. The Putuo District Branch of the Shanghai Drug Company could, according to a visiting team, make technical improvements that would enable it to remit increased taxes and profits.[54] Participation by higher levels reduced the possibility of participation by lower levels. Such interventions also caused a good deal of resentment, which found public expression during the Cultural Revolution.

Many managers had less financial autonomy by the middle of the 1960s than in 1956-57. The main cause of this change, and of the shift in the pattern of participation it implies, was the expansion of the number of socialist accountants.

Personnel

After 1963 China's industrial economy expanded, and more managers were needed by the state. Business training programs had been extensively sponsored during the previous three years, when workers could be spared from their factory posts because of a shortage of materials to process. Considerable numbers of workers studied management, although their qualifications varied a good deal. Shanghai's capitalists, still officially labeled, were increasingly joined in management by ex-laborers, especially in the large plants from which statistics to confirm this are available. In the famous Shanghai Machine Tool Factory at the middle of the decade, 37 percent of the plant's technicians were originally workers. In a sample of large model factories in several cities, 40 percent of the managers and 31 percent of the party secretaries had worker backgrounds. Another 33 percent of the managers and 45 percent of the party secretaries in these favored factories claimed to be from peasant families.[55]

The managers were mixed not only in their family origins, but also in their previous jobs and schooling. This was particularly true in coastal cities such as Shanghai, where the number of important plants having managers with relatively little formal education (but often with experience in the "university of revolution") was surprisingly large. It can be calculated, from data on one sample of showcase firms, that in both large and small enterprises the portion of employees having higher degrees was slightly lower in Shanghai than in similar showcase firms in other large cities. The number who had specialized secondary educations, however, was slightly larger in Shanghai than in other big cities.[56] This may seem surprising until it is realized that important parts of the managements of some large Shanghai firms were recruited from demobilized soldiers and workers, who were trained and assumed major titles in the late 1950s. These people worked with, and generally cooperated with, older administrators from pre-1949 managerial families. Tension between these two groups of staff certainly existed, but it was muted for several years before 1967.

In the mid-1960s, more than ever before, economic decisions were separated from personnel decisions. Managers' participation in production decisions was somewhat divorced from their own careers. The conventional term used for this system was "double leadership" (*shuangzhong lingdao*). For example, the Shanghai Commerce Bureau was formally subject to administrative directions from the central Ministry of Commerce, but its head was appointed by the Shanghai Municipal People's Committees, the leading local organ of which it was a branch (*fenju*). The Shanghai party and government were supposed to lead in organizational matters, and non-local agencies were supposed to set forth policy lines. But when these commitments were in conflict, line leadership was supposed to obey local leadership.[57]

This strongly affected managerial participation at many levels. Collegiality within firms had become a prime value. Bureaucrats at high local levels trying to pursue their own policies had considerable power to do so. The trend toward dual leadership was clearly encouraged by the army and by Mao Zedong, who disagreed with many policies then being sponsored by the central government in Beijing. The rise of political departments in 1963-64 need not be discussed in detail here,[58] but they allowed some socialist managers a great deal of freedom. Interviewees assert that political departments could authorize local economic authorities temporarily to ignore or appeal instructions from higher authorities, and to jump usual bureaucratic channels freely. For example, the Shanghai Textile Industry Bureau was under the administrative leadership of the Industry and Communications Office of the Shanghai Municipal People's Committee. For purposes of trade, production plans, and financial management, it was supposed to obey this office. But it was also under the Party for purposes of staffing, worker relations, and political education. In June, 1964, when political departments were established in the Bureau, they allowed relatively local levels a good deal of leeway to resist central decrees. For example, if the Ministry of Textiles dispatched instructions to Shanghai's Textile Bureau, it also had to send copies to the Political Department of the Industrial and Commercial Office of the Municipal Party (as well as to the corresponding office of the Municipal Committee). If the political department felt the decree was inappropriate for Shanghai, it could instruct the local bureau not to follow it. This was supposed to be reported upward—but any central decree could nonetheless be legitimately disobeyed, at least on a temporary basis. This greatly expanded the possibilities of influence among mid- and high-level economic leaders in the city.

Markets

The sharp depression after the Great Leap Forward caused many economic planners to condone almost any trade pattern that delivered necessary goods. But control of access to markets, particularly during the depression, was the political key to planning. By early 1963, with economic recovery, officials hoped to control the new increases of trade. Early in that year the main planning politician in Shanghai, Cao Diqiu, addressed a rally of 10,000 cadres to call for more austerity, better-regulated markets, and more sales to rural areas outside the big city.[59] Cao called for tighter responsibility systems (*zeren zhidu*) and less enterprise autonomy.

Shanghai's market patterns were complicated, however, and this increased the power of managers. As the economy improved, alternative ways of attempting to procure needed goods multiplied. By 1964 the Socialist Good Shop movement continued the exhortations, warehouse-cleaning campaigns, and other inspection visits that affected small-scale managements sporadically rather than systematically.[60] The planners also had incentives to make sure businesses received materials, and these motives often conflicted with policies of control. This was a period of economic recovery, in which centrally-run markets were more important than ever before, even though non-planned sources of supply were more plentiful than in the earlier depression.

Sales conferences were encouraged among enterprises. Individual plants might send representatives to conclude major materials purchases, to be approved later by umbrella corporations. Often different levels of a company would be responsible for providing different inputs. For instance, the Shanghai No. 3 Steel Mill haggled at supply meetings for the necessary coke, equipment, scrap metal, and pig iron, but its direct superior, the Shanghai Metals Industry Bureau, was responsible for negotiating the supply of coal.[61] Access to markets for the sale of finished products was similarly organized; sometimes the factory-level managers had no responsibility for it at all. In firms as different as the truck and pharmaceuticals companies, selling was entirely the task of higher administrative levels. Production was separated from sales. Potentially, this pattern increased the likelihood that managers would complain ("exercise voice," to use Hirshman's words) about other managers in the same large organizations, when the performance of tasks fell short. The need for some collegiality and the determination and capacity of municipal planners to control whatever they could made this an era of considerable unreported tension in Shanghai's businesses. On the whole, the forces of municipal centralization were strengthened.

Summary of the Consolidation Period

In the mid-1960s firm-level managers became constrained by the recent consolidation of the economic reforms begun in the mid-1950s. It is unrealistic to talk about participation only as a matter of individual initiatives when it was in fact so deeply influenced by institutional changes. Organizational campaigns, especially in 1964-65, strengthened horizontal links within industries and firms, which were increasingly able to manufacture the inputs they needed.[62] Other campaigns of the same period emphasized that firms should "obey central orders" (as Cao Diqiu put it in one speech).[63] In either case, the main issue of participation was not its general extent. It was far simpler: which institutions made the most important decisions?

This problem can be roughly described in terms of the centralization and decentralization of authority at various political levels. Many changes of this period gave great authority to managers at the urban-district and municipal levels. For example, the Shanghai First Department Store could not expand its operations, cover unplanned costs, or make other changes without approval of the Shanghai government's Commerce Bureau.[64] Some corporations, however, could not steward their subordinate firms very closely, because span-of-control and staffing problems remained important. The Shanghai Daily Use Products Corporation, for example, was supposed to supervise forty firms producing very disparate products. The local branch of the China Pharmaceuticals Corporation controlled fifty plants within the city, the Shanghai Machine Tool Corporation administered thirty, and the Shanghai Cotton Textile Corporation had at least thirty large mills, with subcontracted operations in many more places. These companies could make contracts, sue, be sued, deposit money, and make profits or losses. The managers and committees under them, however, also had much actual power because of the complexity of their operations and the practice that policies should fit local situations. On the whole, mid-level managers in bureaus and corporations became very powerful in the mid-1960s.

These same bureaus and corporations were also the main sources of pressure for production. They were generally autonomous of the distant ministries in Beijing. Barry Richman, visiting various enterprises in 1965, provided useful estimates of their independence. Only one of the nine Shanghai firms he visited was even nominally under the direct supervision of a central ministry, and Richman rated that one the most autonomous of the group. Clearly, enterprise-level independence was mainly lost to city agencies, when it was lost at all.[65]

Campaigns by political departments in Shanghai factories could limit the powers of local branch secretaries and give other CCP members greater influence over decisions.[66] Participation was nonetheless increasingly structured by heavy demands for production and by the specialization of different risks in different agencies and levels. A striking example is the procedure for pricing retail commodities in department stores: some of the tags were set by the stores themselves, some by the Department Store Corporation, some by the Ministry of Commerce, some by the Municipal Price Committee, and some by the manufacturing companies. Interviews have shown that economic organs even issued written orders encouraging managers under their jurisdiction to seek raw materials on black markets, if production quotas could not be met in any other way.[67] The socialist economy in Shanghai during the mid-1960s was strained because planning conflicted with production.

From the start of the Cultural Revolution, these anomalies in the system became evident. Economic "trusts" were castigated, partly because low-level managers had lost power to them during previous years and partly because the production pressure they exerted had created resentment. The trusts had advocated "six-unified" systems for supply, marketing, transport, storage, procurement, and accounting. Radicals excoriated the attempts of the bureaucrats to enforce all this.[68] The idea of profit was denounced because of its use as a summary index (along with production) to test low-level managers' efficiency. Profit was seen as a means of control by higher economic authorities over lower ones.[69] Even the revolutionary committees, which attempted to reunify Shanghai's economy after the Cultural Revolution temporarily destroyed control, could not easily obtain information from lower organizations — especially from the revolutionary committees of plants.[70] When teams led by soldiers and workers came into factories, they were often resisted or snubbed.[71] Zhou Enlai, Chen Boda, and various other officials periodically pleaded for managers to reassert themselves, and for revolutionaries to attempt only broad supervision of economic work.[72] But the business of restoring a degree of coordination in this economy took several years.

Conclusion: Chinese Management and the Idea of Participation

Reforms since the death of Chairman Mao have increased the stability of managers' careers, and contrasts of the present period with the Cultural Revolution are much clearer than with the mid-1960s or most of the 1950s. Real issues of production and control and the distribution of real resources have changed less suddenly than policies.

Official interest in foreign management styles has been obvious since 1978. The shelves of China's bookstores are now filled with analyses of economic practices in foreign countries, especially socialist ones. Experts from abroad have come to give lectures at Chinese business schools.[73] Many analyses and translations of policy documents from the PRC's third period of experiment have now been published in English.[74] As Andrew Walder has written, "Continuing ambiguity in administrative reward systems, and persistent patterns of factional conflict, will hinder efforts to overcome the demoralization of staff experts . . . it is, after all, what people *do* that determines whether or not a good policy will come to naught."[75]

Our evidence on participation in revolutionary China mostly concerns issues and institutions, not open politicking. The matter is presented in those terms by the Chinese press, and the reason is not simply that an official press has things to hide. The main conclusion here is not that wary liberals in a non-liberal country are terrified to speak out (even though they are). Instead it is that participation is much more than expression in speech, rallies, voting, or other obvious modes. Participation refers to patterns of political action that are not basically different from leadership or other forms of influence. The sole proviso is that participatory influence is intended, though not necessarily effective.

This situation has been obscured by many recent treatments of the subject. The most important of these is by Samuel P. Huntington and Joan M. Nelson,[76] who define participation as "activity by private citizens designed to influence governmental decision making." This is a possible definition—at first, it sounds like "intended influence." It would be more generalizable, though, if clear distinctions between private citizens and government could be drawn universally. "Activity" and "decision making" are a single process here, and a participatory activity by a citizen involves a personal decision that is as fully political as any government can make. The distinction between private and public in the Huntington-Nelson definition seems to be based on a mere legalism: the government imagines itself sovereign and imagines that other agents are not. But many levels of collectivity, and individuals and leaders in many authority structures, behave as if they were so. Heavy reliance on this distinction, which implies a primacy among levels, is unrealistic. It may not serve to illuminate much about politics in non-liberal states and non-state organizations, because in these cases unsovereign agents are more important than it can allow. And some scholars think this definition is inadequate even as an expression of liberal values, if that were its aim. As Huntington and Nelson point out, their definition also excludes the acts of revolutionaries from "political participation," although hopes for reform are often held concurrently by radical discontents, in case their revolution fails. Revolutionaries are, in common sense, certainly political participants of their communities. Also, Huntington and Nelson regard participation as "usually avocational."[77] In that case, most attempted influence on policy decisions by Chinese managers would not be participation. But these businessmen know what they are trying to do.

This way of defining participation is consistent, even careful, but it omits too much. Governments are not unitary actors; their members participate by leading various parts, sometimes in contradictory directions. Those with no official role may participate in ways that are just as public. In large countries that have imperfect communications and important regional cultures, it is hard to decide which actions are governmental, and which are related to community but nongovernmental.

Most basically, the problem is that participation has too often been defined as noninstitutional and as a general patterned activity that can affect institutions but does not also become what it affects. This concept falls down, because institutions are general patterned activities too. The Huntington-Nelson concept of participation had to be separated from their concept of institution, because their main thesis has been to show a relationship between the two. In setting the stage for this, the similarities were lost.

It is unclear how a behavioral distinction might be made between participation and leadership. It is also unclear what use such a distinction might have, if one were made. Surely a more important contrast, if some criterion for it were found, would distinguish good and bad influences in community life. Common speech uses the word "leadership" in two senses: it can refer to large influence and to the group of people who have that kind of power. Or alternatively, it can refer to a high quality of political action.

Similarly, the word "participation" has two popular implications which, not surprisingly, are related to the two senses of "leadership." On the one hand, participation is a kind of influence, and, on the other, it suggests that intended influence should be normatively good for the community in which it is exercised.

Managers in China have not often engaged in activities that can be likened to the most obvious forms of political participation in liberal countries. If their vocational attempts to shape their political system at its many levels were excluded from "participation," then practically all of their efforts to influence authority structure would be cast out of consideration. If, on the other hand, their participatory activities (and all participatory activities, not just in China) are seen as partly institutional, then their intended influence is a rich subject. The main question is whether their actions will be effective in developing future opportunities for China and the Chinese.

CHAPTER 8

The Role of the Military in Chinese Politics

Harry Harding

The role of the People's Liberation Army (PLA) in Chinese politics over the past thirty-five years has been characterized by an intriguing paradox.[1] On the one hand, the Chinese high command has an impressive array of resources with which to influence national policy: it heads a large organization with a respected place in the Chinese Communist movement, has regular access to all the major bodies that determine party and state policy, enjoys personal connections with key civilian leaders at both the national and local levels and, last but not least, exercises control over substantial coercive power. In fact, the Chinese military has more political resources at its disposal than any other interest group in China, except for the party apparatus itself.

But despite the influence these political assets have sometimes provided, the PLA has not been an omnipotent force in Chinese politics. Its preferences have dominated neither domestic policy nor foreign affairs. It has often been persuaded to accept personnel assignments and policy decisions with which it disagrees. Indeed, even on matters directly related to national defense, the influence of the Chinese military has been surprisingly limited, unable to secure from civilian leaders a sustained commitment to military modernization. The PLA has suffered, in short, from a wide gap between its potential power and its actual influence.

To illustrate this paradox, one can imagine two divergent, but equally plausible, histories of the People's Republic. The first would stress the role of the PLA at nearly every critical juncture in the evolution of contemporary China. In the early 1950s, it was the PLA that helped the Party to consolidate political control, implement land reform, and rehabilitate a war-torn economy. During the Great Leap Forward, it was the minister of defense, Marshal Peng Dehuai, who took the lead in criticizing the shortcomings of the rural communes and the irrationalities of the backyard steel furnaces. And following the death of Mao in October, 1976, it was the support of senior military commanders that made it possible for Hua Guofeng to launch a successful palace *coup* against the Gang of Four. Above all, this first history would emphasize the PLA's involvement in the Cultural Revolution of the late 1960s: its dispatch of military work teams totalling some two million men to restore order in urban schools, factories, and offices disrupted by the Red Guard movement; its establishment of military governments in nearly every province and major city; and then its attempt to perpetuate its newfound control over Chinese society by institutionalizing military participation in civilian politics.

The second history, in contrast, would highlight the occasions on which the PLA loyally submitted to civilian authority and the times when its policy proposals were rejected by party leaders. In the early 1950s, after its extensive involvement in civil affairs, the PLA obeyed party orders to go back to the barracks and return its administrative responsibilities to civilian hands. In 1965, in measures intended to "revolutionize" the PLA, generals and admirals took substantial cuts in pay and were stripped of both their insignia and their formal military ranks. In 1973, 1980, and 1985, regional army commanders accepted a series of reassignments and transfers that were clearly intended to limit their potential political power. On repeated occasions in the 1950s, 1960s, and 1970s the army's requests for more rapid military modernization and higher defense expenditures were rejected by party leaders. And in 1985, the PLA acquiesced to a Party decision to reduce its troop strength by one million, or nearly 25 percent. What is more, this second history would stress, Peng Dehuai's criticism of the Great Leap Forward cost him both his position as minister of defense and his place on the Party Politburo. Similarly, Lin Biao's attempt after the Cultural Revolution to institutionalize military control over China was foiled by a coalition of civilian and military leaders assembled by Mao Zedong, and resulted merely in Lin's death in a futile attempt to flee by air to the Soviet Union.

In this chapter, we will attempt to explain the complicated combination of influence and impotence that has characterized the PLA's role in contemporary Chinese politics. Our explanation will focus on the fine balance between the political resources available to the army and the constraints on the military's exercise of political power. We will see that, despite the political assets already mentioned—its access to the arenas of national policy-making, its institutional legitimacy, its coercive potential, and so forth — the PLA also suffers from two important political liabilities.

First, the army's potential influence has been dissipated by serious divisions within the Chinese military establishment: among the various branches of military service, different generations of officers, political commissars and troop commanders, and competing personal factions. There are, of course, a number of policies and values spanning a wide range of issues that have attracted substantial support across these cleavages. These include maintaining the status and perquisites of military service, protecting the autonomy of the PLA from civilian interference in professional issues, and pursuing conservative policies in economics, political matters, and foreign affairs. But on other issues, even those concerning military modernization and professionalization, the army has been deeply divided, and has been unable to present civilian leaders with single counsel or a unified set of demands.

Second, the PLA is subject to an impressive web of civilian controls, including not only the formal network of party committees and political departments inside the army, but also the personal loyalties binding military commanders to their civilian superiors and powerful ideological constraints against military involvement in politics. These controls not only explain the ability of civilian leaders to reject the demands of the PLA and to disengage the army from its periodic involvement in civilian affairs. They also help explain why military intervention in Chinese politics has almost always occurred at the behest of civilian government, or at least of factions within the Party, rather than at the PLA's own initiative.[2] If the level of military influence and involvement in Chinese politics has varied considerably over the last thirty years, this has been the result of choices made by civilians rather than decisions taken by the high command.

From 1949 until the present, then, the PLA's impressive political resources have been largely, although not entirely, counterbalanced by its subservience to civilian authority, and its wide range of political interests have been substantially, although not completely, vitiated by the divisions within the military establishment. Since the death of Mao, however, Chinese leaders have encouraged the modernization and professionalization of the military. This process should gradually build greater consensus within the PLA behind many of its corporate and programmatic interests and create a sharper distinction between military institutions and civilian society.

The political effect of a more unified and professionalized PLA
will depend largely on developments in the civilian sector, particularly the Party. If, on the one hand, there is greater institutionalization and stability in Chinese politics, the PLA may be
relegated to the role of an influential bureaucratic opinion group that
must compete for resources with other powerful civilian agencies and
interests. If, on the other hand, there is renewed political instability
in China, reflected perhaps in leadership disunity, social unrest, and
declining party legitimacy, then the PLA might be inspired to resume
the more interventionist role that it played in the 1960s and 1970s.
But this military intervention might occur at the initiative of the high
command, rather than only at the instigation of civilian leaders.
What is more, a more unified and professionalized army might be
more difficult to dislodge from civilian affairs than has been the case
in the past.

Resources and Constraints

The PLA possesses substantial resources with which to pursue
its political interests. Some of these resources, such as a relatively
high degree of discipline and control of deadly force, are characteristic of military organizations in all societies. But in other respects the
Chinese army is unusual. For more than thirty years, the PLA has
consistently enjoyed a degree of political legitimacy and a level of
access to national policy-making that are unique among armies in
Communist states.

The first political resource of the army is its size and power as
an organization. Even after the projected force reductions, the PLA,
with about 3.5 million men and women under arms, will be the fifth
largest organization in China, exceeded in size only by the Party, the
Youth League, the state bureaucracy, and the trade unions. Its
budget, at about 12 percent of projected state outlays in 1985, is
greater than that of any other government agency. Its military
discipline and regular political indoctrination give the PLA a level of
organizational cohesiveness that surpasses not only the mass
organizations, but also the state bureaucracy and the Party. And,
more than any other organization in China, it possesses the armed
force to coerce others to comply with its wishes. As in other
countries, then, the numerical, organizational, economic, and
coercive weight of the army make it a force to be reckoned with.

Second, in comparison with the armed forces of the Soviet Union and most of Eastern Europe, the PLA commands an unusual measure of political legitimacy.[3] In the Soviet Union, the Communist Party came to power without an organized military force. The Soviet Red Army was formed only after the Revolution and was distrusted for decades because so many of its commanders were retained from the Tsarist armed forces. In China, in contrast, the Communist Party came to power after more than two decades of protracted guerrilla war. The Red Army was organized as the military arm of the Communist movement shortly after the formation of the Party itself, and most top party leaders held concurrent positions as either commanders or commissars in the Communist armed forces during the revolution. As a result, when the CCP came to power in China, comparatively little suspicion existed between the party center and the military high command. Instead, there was a single elite, in which a relatively small and cohesive group of men shared both military and civilian responsibilities.[4]

After the Communist seizure of power in 1949 there was, of course, a growing division of labor between military officers and civilian officials. But this did not immediately erode the special political legitimacy of the PLA. Indeed, in a country that was undergoing rapid economic modernization and social change many civilian leaders, including Mao Zedong himself, saw the People's Liberation Army as an unbroken link to the simple and egalitarian life of the guerrilla warrior and the peasant revolutionary. Compared with the civilian bureaucracy, which often appeared to be plagued by corruption, inefficiency, and incompetence, the PLA was frequently regarded as an example of the proper combination of technical expertise and ideological commitment. On repeated occasions after 1949, the army was described as the "reliable pillar of the dictatorship of the proletariat," giving it a standing in Chinese politics that was second only to that of the Party itself. As much as the Party, the PLA could characterize itself as the repository of revolutionary values in a modernizing society.

As a result, the PLA has been assigned a wide range of roles in Chinese life which have made it indispensable to the survival and success of the Communist government.[5] The army has been charged with the national security of a country which ever since 1949 has been threatened by either the United States or the Soviet Union or both. It has had to develop and maintain the capability to launch a military attack against Taiwan or the Nationalist-held offshore islands as part of Beijing's pursuit of the unification of China. The

PLA has had ultimate responsibility for internal security in China—not an unimportant assignment in a regime which overthrew its predecessor through revolution, sought to increase agricultural productivity by radical and repeated reorganizations of the country side, and then brought the country to the edge of anarchy in an attempt to ensure the ideological commitment of the urban bureaucracy. Beyond this, the PLA has at various times also been given the tasks of assisting in economic construction projects, conducting ideological education in both city and countryside, aiding the state bureaucracy in civil administration, and even producing model plays and operas. The PLA has assumed a wider range of roles than armies in most other societies, and this has given it a stake in a wider range of policy issues.

Moreover, the PLA has enjoyed an access to policy-making in China that is unmatched by any other interest group under consideration in this volume. At the central level, for example, the PLA has consistently had significant representation on both the Central Committee and the Politburo. The degree of representation has fluctuated substantially, rising as a result of military intervention in the Cultural Revolution, and declining again once the Cultural Revolution had subsided. Setting such variations aside, however, the PLA has generally constituted about 20 to 30 percent of the Central Committee (as compared to about 5 to 10 percent in the Soviet Union), and has occupied an average of seven seats on the Party Politburo.[6] Neither of these formal bodies, to be sure, has been the true locus of national decision-making in China. But membership on the Politburo and the Central Committee has guaranteed the PLA admission to the *ad hoc* central work conferences at which national policy is usually made.[7]

In a similar fashion, the PLA has also had regular access to the central party and state bodies that turn general policy guidelines into specific bureaucratic directives and that supervise the implementation of national policy. Traditionally, at least one member of the party secretariat and at least one vice premier have been active duty military officers.[8] Through the minister of national defense, who with only one exception (Geng Biao, 1980-82) has always been a military officer, and through the ministers responsible for the production of military equipment, who have also often come from military backgrounds, the army has enjoyed additional representation on the State Council. Military delegates also serve in the National People's Congress, the country's nominal legislature.

The army's formal access to policy-making in the provinces has been more variable than in Beijing. In the early 1950s the PLA directly administered much of China through its leadership of temporary military and administrative committees that were formed immediately upon the seizure of power by the Communist Party. Then, between 1952 and 1954, with the establishment of civilian administration in the provinces, the role of the PLA in local affairs was substantially reduced. From then until the mid-1960s, the army played little role in the provincial government or party apparatus in most parts of the country. Military officers did, however, retain membership on some provincial party committees, particularly in such strategically sensitive border areas as Xinjiang and Tibet.

With the turmoil of the Cultural Revolution, the PLA was required once again to serve as the instrument of central authority in the provinces, and regained substantial representation in the provincial party and state apparatuses. When provincial revolutionary committees were established in 1967-68 as temporary organs of state power, replacing the government agencies and party committees overturned in the Cultural Revolution, military officers held nearly half of the leading positions. And when provincial party committees were reestablished in 1970-71, the PLA received 62 percent of the secretaryships and provided twenty-one of twenty-nine first secretaries. After the purge of Lin Biao in 1971 that ratio gradually declined, so that the army occupied 44 percent of the provincial party secretaryships in 1975.[9] More military representatives were removed from civilian party and government positions in the provinces in the post-Mao era, until the level of formal military participation in provincial affairs returned to that of the late 1950s and early 1960s.

But the army's access to civilian policy-making does not depend exclusively on military representation in such bodies as the State Council, provincial party committees, or even the Politburo. The PLA also benefits from the personal contacts between its high-ranking officers and civilian leaders in Beijing and the provinces. At the national level bonds of common service in the Red Army during the revolution have, until recently, linked all of the high command with the party elite. And at the provincial level similar connections have been formed between civilian and military leaders, if only because the first party secretary has usually been the political commissar of the local military forces and the PLA has often been assigned to cooperate with the Party in numerous civilian projects. These personal connections have given the army an access to party officials that few other interest groups enjoy.

These four factors — size, legitimacy, organizational indispensability, and access to the arenas where decisions are made — provide the PLA powerful resources with which to pursue its political interests. But these political assets are offset, to a significant degree, by two liabilities that limit the military's influence in civilian affairs. One is the system of party control over the military; the other is a complex network of cleavages and divisions within the military itself.

The principle of civilian supremacy over the PLA is embodied in Mao's famous dictum, dating to 1938, that "the Party should command the gun . . . the gun should never be allowed to command the Party."[10] In part, this doctrine reflected the Leninist concept that only the Party could be the legitimate leader of a communist movement. But it also had roots in the experience of the Chinese Revolution. Communist leaders believed that warlord forces had been unable to unite the country after the collapse of the Manchu dynasty largely because they did not represent any compelling political program or ideology. Only if military force were subordinated to some civilian purpose, as embodied in a political party, could it acquire political legitimacy and attract popular support.

The abstract principle of civilian control over the armed forces has been realized through a variety of formal organizational mechanisms, many of which were established during the Communist Revolution and maintained in effect after 1949.[11] To begin with, the army, like all other organizations in China, is penetrated by a network of party committees which are ultimately responsible to the Party's Military Affairs Committee. Virtually all officers above company level are party members, and therefore subject to party discipline as well as to the military chain of command. In addition, there is a network of political departments in the army that conducts political education programs designed to maintain the commitment of the troops to party policies. During most periods, the post of first political commissar at the military district and military region levels has been held concurrently by provincial or regional civilian party officials. And since 1975, the directorship of the army's General Political Department has also been held by a civilian, although usually one with past military experience.

The Party also maintains close control over military appointments. The high command, including the minister of defense, the chief of staff, and the director of the General Political Department, are selected by the Party Politburo and are expected to be the representatives of party leadership over the armed forces. Other key military appointments, probably as low as divisional commanders in the main forces,[12] are approved by the Party's Military Affairs Committee. And, as demonstrated by the dismissals and reassignments of defense ministers in 1959 and 1971; chiefs of staff in 1959, 1965, 1968, and 1971; heads of the General Political Department in 1967 and 1982; and regional commanders in 1967, 1973, 1977-78, 1980, and 1985, the Party has employed its power of appointment and purge to ensure the loyalty of the high command.

The very nature of the military command structure provides yet another bulwark against unauthorized military intervention in politics. Military region commanders are given control only over the lightly armed garrison, border, and security forces stationed in their territory. Main force units, including all the naval and air forces and the most modernized ground forces, are commanded directly by the chief of staff. The result, as Harlan Jencks puts it, is that "no one in the PLA, short of the chief of staff—not even a service arm commander—has direct control of more than four or five combat divisions."[13] This division of command means that it would be difficult, if not impossible, for any regional commander to assemble the forces necessary to carry out a *coup d'état*. It also means that in extreme cases, such as the Wuhan mutiny of 1967, main forces can be ordered to suppress insubordination or insurrection in any of the regional forces.

The formal structure of civilian control over the PLA has been reinforced by the personal connections that, as previously noted, link senior civilian officials and veteran military commanders in China. In some ways, in fact, the subordination of the Chinese armed forces to the Chinese Communist Party has been as much a matter of personal friendship and political loyalty as ideological principle or organizational control. In 1959, for example, Mao did not gain the PLA's support for his dismissal of Defense Minister Peng Dehuai by invoking the principle of party leadership over the armed forces, but by asking military commanders for a display of their personal loyalty. Similarly, Deng Xiaoping's ability to secure the PLA's tolerance of his economic programs and political reforms, many of which run counter to military preferences, can also be traced largely to his long-standing personal connections with key military commanders. The same associations that give the Chinese military unusual access to the arenas of national policy-making, in other words, have also helped ensure ultimate civilian control over the PLA.

These control mechanisms are not, to be sure, as stringent as they first appear, if only because the levers of "civilian" leadership are largely manipulated by military officers.[14] A network of party committees may penetrate the armed forces, but troop commanders usually occupy key positions in the party organs of their units. Except at the highest levels, political commissars are not civilian party cadres acting as watchdogs over the military, but are professional military officers who are probably committed as much to the PLA as to the civilian party apparatus. Similarly, the Military Affairs Committee, nominally the Party's principal instrument for day-to-day control over the armed forces, is composed primarily of military officers. Nonetheless, these organizational devices do provide a high degree of civilian control over the PLA, especially when coupled with the more general principle of party leadership over the armed forces and the personal relations between military leaders and civilian officials.

Moreover, there is a second constraint on military participation in Chinese politics that has nothing to do with the concept of civilian supremacy. A lack of unity within the PLA has limited its ability to mobilize all potential resources in pursuit of its political interests. Four major cleavages have divided the Chinese officer corps: cleavages among various military services and commands, between political commissars and military commanders, among different generations of military officers, and among factions loyal to different civilian and military leaders.[15] As a result of these cleavages the PLA has offered divided counsel to civilian leaders on virtually all major issues. Inability to speak with a single voice has rendered the Chinese army unable to use its impressive political resources to full effect.

Like all large military establishments, the Chinese armed forces are divided into a number of different units and commands, each of which has a different set of responsibilities, possesses a distinctive set of organizational outlooks and interests, and competes with the others for the resources with which to perform its tasks.[16] As in other countries, one of the most important of these bureaucratic cleavages has been interservice rivalry: the competition among the ground forces, the navy, the air force, and the nuclear forces for a larger share of the military budget, and for adoption of a national security strategy in which they would play the leading role. In China, however, two other organizational cleavages have also been apparent within the armed forces. One is the tension between the agencies responsible for the production and deployment of current weapons (such as the Ministries of Aeronautics and Ordnance), and those responsible for the development and testing of more advanced designs (such as the National Defense Scientific and Technological Commission).[17] The other is a cleavage between the main force units (the elite divisions of the ground forces and most of the navy and air force), which are commanded by the general staff in Beijing, and the regional forces (less well-equipped ground forces), which are controlled by the country's military region commanders.[18]

These cleavages have been especially visible during discussions of the military budget over the past thirty-five years. In the 1960s, the ground forces and the air force competed for increased procurements. Just before the Cultural Revolution, the service arms criticized the National Defense Scientific and Technological Commission for spending substantial sums of money on research projects that produced few results. Deng Xiaoping's proposals to reduce the size of the PLA, first put forward in 1975 but not adopted until a decade later, aroused stiff opposition from the regional forces, which will suffer the bulk of the cuts in budgets and staff. Interservice rivalries were also evident in the political turmoil of the Cultural Revolution, during which the main ground forces and the regional forces stationed in the same province often competed for representation on the revolutionary and party committees.[19]

A second division within the Chinese army is between the commanders and the political commissars.[20] Commanders are principally responsible for military preparedness and training and for the performance of their units in combat. Commissars, in contrast, are responsible for political education, unit morale, internal security, the welfare and recreation of soldiers, and relations with the local civilian population. As a result, the role of the commander tends to emphasize technological and material factors, while the commissar's responsibilities lead to a stress on political commitment and human will. The friction created by the different perspectives and assignments of the two groups of officers is heightened by an ambiguous organizational arrangement. At most levels of the Chinese armed forces, commanders and commissars are of roughly equal rank, are jointly responsible for the performance of their units, and are supposed to reach agreement on major decisions.

As in the case of the Soviet army, it would be wrong to exaggerate the conflict produced by the shared powers and divergent responsibilities of the commanders and commissars.[21] Both groups are, in the main, professional military officers, and committed to building the PLA into a strong and effective fighting force. The relationship between them is, accordingly, usually a cooperative division of labor rather than a competitive struggle for power. Nonetheless, commanders have in the past often been more willing than commissars to sacrifice some of the traditions of the PLA for the sake of modernization of the armed forces.

Third, the officer corps of the PLA can be divided into a number of military generations, based on the date of joining the army and the training and experience received as young officers.[22] The most senior officers, now being persuaded to retire, are those who organized and led peasant guerrillas against the Guomindang and the Japanese in the 1930s and 1940s. Their initial training and experience was with large numbers of poorly-armed but highly-committed volunteers, using strategies of retreat and deception to defeat much better equipped but less well-motivated opponents. The middle-aged officers now emerging in the high command, especially those who joined the PLA during the Korean War or during the mid-1950s, were trained at a time when the Chinese army was undergoing rapid professionalization and modernization and was being reorganized and reequipped along Soviet lines. Younger officers, such as those trained in the early 1960s, were taught to strike a balance between "redness" and "expertise" and to lead an army equally adept in helping to administer domestic civilian programs and in defending the country against external threat.

Obviously, these early experiences merely create predispositions which can change with the passage of time. Old lessons can be unlearned by practical experience, changing circumstance, and political reeducation. Nonetheless, there is reason to believe that, generally speaking, younger officers in China are more comfortable with extensive military modernization than their more senior colleagues, and are eager for it even at the cost of much of the PLA heritage.

Finally, like all Chinese organizations, the PLA is divided into factional networks based on personal comradeship and on mutual political support.[23] The earliest factions emerged from the widely dispersed operation of individual Red Army units during the revolution and then by the division of the PLA into five large regional "field armies" in the late 1940s. The personal ties forged by these common experiences still form, to a degree, the basis of the factional network within the PLA. But they have been sustained by an additional consideration. An officer's career is more likely to consist of a gradual series of promotions within a particular military unit or region than a series of transfers from one unit to another. As a result, an officer can expect to serve for most of his career under the same set of superiors. He soon comes to realize that personal loyalty to those commanders is a prerequisite for advancement. In turn, the superiors rely on the support and cooperation of their subordinates to perform their assignments successfully, to win promotions, and to avoid dismissal or transfer.[24]

Factional considerations have, of course, been reflected most frequently in controversies over personnel appointments. Some scholars have suggested that the selection of unit, regional, and service commanders has reflected an elaborate effort to maintain an acceptable balance among representatives of the five original "field armies" of the 1940s. There is even greater evidence to suggest that attempts by one faction to establish dominance over the army have engendered substantial opposition from other senior military commanders with personal followings of their own. This is particularly clear in the case of Lin Biao's efforts to place his subordinates in positions of authority in the late 1960s.

These four sets of cleavages imply that the PLA, although an active and influential voice in Chinese politics, is likely to express a wide range of opinions on many significant policy issues. They also suggest that debates over military policy rarely pit a bloc of civilian officials against a comparable bloc of military officers. Instead, civilians are likely to look for, and find, supporters within the PLA on many issues. Similarly, groups within the military will form tactical alliances with civilian interest groups to pursue common political interests. Chinese politics, accordingly, is not a series of "party-army debates." Instead, it generally consists of disputes between complex political alliances, each of which has military and civilian members.[25]

The Political Interests of the Chinese Military

The array of bureaucratic, functional, generational, and factional cleavages within the PLA indicates the difficulties in trying to identify a set of common military interests. Nonetheless, the available evidence suggests that such interests do exist, and they provide the framework within which different groups within the military may adopt somewhat divergent positions.

The interests of the PLA are by no means confined to purely military matters. Because so many policies have an impact on military affairs and because the PLA has so many non-military responsibilities, its interests span a broad range of organizational, economic, social, political, and international issues. These interests can be divided into four interrelated categories: the personal interests of the Chinese officer corps, the army's corporate interests as a

professional military establishment, the PLA's programmatic
interests in the areas of foreign and domestic policy, and the
military's interests in the selection of the nation's civilian
leadership.[26]

Personal Interests

Every member of the PLA has an interest in maintaining and
increasing his standing in society, his family income, his job security,
and his chances for promotion. Military officers are particularly
interested, of course, in their own status and welfare. But since the
officer corps is also concerned with the morale of its troops, it tends
to reflect the personal interests of the common soldier as well as its
own.

The most fundamental personal interest of the PLA concerns
military salaries. Through most of the history of the People's Republic, however, this interest has been of relatively little concern to the
high command. Military salaries have been relatively high — equal to
if not higher than those paid to civilian officials. Furthermore,
military officers have received non-wage benefits and perquisites
fully comparable to those available to civilian bureaucrats, including
access to better hospitals, schools, stores, and resorts, and first-class
accommodations in railroads and hotels.[27]

More recently, the issue of military pay has begun to assume
somewhat greater importance. Since the death of Mao Zedong,
greater opportunities for private farming, promotions for large
numbers of factory workers, and the reinstitution of industrial
bonuses have led to substantial increases in both peasant incomes
and worker salaries, and to significant disparities between military
and civilian pay. For the first time since the institution of military
ranks in 1954, therefore, there has been some dissatisfaction with
the level of military salaries. One divisional officer is recently quoted
as complaining:

> The pay in the army is lower than in the towns
> now. . . . They eat better, dress better, everything
> they have is better. Televisions, tape recorders, elec-
> tric fans — they've got them all! How can I afford
> things like that at today's prices when I make only a
> few hundred *renminbi* a month? My wife and my kids
> all live in Swatow. I can just barely save up enough
> money to visit them once a year, and when I get

home all they do is complain about how little I make
and how destitute they are compared to the neighbors. That's why all the army cadres want to get out
and work in the towns.[28]

Closely related to military salaries is the problem of the welfare
of military dependents. Most soldiers and officers are recruited from
the countryside. Most of their families remain in their native
villages, where their income and well-being are directly dependent
upon rural economic conditions and agricultural policies. One particular problem is that military dependents in the countryside are
denied the labor power of one of their strongest family members, who
is away from home serving in the armed forces. When rural income
is tied directly to the productivity of each individual household, as
became the case in the post-Mao era, families of soldiers are likely to
receive proportionately lower incomes than their neighbors. As a
result, the PLA favors policies that either provide for a more
egalitarian distribution of rural income, or else provide state or
communal subsidies for military dependents.

Another major interest of the high command is in preserving
their own privileges as members of a military elite. Professional
officers opposed, for example, some of the egalitarian reforms which
were instituted in the PLA during the Great Leap Forward, such as
the provision that officers serve as ordinary soldiers at regular
intervals, and secured their elimination as soon as the Leap ended.
Conversely, the professional officer corps has favored the restoration
of formal military ranks, which were eliminated in 1965 as part of
Lin Biao's effort to "revolutionize" the PLA.

More generally, the PLA has supported programs and policies
that have increased the prestige and status of the army, and opposed
those that have reduced it. The military, for example, favored the
nationwide propaganda campaign in 1964-65 to "learn from the
People's Liberation Army," because it lauded the accomplishments of
the army and the achievements of several of its model soldiers. In
contrast, it has opposed any public criticism of military shortcomings, such as the 1970-71 campaign against "arrogance and com-
placency" in the PLA, or the poems and stories exposing the abuse of
privilege by military officers that appeared during the "Beijing
Spring" of 1979-80. Even the trial of some of the conspirators in Lin
Biao's alleged *coup* attempt aroused some discomfort among PLA
officers, who would have preferred not to see their colleagues
subjected to public humiliation.

The Chinese officer corps also has an interest in securing responsible, well-paying urban jobs for the troops upon separation from military service. The overwhelming majority of soldiers come from rural areas, serve one tour of duty, and are then discharged to civilian life. To them, and to many officers as well, military service is both a door to an attractive civilian career and an avenue of mobility from the countryside to the city. Military morale, as a result, depends to a large degree on the soldiers' assessment of their job prospects after demobilization.

The military's interest in the fate of demobilized servicemen can be illustrated by two episodes. In the early 1960s Lin Biao tried hard to find positions for demobilized soldiers in the party and state bureaucracies, accusing Liu Shaoqi and An Ziwen, the party officials then in charge of organizational work, of discriminating against former soldiers when staffing civilian positions. The creation of political departments in state economic bureaus in 1964 was thus a major victory for Lin, in large part because the new agencies were staffed primarily by cadres transferred or discharged from the PLA.[29] In the early 1980s there have again been complaints about the career opportunities for demobilized servicemen. Traditionally, peasant recruits could expect to receive positions in urban industry or administration after completing their tours of duty. Recently, however, soldiers from rural areas were told that they would have to return to their native villages after demobilization, and should not expect city assignments after fulfilling their military service. Press reports have indicated that this change in policy has produced serious morale problems within the army, and has complicated military recruitment in rural areas.[30] One can anticipate that the massive force reductions announced in 1985 will further heighten concern about the opportunities offered to retired military personnel.

Finally, the officer corps has an active interest in its own job security and in the opportunities for promotion. But this common interest has very different implications for senior and junior officers, and has produced serious tensions between them. Veteran military officials, like their civilian counterparts, have been interested in maintaining the practice of appointment according to seniority and have opposed the Party's recent attempts to establish a mandatory retirement age. They would probably also prefer to preserve a personnel system in which reassignments to new units are relatively infrequent, for it is this practice that has enabled them to build solid networks of loyalty and support among their subordinates.

Junior officers, in contrast, have been frustrated at the limited opportunities for career advancement in the PLA. Without a major war since the early 1950s, and with no significant increase in the size of the armed forces, promotion opportunities have been slow. Only the death, transfer, dismissal, or retirement of a senior officer can create a vacancy which a younger man can fill. This has produced a resentment and frustration among younger officers that exploded during the Cultural Revolution, when junior officers criticized senior commanders as disloyal and incompetent in an effort to secure their transfer or demotion.[31] Similarly, during the mid-1970s many younger officers were attracted by the Gang of Four's promise to give talented junior cadres rapid promotions to positions of responsibility within the PLA. More recently, junior officers have favored the compulsory retirement of superannuated veterans and the adoption of policies of advancement on the basis of merit rather than seniority.

Corporate Interests

A second broad category of military interest is the maximization of the organizational resources provided to the PLA and the prevention of civilian encroachment on the army's organizational prerogatives.[32] Within the PLA there appears to be agreement on the general nature of these corporate interests. But the deep cleavages within the Chinese armed forces have led to substantial disagreement on how best to achieve them.

The PLA's most basic corporate interest, for example, is the effective performance of its primary mission: to secure China against both internal and external threat. No member of the Chinese officer corps has ever argued that the PLA should not be well trained to defend against a foreign invasion, or well prepared to maintain the internal security of the regime. But there has occasionally been disagreement about the relative importance of these two threats, as in 1965, when Luo Ruiqing argued that the American escalation in Vietnam posed a direct threat to the security of China and Lin Biao countered that the American threat was not so serious that it should prevent the PLA from helping combat revisionism at home.[33] There has also been disagreement over the importance of the PLA's sideline occupations as an economic construction force and political work team. Some officers, especially those in the main forces, have apparently proposed that the PLA gradually withdraw from its involvement in routine civilian affairs so as to increase its

professionalization and modernization. Others, especially those connected with the political commissariat and the regional forces, have
insisted that such service is an important part of the role of a
"proletarian" army.

Second, the PLA also has a corporate interest in upgrading its
capabilities, equipment, training, and strategy, so as to be able to
meet the challenge of an external attack. Again, there has been near
unanimity on the desirability, in principle, of military modernization.
But this has not prevented serious disagreement about the degree to
which modernization requires a sacrifice of the values and institutions associated with the PLA's revolutionary traditions and the
development of a new set of military strategies to replace those of
people's war. In both the mid-1950s and the late 1970s, for example, the officer corps divided between those who believed that
modernization and professionalization would require a radically
different set of strategies, organizational arrangements, and
equipment, and those who were convinced that relatively modest
changes would suffice to fight a "people's war under modern
conditions."[34]

The PLA's third corporate interest is securing increases in the
budget of the armed forces. In part, this is because additional funds
are necessary to finance a program of military modernization; it also
stems from the high command's realization that morale and management problems are eased when budgets increase. But despite general
agreement on the desirability of expanding budgets, there has been
no unanimity over the proper size of budgetary increases, the allocation of the budget among the various services and components of the
PLA, or the rate at which military modernization can be successfully
undertaken. In 1955, 1965, and 1977-78 some officers proposed
rapid increases in military expenditures, on the grounds that China's
security required a "quick fix" of China's defense and deterrence
posture, while others insisted that only more gradual increases
would be financially and technologically possible. In the mid-1960s
and again in the early and mid-1970s, there appear to have been
serious debates over the allocation of resources among the major
services, with the ground forces expressing dissatisfaction with the
emphasis then being placed on the air force, the strategic nuclear
program, and the navy.[35]

Fourth, like most professional institutions, the Chinese military
has tried to protect its autonomy against unwarranted civilian interference in its operations and management. The PLA tried
strenuously to keep civilian Red Guards out of military units and

installations during the Cultural Revolution and resisted attempts by the Gang of Four during the mid-1970s to control decisions affecting military budgets, strategy, training programs, and personnel policy.[36] But despite consensus on these extreme cases, there has been disagreement over the more routine mechanisms of civilian control over the PLA. Professional officers, such as Peng Dehuai, have occasionally been accused of resisting the leadership of the Party's Military Affairs Committee and of permitting, if not encouraging, the decay of the party committee structure within the army. In so doing, Peng presumably encountered resistance from officers in the PLA's General Political Department, whose careers depended in part on the strengthening of these control mechanisms.

Fifth, the PLA has also sought to preserve its organizational exclusivity—to prevent its military responsibilities from being assigned to any other organization. It vigorously opposed the Gang of Four's proposal in the mid-1970s to create an urban militia force that would fall solely under municipal party leadership, outside of military control. Again, however, while there has been agreement about the unacceptability of a totally independent civilian militia, there has been substantial disagreement within the PLA over the extent to which a popular militia would be desirable if kept under military command. Some high-ranking professional officers, such as Peng Dehuai and Luo Ruiqing, allegedly sought to abolish the militia altogether, or at least to transform it into a smaller and more regularized reserve force. Others, such as Lin Biao, have seen a greater role for a larger popular militia, trained to serve as guerrillas and auxiliaries in the case of an invasion of China.

Finally, the PLA has an interest in preserving its access to arenas of national policy-making, a prerequisite for pursuing its other political interests. As Lynn White has put it, "the soldiers of the Chinese People's Liberation Army are unlikely to regard any government over them as fully legitimate unless they participate in constituting it."[37] But there has been disagreement over the extent of involvement in civilian affairs that the PLA should undertake. Some officers have wanted the army to have more extensive representation in party and state agencies, while others have been willing to accept a more modest role as long as military opinion receives proper attention from civilian leaders.

The range of opinion within the PLA on these corporate interests may seem puzzling at first. How could the Chinese army be so divided on such basic organizational interests?

The answer rests in part with the factional divisions and service rivalries within the PLA. The competition among the air force, the navy, and the ground forces has been repeatedly reflected in debates over the military budget. Similarly, the controversy between Lin Biao and Luo Ruiqing over China's response to the escalation of American involvement in Vietnam, and the differences between Lin and Peng Dehuai over the proper role of the militia, probably had much to do with the personal rivalries among these three military commanders.

A more fundamental explanation, however, lies in the fact that performance of mission, modernization of equipment, maximization of budget, preservation of organizational autonomy, and maintenance of organizational exclusivity are all interests that develop together with the professionalization of an organization. And the PLA, despite a history of more than sixty years, remains only partly professionalized. Only the more technologically sophisticated services — the navy, air force, and the main force ground units — have been trained in the principles of modern warfare in a post-revolutionary environment. And only younger officers, in part under Soviet influence, have absorbed a professional military ethic and become committed to the corporate interests of a modern military force.

In contrast, the oldest generations of officers, the regional ground forces, and, to a lesser degree, the political commissariat, all represent the pre-professional army of the revolutionary period. Older officers fear that professionalization would, with one stroke, make much of their own training and experience irrelevant. Commanders of the regional forces suspect that, with modernization, the PLA would place much less emphasis on regional forces and militia than in the past, and would stress instead the strengthening of the centrally-commanded main force units and the development of a regularized system of military reserves. Political commissars, especially those of an older generation, may worry that professionalization would mean a widening gulf between military and civilian life, the abandonment of the sideline civilian roles once assigned to the PLA, a reduction in the time devoted to political and ideological training, and thus a weakening of the powers and responsibility of the army's political departments. All these officers, in short, oppose those aspects of professionalism that challenge the revolutionary heritage with which they are familiar.

This is not to say that the army's older officers, or the political commissariat, oppose all aspects of professionalization. They, too, desire a PLA that is strong, modern, and capable of defending China against external attack. Nor is it to say that younger officers or main force troop commanders oppose all elements of the PLA's revolutionary heritage, for most of them probably appreciate the role that ideological and political work can play in maintaining morale and discipline. The question is not, in other words, a choice between professionalization and "revolutionalization," but rather the balance to be struck between them. But it has been no less controversial for being so. It is on the basic corporate interests of the PLA, in fact, that the Chinese military has been most deeply divided.

Programmatic Interests

The constraints on the expression of political interest in China make it difficult to identify the preferences of the Chinese army on matters other than national defense. Nonetheless, the available evidence does suggest that the PLA has an interest in a wide range of foreign and domestic policies that would facilitate the effective accomplishment of its principal missions, the pursuit of the personal interests of its officers and men, and the achievement of its corporate interests as a professional military establishment. It also indicates that, overall, the PLA's policy preferences are conservative. The army, in other words, appears to oppose programs that move either far to the left or far to the right of the mainstream of Chinese political life.[38]

In foreign affairs most of the PLA high command appears to favor what might be described as "cautious nationalism."[39] It is willing to use force to pursue China's national interests and to defend China's sovereignty and integrity against external pressure. It also seems to believe that, as a general proposition, China's security should be assured by independent military preparations, rather than through reliance on the diplomatic support of an external power. It is for this reason that important segments of the PLA appear to have opposed China's opening to the United States in the late 1960s and early 1970s.[40]

On the other hand, the military also opposes foreign policies that would increase the external threat to China. In 1959, for example, it seems likely that Peng Dehuai resisted any serious deterioration of Sino-Soviet relations, on the grounds that this would seriously jeopardize China's security against the United States. The PLA has also opposed the deliberate provocation of China's enemies, lest such a strategy generate counterpressure against which Peking could not effectively cope. Accordingly, many PLA officers seem to have opposed the proposals made by civilian radicals in the mid-1970s for a confrontation with the Soviet Union. The radicals argued that a tough stance on the border and toward alleged Russian spies captured inside China would demonstrate to Moscow the strength of Chinese resolve. The military, in contrast, feared that such measures would be unnecessarily provocative and would only lead to embarrassing Soviet retaliation.[41]

In domestic affairs, much of the PLA has an interest in policies that would ensure a sound economy, promote steady economic development, and facilitate military modernization. First and most obviously, the army has a stake in China's industrial and scientific policies. Heavy industry produces the equipment that the army needs if it is to modernize, while the scientific establishment provides the basis for research and development of new weapons systems. As a result, professional officers have opposed not only leftist policies, such as the Great Leap Forward, that sacrificed economic rationality and scientific development for the sake of ideological goals, but also rightist reforms, such as those undertaken in the early 1980s, that assigned lower priority to heavy industry than to consumer goods. The PLA, in other words, has been a firm advocate of what Robert Dernberger calls the Stalinist model of economic planning and development.[42]

Because it draws its recruits mainly from the countryside, the PLA is also deeply concerned with agricultural issues and here, too, it has generally stood at the middle of the Chinese political spectrum. It opposed the leftism of the Great Leap Forward when it became clear that it was undermining the agricultural economy, causing great hardship among the families of servicemen and thus damaging troop morale within the PLA itself. But it has also opposed the rightism of Deng Xiaoping's new agricultural program on the grounds that remuneration according to productivity will punish those peasant families whose strongest members are away from home serving military duty.

Third, the PLA has an interest in political stability. All Chinese leaders, military and civilian alike, tend to assume that internal instability is closely correlated with external crisis. In other words, a serious disruption of China's domestic social and political fabric might well invite China's enemies to increase military and political pressure against China, or even to intervene in China's internal affairs. What is more, widespread internal instability might also require the military to act to restore political order, possibly involving the use of force against other Chinese, and might draw the army into politics in ways that would damage the internal unity and discipline of the PLA itself.

Fourth, the PLA appears strongly disposed to cultural and political orthodoxy and opposed to any significant loosening of the restraints on political and intellectual life. There have been two such periods of liberalization in China: the Hundred Flowers movement of the mid-1950s and the movement to "emancipate the mind" in the post-Mao years. In each case, the PLA expressed skepticism about the desirability of liberalization and warned against the process being carried too far.

During the Hundred Flowers period, for example, officers in the General Political Department were among those who most staunchly insisted that Chinese intellectuals should accept party leadership and that criticism of the Party should be limited in scope and duration.[43] Much of the PLA has also been dissatisfied with the recent reassessment of Mao Zedong's place in modern Chinese history and has criticized the political and intellectual dissent that has accompanied the movement to "emancipate the mind." As one officer put it:

> Only through Mao Zedong Thought can unity be preserved in the military. The way the country is being run now, Mao Zedong Thought no longer has any authority at all. It's a terrible situation. The army needs to have a credo; that's the only way they can unify their thinking, the only way they can become an effective fighting force.[44]

The *Liberation Army Daily* carried an outspoken article in August, 1982 that condemned "bourgeois liberalization" and called for a reemphasis on "communist spiritual civilization." The essay was considered so egregious a departure from established party policy that within two months it led to the dismissal of Wei Guoqing, the head of the Party's General Political Department.[45]

Why does the PLA represent such a conservative force in Chinese politics? The army's responsibility for national security, its desire for modern weapons, its concern with the welfare of military dependents, and its reluctance to become involved in domestic political turmoil all help to explain its interest in political stability, economic equilibrium, and nationalism. In addition, the army's desire for political and intellectual orthodoxy can be traced to the traditional values of unity, *esprit,* discipline, and community that are characteristic of most military forces.[46] And the PLA's conservatism is also the result of the social background and career patterns of the officer corps. Most are from rural backgrounds; most are relatively uneducated. As a result, the PLA is characterized by the same basic conservatism as the Chinese peasantry. In the unflattering words of a Hong Kong magazine that favors reform and liberalization on the Mainland, the Chinese army is "seriously affected by feudalism" and by the "narrowmindedness and passion of peasants engaged in small-scale production."[47]

Leadership Interests

Finally, the PLA has an interest in seeing that China's national political leaders are attentive and responsive to all the concerns discussed above: the personal interests of the army's troops and officers, the corporate interests of the PLA as a professional military organization, and the programmatic interests of the high command. In practice this has meant that military officers have favored as national leaders men who represent bureaucratic stability and political orthodoxy, rather than either continuous revolution or radical reform. When given a choice, in other words, the PLA has generally supported leaders whose political and economic conservatism has echoed their own.

This interest has been most clearly manifest on the two occasions when the PLA had the greatest influence over the selection of civilian leaders. During the Cultural Revolution, the military was largely responsible for assembling the revolutionary committees that temporarily replaced the discredited party apparatus in the provinces. In so doing, the commanders of the regional forces consistently supported veteran party officials, even those who had been criticized as "capitalist roaders," over the Red Guards and revolutionary rebels put forward by the left. In the mid-1970s the military had the decisive voice in the struggle to succeed Mao Zedong. And here, too, the PLA threw its support to the forces of bureaucratic stability symbolized by Hua Guofeng over the forces of revolutionary convulsion represented by the Gang of Four.

And yet the military's interest in a conservative national leadership has often been qualified by the ties of personal loyalty and friendship that link top army officers to each other and to their civilian counterparts. If, for example, the military's position in the 1959 confrontation between Mao Zedong and Peng Dehuai had been determined by considerations of policy alone, then the PLA might have given its minister of defense much greater support for his criticism of the Great Leap Forward. But the situation was complicated when Mao Zedong decided to redefine the issue as a vote of confidence in his own leadership. Faced with that choice, the members of the high command found it difficult to oppose a man to whom most had deep ties of loyalty and affection. In the same way, if rational calculations alone had determined the PLA's position in 1966, when Mao decided to launch his Cultural Revolution, the army might have concluded that their interests would be better served by the bureaucratic stability of Liu Shaoqi. But, once again, the PLA's loyalty to Mao overrode many of its own corporate and programmatic interests.

Roles and Strategies

Compared to other societal interest groups, or even to other bureaucratic interest groups, an army can play a wide range of roles in the political life of a society.[48] At one extreme, it can be a neutral instrument of civilian leaders, faithfully implementing the duties assigned to it and exerting virtually no political influence whatsoever. At the other extreme, an army, because of its possession of both military force and administrative skills, has a unique ability to seize and exercise political power, sometimes allowing only limited civilian participation in the military government.

The PLA has never been merely a neutral instrument of civilian authority. Its legitimacy, its size, its range of responsibilities, and its access to leadership have enabled it to seek and obtain more political influence than that. Instead, at various times over the past thirty-five years, the PLA has played four more active roles in Chinese politics. In "normal" times—from the mid-1950s through the mid-1960s, and from the late 1970s onward—the PLA has been a powerful bureaucratic lobby, articulating and pursuing its political interests through the regular Chinese bureaucratic policy-making process. The PLA moved more deeply into politics on two other occasions in the early 1950s and late 1960s, serving as a part of a coalition regime in periods when the party and government were unable to maintain political order without military assistance. In the mid-1960s on the eve of the Cultural Revolution, and again in the mid-1970s at the time of the succession to Mao Zedong, the army assumed the role of political arbiter, playing a decisive role in determining the outcome of intense struggle between competing civilian leadership factions. Finally, in the early 1970s, under the leadership of Lin Biao, a group composed of elements of the PLA became an active contender for political power, trying to institutionalize and perpetuate the leading role in politics that the army had acquired during the Cultural Revolution.

Bureaucratic Lobby

During periods of relative political stability in China, the PLA has acted as a bureaucratic lobby, pursuing its interests through its normal representation on national policy-making bodies, rather than seeking any further political power.

When acting as a lobby, the PLA relies on the familiar strategies of modern Chinese bureaucratic politics. It uses political argument, with military officers making speeches and presenting reports at a wide range of party and government meetings, including the National People's Congress, national party congresses, plenary sessions of the Central Committee, central work conferences, meetings of the Party's Military Affairs Commission, and specialized work conferences on military affairs.[49] In addition, military officers write articles in the public media, often under pseudonyms, to gain further publicity and support for their proposals. At times these articles have addressed contemporary military matters and policy issues directly; more frequently, however, the authors have used historical analogy and allegory to express their views in more veiled terms.[50]

The PLA occasionally employs strategies of bureaucratic delay to influence policy implementation. Like all bureaucratic organizations, the PLA understands that the pursuit of political interest does not end when a policy is formulated. The PLA may respond quickly and efficiently to policy directives with which it agrees, but drag its feet on decisions of which it disapproves. One example is the alleged refusal of Chief of Staff Luo Ruiqing to implement a directive from Mao Zedong in the early 1960s to dispatch elements of the main ground forces to strengthen the organization and training of the militia; another is the protracted delay in the early 1980s in restoring the system of military ranks.

The PLA also forms bureaucratic alliances, finding support for many of its programmatic interests in civilian party and government agencies. Those commanders interested in higher levels of military procurement, for example, can cooperate with the metallurgical ministries that produce the raw materials for national defense, and with the machine-building industries that produce military equipment. The political commissars concerned about political and intellectual liberalization may seek an alliance with the party *apparatchiks* responsible for political controls over literature and art. When the issue is whether or not to undertake a provocative strategy toward one of China's principal adversaries, the cautious nationalists in the armed forces may find common ground with the officials in the Ministry of Foreign Affairs. And most generally, the younger generations of military officers are professional, pragmatic, and impatient, and may hold views quite similar to those of younger reformers within the state bureaucracy.

On occasion, the PLA has even looked for allies outside of China. It is possible that Peng Dehuai, in planning his criticism of the Great Leap Forward in the summer of 1959, discussed his position with Nikita Khrushchev in the hope of receiving some kind of support from the Soviet leader.[51] In the middle and late 1970s the PLA seemed eager to allow foreign officials and correspondents to inspect its facilities and equipment, perhaps in the expectation that reports of China's military backwardness appearing in the western press would place greater weight behind their own proposals for military modernization.

The PLA has played this role of a bureaucractic lobby during two periods. During the mid-1950s and early 1960s, when Chinese politics were still relatively orderly and institutionalized, the PLA took an active part in discussions of military strategy, foreign affairs, and national economic policy. In 1954-55, for example, military officers argued that the PLA would have to modernize its equipment and its doctrine if it were to have any hope of defending the country's interests against a technologically superior United States, and would need substantial increases in its budget to do so rapidly.[52] In July 1959, Minister of Defense Peng Dehuai sharply criticized the failures of the Great Leap Forward, speaking not only as a member of the Politburo, but also as the representative of an army whose morale depended to a great degree on economic stability and prosperity in rural areas.[53] In 1965 Chief of Staff Luo Ruiqing warned that the escalation of American involvement in Vietnam might bring war to China and proposed a reduction in the civilian responsibilities of the PLA, a redeployment of forces toward the south, and more rapid procurement of weaponry.[54]

The PLA again acted as a vocal lobby for its political interests after the reestablishment of a more regular system of bureaucractic policy-making following the Cultural Revolution. As before, high-ranking military officers argued that the international situation—in this case the threat presented by Soviet forces in Mongolia and Siberia—was such that China needed to increase military spending to prepare for war. Many of them also insisted that the time had come to resume the modernization and professionalization of the armed forces that had almost stopped during the Cultural Revolution decade and to revise Chinese military doctrine and strategy so that the PLA would be prepared to fight a war "under modern conditions."[55]

But the PLA also expressed its views on issues other than military strategy and budgets in the late 1970s and early 1980s. Military officers were reportedly among the most vocal critics of some of the reform policies associated with Deng Xiaoping, including the reassessment of Mao Zedong, relaxation of restrictions on cultural life and political dissent, election of managers and foremen in factories, reduction of the share of national investment allocated to heavy industry, and modification of agricultural policies to permit contracting production quotas to individual households. All of these, the PLA allegedly argued, represented an unacceptable abandonment of party leadership and an unnecessary weakening of party authority. Moreover, the adjustment of economic priorities at the expense of heavy industry threatened the military's industrial base and the reform of agricultural policy threatened army morale by reducing the relative income available to the dependents of PLA soldiers.[56]

It is difficult to measure precisely the political influence of the Chinese armed forces when they have acted as a bureaucratic lobby. On balance, however, the PLA's record has been mixed: it has been much more successful when it has pursued its programmatic interests in conjunction with other powerful bureaucratic interest groups than when it has pursued its corporate interests alone.

On the three occasions when military spending has been a major issue in Chinese politics—1955, 1965, and the early 1980s—the PLA has been unable to win substantial, sustained increases in the military budget. The military was split, with less professionalized officers either unenthusiastic or openly skeptical about the consequences of the ambitious modernization programs being proposed by their more professionalized colleagues. In addition, the magnitude of the budget increases threatened a wide range of civilian programs, from investment in agriculture to public health. In each case, therefore, planners and bureaucrats concerned with preserving civilian programs were able to join with military officers concerned with the consequences of rapid military modernization to defeat proposals for dramatic increases in military spending.[57]

The PLA was more successful in its criticism of the Great Leap Forward in 1959 and elements of Deng Xiaoping's reforms in the early 1980s. In both cases, these radical programs were modified in favor of policies closer to the center of the Chinese political spectrum. But these apparent successes should not be credited to the PLA alone. In both instances, the PLA's call for economic or political orthodoxy was echoed by powerful segments of the party and state bureaucracies. It was a combination of military and civilian pressure, rather than the PLA acting alone, that forced Mao and Deng to return to the mainstream of Chinese political life.

Coalition Partner

On two occasions, the Party has given the PLA an extensive role in civilian administration as the Party's partner in what was tantamount to a military-civilian coalition regime in China. In each case, military participation in government proved necessary because the party and the government bureaucracies were too weak to provide orderly administration or promote political stability. And in each case this higher level of military involvement in politics occurred at the behest of civilian leaders rather than at the instigation of the military itself.

The first of these was in the early 1950s, immediately after the establishment of a national Communist government. Except for those parts of the country which had been under Communist administration for some time, particularly North China and Manchuria, China came under Communist control through rapid military conquest. The Party had about 4.5 million members in 1949, but only some 720,000 were considered even minimally qualified to hold administrative positions. While some officials from the Nationalist government were asked to stay on in lower-level positions, the Communist regime clearly did not want to rely on its former enemies to administer "New China." The answer, at least in the short run, was to ask the PLA to govern the "newly liberated" parts of the country. The Party established military governments, called military and administrative committees, in four of the six

multiprovince regions established in 1949 and gave them substantial
leeway to adapt broad central policies to local conditions.[58]

It would be totally wrong to see this period as reflecting some
kind of military *coup d'état* in China. The army was still serving as
an integral part of the broader Communist movement as it had in the
1930s and 1940s. The same group of men who had served in the
revolution simultaneously as civilian party cadres and military
leaders still occupied concurrent positions in the Party and the PLA.
The only difference was that before 1949 the army's principal task
was to be the military wing of a revolutionary movement, while one
of its major assignments in the early 1950s was to serve as the administrative arm of a Communist government. Once the Party had
begun to recruit and retrain enough civilians to serve as
administrators, the PLA was quickly and smoothly withdrawn from
government.

The second occasion on which the military participated in a
coalition government in China was the early part of the Cultural
Revolution decade, from 1967 to the mid-1970s.[59] Originally, Mao
Zedong's program for the Cultural Revolution was to mobilize
ideologically committed young people, particularly high school and
university students, to criticize revisionist tendencies in the Party
and government. But growing resistance to the Red Guard movement by Mao's opponents made it impossible to achieve Mao's original vision. Ultimately, Mao felt compelled to order the military to
intervene in the Cultural Revolution, first to displace the party and
government officials who were resisting him, and then to restore
social order through what amounted to martial law.

The Military Affairs Committee, staffed almost entirely by
military officers; the Party's Cultural Revolution Group; and what
was left of the State Council became the most influential central
decision-making bodies in the country. Together, these three committees supplanted the Politburo as the peak of the Chinese political
pyramid. At the provincial and municipal levels, the PLA ultimately
joined with selected civilian officials and mass representatives in
forming "revolutionary committees," temporary administrative
structures that would govern China while a new civilian structure
was rebuilt. Once again, civilian institutions proved too weak to
govern the country and the PLA was the only organization with
enough administrative skill and discipline to take their place.

During both of these periods the military could pursue its
political interests as an active component of government, rather than
simply as a lobby. It could, in other words, employ tactics beyond the

bureaucratic strategies of argument, delay, and alliance described above. As a coalition partner of the Party, the PLA had even greater regular access to national and local decision-making and could shape policy implementation at the regional and provincial levels. And it was in a position to demand from the Party some special payments for its participation in state administration and its ultimate return to the barracks.

In 1949 and 1950, to be sure, the military does not appear to have used this additional leverage to pursue its own interests. At that point, the PLA was still closely intertwined with the Party and may not have developed distinctive organizational goals of its own. In the late 1960s, however, the military had become a more specialized institution with distinct corporate, programmatic, and leadership interests. It took advantage of its position as a coalition partner to pursue those interests actively. It used its power in Beijing to double the military budget between 1965 and 1971 – an increase that it could not possibly have obtained through the lobbying tactics it normally employed.[60] And it used its power in the provinces to exclude radicals from local revolutionary committees in the name of order and stability, even when this meant defiance of instructions from Beijing.

The disengagement of the military from participation in government has provided further opportunities to pursue its organizational interests. In the 1950s, for example, the PLA may well have demanded that the Party support the proposals for military modernization which grew directly from its experience in the Korean War as a precondition for the transfer of administrative authority to civilian hands. In the 1970s the PLA may have insisted that the positions it occupied in Beijing and the provinces be turned over to conservative veteran party administrators, rather than to the younger and more radical leaders recruited during the Cultural Revolution. The high command may also have demanded the rehabilitation of Deng Xiaoping, the second-ranking victim of the Cultural Revolution, as a visible symbol that Mao and Zhou were returning to policy decisions and personnel appointments closer to the center of the political spectrum.

Arbiter

The PLA served as an arbiter during two periods of intense political conflict, using its resources to support one group of civilian leaders against another. In both cases, the PLA's control of force and other resources was so great that the army's preferences played the major, and probably the decisive, role in determining the outcome.

The first of these occasions was the mid-1960s, on the eve of the Cultural Revolution.[61] By 1964 Mao Zedong had become locked in confrontation with some of his most senior colleagues over the direction that China had taken after the Great Leap Forward. On issue after issue, from education and public health to agricultural policy, the Party had adopted programs that in Mao's eyes tolerated too much social and economic inequality. On many of these issues, Mao tried to intervene to set new policy directions, but with only partial success. Then he launched a series of rectification campaigns against rural party organizations, and then the urban bureaucracy, but again was unable to achieve any decisive changes in policy.

Ultimately, Mao turned to the army, and particularly to Minister of Defense Lin Biao, for support. Under Lin's leadership, the PLA had established a record of organizational efficiency and ideological commitment in the early 1960s that neither the Party nor the government could match. After assuming his ministerial position in 1959, Lin had invigorated the network of party committees in the PLA, strengthened ideological education, and eliminated formal military ranks and insignia. At the same time, he had presided over the modernization of the air force, a successful border war with India in 1962, and the explosion of China's first nuclear device. Mao could plausibly consider the army to be a model of the proper combination of "redness" and "expertise," and would call on all China to "learn from the PLA" in February 1964.

When the confrontation between Mao and his rivals reached a showdown in 1966, it soon became obvious that the PLA sided with Mao. An army conference on cultural work, with Mao's wife Jiang Qing as an adviser, launched the first attack on revisionism in cultural circles. The PLA newspaper, *Jiefangjun bao*, carried editorials warning of "capitalist roaders" in the Central Committee. And then, in the early stages of the Red Guard movement, the PLA provided transportation, logistical assistance, and military uniforms for Mao's "young generals." Even Mao might have found it impossible to initiate the Cultural Revolution without this kind of military support.

Ten years later, between 1974 and 1976, the PLA played a comparable role in the struggle between radical and moderate civilian leaders surrounding the succession to Mao Zedong.[62] As the health of both Mao and Zhou deteriorated, these two groups, headed by Deng Xiaoping and Jiang Qing respectively, seemed to have reached political stalemate. The moderates had a strong base in the large numbers of veteran officials who had been reinstated in the party and state bureaucracies after the Cultural Revolution. They also enjoyed considerable popular support from those who had either suffered directly from Red Guard criticism and attack during the Cultural Revolution, or who were tired of continued campaigns and chronic political disorder. The radicals, in contrast, had the backing of those who sought to sustain Mao's egalitarian and populist vision after his death and whose careers had benefited from the opportunities for promotion provided in the turmoil of the Cultural Revolution. Neither side had the full support of Mao; neither side was able to establish complete control over the party bureaucracy.

As a way of breaking this stalemate, both radicals and moderates therefore sought to secure the support of the military. The radicals appealed for military cooperation in 1973-74 by proposing to strengthen the nation's defenses against the Soviet Union and by accusing the moderates of appeasing Moscow through negotiation and diplomatic maneuver. The moderates, in contrast, drafted a program of military modernization in 1975 and argued that only the subordination of the radicals could provide the political and economic context in which it could be effectively implemented. Both sides, too, tried to establish firm lines of political control over the PLA. Deng Xiaoping, who served as chief of staff for much of the mid-1970s, proposed a tightening of military discipline, a rehabilitation of senior officials purged during the Cultural Revolution, and a rectification campaign against officers aligned with the radicals. Zhang Chunqiao, a member of the Gang of Four who served as director of the General Political Department, called for an alternative program of rectification that would have promoted younger officers to positions of power and blocked the rehabilitation of veteran commanders.

These maneuvers for military support did not, however, immediately break the deadlock between radicals and moderates. The PLA bided its time, unwilling to move decisively while Mao Zedong was still alive. The continuing impasse was reflected in the fact that neither Deng nor Zhang was able to secure appointment as prime minister upon the death of Zhou Enlai in January 1976. Instead, the position went to a compromise figure, Hua Guofeng, who was closely associated with neither faction.

When Mao died in September 1976, the military was finally in a position to act as arbiter in the struggle for power. Defense Minister Ye Jianying decided to support Hua in launching a palace *coup* against the radicals, and military units played the crucial role in the arrest of the Gang of Four in early October. What is more, by a show of force in Shanghai and other radical strongholds across the country and by fervent expressions of support for Hua Guofeng in the military press, the PLA helped convince the Gang's remaining supporters that resistance to the *coup* would be futile.

Why did the PLA make the choices it did? Why did it support Mao Zedong in 1966 and then turn against his widow a decade later? Why did it support Hua Guofeng in 1976 when it had refused to back Liu Shaoqi ten years earlier? In each case, as suggested above, the PLA's decision was determined by a complex weighing of organizational interests against personal loyalties to the competing civilian factions. In 1966 much of the PLA allowed loyalty and discipline to override its own political interests. In 1976, in contrast, the military's organizational interests overshadowed whatever loyalty it may have had to Jiang Qing as Mao's widow.

On the eve of the Cultural Revolution, to be sure, one group of officers in the PLA did conclude that Mao's initiatives were in their interest. Lin Biao's speeches and actions in the early 1960s suggest that he may have genuinely shared Mao's vision of the proper direction for Chinese society. Even more important, however, Lin clearly believed that if he supported Mao he could expand the material resources available to the PLA, increase the army's status in society, provide greater opportunities for demobilized servicemen, gain power for himself, and promote the careers of his closest associates. From Lin's point of view, in other words, the corporate and programmatic interests of the PLA, as well as the personal interests of his own faction, suggested an alignment with Mao Zedong against Liu Shaoqi and the party establishment.

Much of the rest of the PLA must have disagreed with Lin's assessment. Many professional officers and regional commanders probably suspected that the Cultural Revolution would not promote the organizational interests of the armed forces and might even damage them. Nonetheless, considerations of both organizational discipline and personal loyalty led them to support the Cultural Revolution. The entire officer corps was legally subordinate to Lin as minister of defense and to Mao as *ex officio* chairman of the Military Affairs Committee. And with the dismissal of Chief of Staff Luo Ruiqing in 1965 and the transfer of other high military officers in early 1967, Lin and Mao had made it clear that they would use their authority to reward officers who supported them and demote or reassign those who refused.[63] Most members of the high command were also willing to allow their loyalty to Mao to overcome any reservations they may have had about the wisdom of the Cultural Revolution. They had stronger bonds of fealty to Mao than to any of his rivals on the Politburo.

In addition, the PLA received significant concessions from Mao and Lin in return for its support. Three senior PLA marshals — Ye Jianying, Xu Xiangqian, and Nie Rongzhen — were named to the Politburo in late 1966, in part to increase the military's voice at the highest levels of the Party, but also to ensure that the views of factions other than Lin Biao's would be represented in Beijing. Although the assurances were later violated, the PLA was also promised that the Cultural Revolution would be conducted inside the military through different methods than in the party and state bureaucracies, so that the armed forces would not be disrupted by the activities of civilian Red Guards.[64] And it is not unreasonable to assume that the PLA also received a guarantee that Zhou Enlai would remain in office as prime minister to help restrain Cultural Revolutionary radicalism.

In 1976 the corporate and programmatic interests of the PLA led it to support Hua Guofeng rather than the Gang of Four. The policy preferences of the Gang of Four ran counter to the PLA's programmatic interests in political stability, economic growth, and technological modernization. Furthermore, the Gang had taken a number of positions in the mid-1970s that were diametrically opposed to the corporate interests of the high command. The radicals had favored a policy of confrontation with the Soviet Union, proposed the formation of an independent urban militia, sought to block the rehabilitation of veteran commanders purged during the Cultural Revolution and to replace them with younger officers, and opposed the program of military modernization formulated by Deng Xiaoping in 1975. And, of course, the Gang of Four was closely associated with the radical mass organizations that had fought with the PLA in the provinces at the height of the Cultural Revolution.

Moreover, just as they had when they aligned themselves with Mao Zedong and Lin Biao on the eve of the Cultural Revolution, important elements of the PLA secured benefits for supporting Hua Guofeng in 1976. Both Ye Jianying and Wang Dongxing, the commander of the elite military guard unit that arrested the Gang of Four, gained important promotions when the Politburo was reorganized in 1977. The PLA won Hua's support for a reemphasis on military modernization, as reflected in a rapid increase in defense spending between 1977 and 1979.[65] And an influential regional military commander, Xu Shiyou, who headed the Canton Military

Region, apparently demanded that Deng Xiaoping be restored to a powerful position in the Party as a condition for his support for Hua Guofeng.

But the PLA did not receive all that it asked for. In the months immediately following the purge of the Gang of Four, it was military newspapers such as the *Jiefangjun bao* that took the lead in demanding a vigorous purge of leftists throughout the party and state bureaucracies, so as to prevent any possibility that radicals like the Gang could ever return to power in China. Hua Guofeng, in contrast, advocated a policy of greater leniency towards those who had been "misled" by the radicals, perhaps because he realized that he might need the support of those cadres and party members who had been recruited or promoted during the Cultural Revolution. Hua had his way, at least for a while, and the PLA once again discovered the limits on its political influence.

Contender

Finally, on one critical occasion, a group of officers within the high command of the PLA assumed a role in Chinese politics that went far beyond that of either lobby group or arbiter. In 1969-71, not content with simply pursuing the military's interest through the normal "rules of the game," or even with using the additional resources which had come to the PLA through its involvement in government administration, Lin Biao attempted to secure for the army the preeminent position in the Chinese political system. Through Lin, the PLA became an active contender for civilian political power.

As we have already seen, the army's role in Chinese politics increased steadily during the Cultural Revolution. From serving as a bureaucratic opinion group in the more "normal" years of the early 1960s, the PLA had become an arbiter in the growing conflict between Mao Zedong and the party apparatus, and then a participant in the military-civilian coalition regime which was created to restore order after the turbulent Red Guard movement. In 1969, however, realizing that his own power depended on a perpetuation of military rule, Lin Biao began an effort to make that coalition regime a permanent feature of Chinese politics, and to make the PLA the dominant partner within the coalition.[66]

Lin sought to create a complex set of institutional arrangements by which military officers would dominate both the government bureaucracy and the newly reconstructed Chinese Communist Party. He increased the level of military representation on the new provincial party committees, the Central Committee, and the State Council, so that military men received a higher proportion of appointments on all three bodies than at any time since the early 1950s. In addition, Lin attempted to preserve the independence of military officers serving in state and party agencies from civilian control. In the political system he tried to establish, military representatives would discuss key problems separately from their civilian colleagues, be subject to the military chain of command rather than to party disicipline, and take policy guidance from an expanded staff in the Ministry of Defense rather than from the functional departments of the central government or party apparatus. If Lin's vision had been implemented in its extreme form, the state would have become the administrative arm of the army and the Party little more than a mass organization under military leadership.

As a second strategy, Lin formulated a set of foreign and domestic programs that he believed would attract support from a wide range of civilian leaders, while still satisfying the interests of much of the military. These policies included opposition to the emerging *rapprochement* with the United States, an attempt to weaken the political standing of Premier Zhou Enlai, promotion of a new "leap forward" in the economy, an effort to recreate the alliance of party bureaucrats and political ideologues that had supported the first Great Leap Forward in the late 1950s, and continued high levels of military spending, a measure designed to maximize Lin's support within the PLA.

By the end of 1970, however, Lin's organizational strategy and policy programs had encountered increasing resistance from both moderate and radical civilian leaders. Working together, Mao Zedong and Zhou Enlai announced plans to reduce the military's involvement in civilian affairs. At this point some junior officers associated with Lin, including his son Lin Liguo, began planning a third strategy for consolidating military power: a *coup d'état* aimed principally against Mao and the radicals. This rather naive plot was uncovered before it could be successfully implemented and, realizing that he had lost his struggle for power, Lin tried to flee to the Soviet Union. He died in an airplane crash *en route*.

Lin's failure can be attributed to a variety of factors. For one thing, his economic and foreign policy programs, particularly his advocacy of a new "leap forward," were not sufficiently attractive to assemble the broadly-based coalition of civilian and military leaders that he had hoped for. Even more important, his organizational policy, by threatening to institutionalize military domination of Chinese political life, aroused the opposition of a wide range of leaders who believed in civilian control over the military. And, most significant of all, Lin was never able to gain the complete support of the PLA itself. Although he had placed friends and followers in key positions throughout the military, much of the PLA remained under the leadership of officers from other factions. In the final confrontation between Mao and Lin, many commanders supported the chairman out of a combination of their loyalty to Mao and their distrust of Lin.

Summary and Prospects

As this review suggests, the political influence of the Chinese People's Liberation Army has fluctuated widely over the past thirty-five years. The principal thesis of this chapter is that these fluctuations have been the result of three interrelated factors: the political context, including the organizational effectiveness of the party bureaucracy and the level of conflict among civilian leaders; the role that the PLA has assumed in political life; and the particular set of interests that the army has elected to pursue. The interconnections among these variables can be summarized in the following three summary propositions.

First, the role that the PLA has assumed in China's civilian politics is related to the political context at the time. During periods of relative political stability, such as the mid-1950s and the early 1980s, the PLA has acted solely as a bureaucratic lobby, competing with other interest groups for a voice in national policy. When the civilian bureaucracy has been small and weak, as in the early 1950s, the PLA has been called upon to serve as an active participant in a coalition civilian-military government. When the civilian leadership has been divided and locked into a struggle for political power, as was the case on the eve of the Cultural Revolution in 1966 and at the death of Mao Zedong in 1976, the army has served as arbiter, deciding which of the competing factions would receive its support. And during the Cultural Revolution, when civilian institutions were ineffective and the party leadership fragmented, parts of the PLA sought to create and institutionalize what would have amounted to a military dictatorship over China.

Second, the role that the PLA has assumed in civilian affairs helps determine, in turn, its degree of political influence. When the PLA has been an arbiter between competing civilian factions, as in 1966 and 1976, the PLA has been able not only to select China's national leadership, but also to win significant side payments from the faction it supports. And when the PLA has been a partner in a civilian-military coalition, it has had substantial influence over both the determination of national policy and the implementation of that policy at the local level. In neither role has the PLA completely controlled civilian affairs, but it has obtained substantial influence.

Conversely, the PLA's influence has been somewhat less when it has been restricted to the role of a bureaucratic lobby. At those times, the PLA has been only one of a number of powerful interest groups competing for scarce resources from civilian leaders and it has often seen its proposals rejected, ignored, or substantially modified by civilian leaders. The military has found it particularly difficult in such circumstances to obtain the budgets it has sought. Only when it has been able to forge alliances with other lobbies, usually around broader political and economic programs, has the PLA been able to have a noticeable influence on national affairs.

At the other extreme, active contention for political power has proven to be a risky, and ultimately counterproductive, undertaking for the PLA. In 1970-71, on the one occasion when this strategy was attempted, Lin Biao's bid to consolidate political power generated overwhelming opposition from civilian leaders and from other factions within the military establishment. The results of his failure were a purge of the military from civilian posts, a substantial reduction in the military budget, and intensified civilian controls over the PLA. The influence of the army went into a decline from which it did not recover for about five years.

Our third summary proposition is that the influence of the PLA has also depended on the particular set of interests it has chosen to pursue. In general, it has fared relatively well in attaining its personal and programmatic interests, been somewhat less successful in determining the composition of China's civilian leadership, and encountered the greatest difficulties in the pursuit of its corporate interests.

The PLA has been reasonably successful in securing high salaries, obtaining opportunities for demobilized servicemen, and protecting the status and privileges of the officer corps. It has, in other words, been able to realize its personal interests in ensuring that the PLA preserves its privileged role in Chinese society. Success in this area is due to the fact that the PLA still enjoys substantial legitimacy because of its critical role in the Chinese revolution. What is more, satisfying the personal interests of the PLA has been a relatively inexpensive way for civilian leaders to obtain military support and compliance. Only when the personal interests of the PLA have conflicted with important goals of the civilian leaders, as when the PLA's interest in job stability and security clashed with Deng Xiaoping's desire to reinvigorate the country's aging bureaucracies, has the military encountered difficulty in achieving them.

The PLA has also been fairly successful in pursuing its programmatic interests in nationalism, political stability, economic development, and cultural orthodoxy. While there certainly have been periods when these values have been sacrificed in favor of more radical programs from either the left or the right, the PLA has generally been able to see the restoration of socioeconomic policies and political programs that are more in keeping with its brand of conservatism. The military's success in this area is quite easily explained: not only does the PLA occupy the center of the Chinese political spectrum, it also shares its conservative preferences with important sectors of the party apparatus. And an alliance of military officers with party *apparatchiks*, perhaps China's two most powerful interest groups, is a combination of particular potency.

The PLA has been able to pursue its interests in the selection of China's civilian leaders most effectively when it has acted as a political arbiter. If, in other words, there is a confrontation between competing factions that cannot be resolved through institutionalized procedures and the PLA should decide to intervene, it will almost certainly have the coercive capability to determine the outcome. On the other hand, if the competition among civilian leaders is muted and new leaders are selected through more routine mechanisms, then the PLA will find itself with much less influence. Thus the army, acting as arbiter, was able to see to it that Hua Guofeng and not Jiang Qing would succeed Mao as party chairman; but acting only as a bureaucratic lobby it was not able to prevent Hua's replacement by Hu Yaobang only five years later, let alone the purge of its own defense minister, Peng Dehuai, in 1959.

Finally, the PLA has been least effective in attaining what we have defined as its professional corporate interests. Some, such as PLA control of the militia and a reasonable degree of autonomy in the determination of military programs, have been relatively easy for civilian leaders to accept. But in matters of military modernization and military budgets, the professional sectors of the

PLA have encountered significant obstacles from civilian leaders and those within its own ranks. As we have already noted, an alliance of traditionalists inside the PLA and civilian interests outside the army have, in the past, usually been able to turn back demands from military professionals for rapid military modernization and for greater expenditures on national defense.

The PLA's record in Chinese politics, then, falls somewhere between the record of other communist countries and that of other developing states. Compared with the armies of other communist nations, the role of the PLA seems large indeed. The PLA's role in shaping national policy, in ensuring political stability, in determining leadership succession, and in administering the economy has not been exceeded by the armed forces of any other communist country and has been matched by only a few. In contrast to the armies of other developing countries, the PLA has played a relatively acquiescent role. There have been no successful *coups*, no purely military governments, few cases of overt insubordination to civilian authority, and only one credible report of a planned military uprising. Military praetorianism may be characteristic of much of the Third World, but it has never come to full flower in China.

But what of the future? Will the military continue to play the relatively modest role of bureaucratic lobby that it has assumed in post-Mao China? Or will it be drawn, once again, into deeper involvement in Chinese civilian politics?

The PLA's future role in Chinese politics will be shaped significantly by the process of professionalization and modernization that has accelerated since the death of Mao Zedong in 1976. Inasmuch as the modernization of national defense has been assigned the lowest priority of the Four Modernizations, the process is likely to be slower than many professional officers might wish. Nonetheless, substantial changes are already apparent in the staffing and structure of the Chinese armed forces. Military exercises now feature large-scale, multiservice operations by ground, land, and sea forces. A program to rejuvenate the officer corps has placed younger, better educated officers in leading positions in the Defense Ministry, the service arms, and local military commands. In mid-1985, the PLA announced plans to trim its troop strength by one million soldiers, and reduced the number of military regions from eleven to seven.[67] Over the rest of the century, it is virtually certain that the PLA will receive more sophisticated weapons, concentrate more on its national security responsibilities at the expense of its sideline domestic occupations, and develop new and more modern strategic doctrines.[68]

Over time, professionalization will probably reduce some of the assets that, in the past, the PLA has been able to bring to the political arena. The military, of course, will retain many of its current political resources. It will certainly remain a powerful bureaucracy, continue to command a substantial share of the state budget, and retain regular access to Party and state decision-making bodies. Its other resources, however, may decline. For one thing, the military may well lose its special political legitimacy as memories of its heroic role in the revolution fade and are replaced by the less flattering image of the PLA's involvement in the political struggles of the 1970s. For another, the range of the military's civilian activities should shrink substantially as the PLA gradually becomes more modernized and professionalized. This too should give the PLA somewhat less claim to speak on domestic social and economic issues that are only tangentially related to national security.

Perhaps most important, the death or retirement of the Long March generation in China is steadily removing the party leaders who, during the revolution, simultaneously occupied both civilian and military positions within the Communist movement. These were the leaders with whom the military high command could claim such close personal ties throughout the first thirty years of the People's Republic. As there is greater division of labor between civilians and soldiers, in other words, the PLA will gradually lose the special, informal access to top party leaders described earlier in this essay. It may also see a reduction of its representation on the Politburo, and even the Central Committee.

Professionalization will also reshape the cleavages that now divide the army. The most senior generation of military leaders, who retain a substantial commitment to the revolutionary traditions of the PLA, are already being replaced by more junior officers with a more professional outlook. While there will continue to be generational cleavages within the PLA, they will become more muted, as the officer corps becomes more homogeneous in training and experience and as more regular systems for promotion, rotation, and retirement relieve the tension between junior and senior officers. Professionalization should also alter the relationship between commanders and commissars, molding it, as in the Soviet Union, into a more cooperative relationship in which the commissar gradually becomes a loyal deputy responsible for morale and political training, rather than an institutional rival of the commander. ·

Cleavages will remain, as in any large organization. But they will be largely of two kinds. The networks of personal relationships characteristic of most Chinese organizations will continue to exist, although factionalism could be substantially reduced by a personnel policy that stresses promotion by merit and regular rotation. Above all, there will be intra-bureaucratic rivalries among the major services. Increasingly, however, these cleavages will focus on budgetary and strategic priorities rather than on the desirability of modernization and professionalization: on *what* and *when* to modernize, not *whether.*

This suggests, in turn, that professionalization will have a considerable impact on the political interests of the PLA. The personal interests of the officer corps in material benefits for themselves and their families will remain strong and may even become more salient if economic liberalization produces greater differentiation within Chinese society. Professionalization may also mean that the high command will become even more concerned with maintaining the economic rationality, political stability, and secure international environment that would be most conducive to military modernization. Above all, professionalization should produce a growing consensus that the corporate interests of the PLA require steady modernization, larger budgets, greater autonomy, guaranteed exclusivity, and deference to the officer corps. All this should mean that the PLA will come to resemble the Soviet Red Army more closely, divided perhaps on questions involving the allocation of scarce resources within the military, but increasingly united on the definition of the army's basic corporate and programmatic interests.

Finally, professionalization may also affect the Party's ability to maintain control over the Chinese armed forces. In formal terms, the structure of civilian control will likely remain unchanged. Professionalization may also increase the PLA's fear that involvement in civilian politics would have a detrimental effect on its military preparedness. On the other hand, professionalization will also mean that the PLA will no longer be held in check by the personal ties between military and civilian leaders that have been so important in the past.

Our prognosis, then, is that the PLA will become more professionalized and more unified than in the past, but will also lose some of the special political resources it enjoyed during the first thirty-five years of Communist rule in China. Taken together, these factors point in two possible directions. If the Party engages once again in a debilitating succession struggle, is unable to formulate a convincing political doctrine to justify its rule, fails to define its role in an increasingly complex and technocratic society, and proves unwilling to root out corrupt and incompetent civilian officials – if, in other words, there is a general decline in the Party's legitimacy – then the chances for more extensive military participation in Chinese politics will be substantially increased. The army may, as in the late 1970s, become an active arbiter among civilian factions, or even a contender for national political power. And the growing unity of the PLA around a common set of professional interests may make it a more effective political force than ever before.

If, however, the Communist Party can recover from the trauma of the Cultural Revolution, invigorate itself organizationally and ideologically, restore its internal unity, and promote China's modernization effectively, then it should be able to retain its control over the armed forces. In this more plausible scenario, the PLA will continue to be actively involved in Chinese politics, but only as a lobby, competing with a growing array of other social and bureaucratic interest groups for influence and resources. The growing unity of the army will probably help increase its bureaucratic influence. But, in the years to come, the PLA will simultaneously lose the advantages that accompanied its personal ties to the current generation of civilian leaders and the special political legitimacy that it has enjoyed in the past.

NOTES

List of Abbreviations

CPCC	Chinese People's Political Consultative Conference
DGB	*Dagong bao* [Impartial news], Hong Kong
FBIS	Foreign Broadcast Information Service Daily Report: China
GMRB	*Guangming ribao* [Bright daily], Beijing
JFRB	*Jiefang ribao* [Liberation daily], Shanghai
LDB	*Laodong bao* [Labor news], Shanghai
NCNA	New China News Agency, Shanghai
NFCPRS	News from Chinese Provincial Radio Stations
NPC	National People's Congress
RMRB	*Renmin ribao* [People's daily], Beijing
SCMP	Survey of China Mainland Press
SCMPS	Survey of China Mainland Press (Supplement)
SHGSZL	*Shanghai gongshang ziliao* [Shanghai industrial and commerical materials], Shanghai
SN	*Shanghai News*
SPRCP	Survey of People's Republic of China Press
WHB	*Wenhui bao* [Culture news], Shanghai
XDRB	*Xingdao ribao* [Singapore daily], Hong Kong
XMB	*Xinmin bao* [New people news], Shanghai
XWRB	*Xinwen ribao* [News daily], Shanghai.

Chapter 1

1. Archie Brown, "Policy Making in Communist States," *Studies in Comparative Communism* 11, no. 4 (Winter 1978).
2. Robert A. Dahl, "Pluralism Revisited," *Comparative Politics* 10, no. 2 (January 1978): 191-203.
3. Franz Schurmann, *Ideology and Organization in Communist China*, rev. ed. (Berkeley: University of California Press, 1968), iv.
4. James Townsend, *Political Participation in Communist China*, new ed. (Berkeley and Los Angeles: University of California Press, 1968), xii-xiii.
5. Michel Oksenberg, "Occupational Groups in Chinese Society and the Cultural Revolution," *The Cultural Revolution: 1967 in Review*, Michigan Papers in Chinese Studies, no. 2 (Ann Arbor: University of Michigan Center for Chinese Studies Publications, 1968).
6. See for example, Byung-joon Ahn, *Chinese Politics and the Cultural Revolution* (Seattle: University of Washington Press, 1971); *China's Quest for Independence: Policy Evolution in the 1970s*, ed. Thomas Fingar (Boulder: Westview Press, 1980).
7. See for example, David M. Lampton, *The Politics of Medicine in China: The Policy Process, 1949-1977* (Boulder: Westview Press, 1977); Dorothy Solinger, *Chinese Business under Socialism: The Politics of Domestic Commerce, 1949-1980* (Berkeley: University of California Press, 1985).
8. Alan P. L. Liu, *Political Culture and Group Conflict in Communist China* (Santa Barbara: Clio Books, 1976); Hong Yung Lee, *The Politics of the Chinese Cultural Revolution: A Case Study* (Berkeley: University of California Press, 1978); Gordon White, *Party and Professionals: The Political Role of Teachers in Contemporary China* (Armonk, N.Y.: M.E. Sharpe, Inc., 1981); *Groups in the People's Republic of China*, ed. David S. G. Goodman (Armonk, N.Y.: M.E. Sharpe, Inc., 1984).
9. Andrew Nathan, "A Factionalism Model of CCP Politics," *China Quarterly*, no. 53 (1972); see also his "Clientelism in Communist Systems: A Symposium," in *Study in Comparative Communism* 12, no. 223 (Summer/Autumn 1979); Jean C. Oi, "Communism and Clientelism: Rural Politics in China," *World Politics* 37, no. 2 (January 1985).

10. *Interest Groups in Soviet Politics*, ed. H. Gordon Skilling and Franklyn Griffiths (Princeton: Princeton University Press, 1971).
11. Zbigniew Brzezinski and Samuel P. Huntington, *Political Power: USA/USSR* (New York: Viking Press, 1964), 195-96.
12. Seweryn Bialer, *Stalin's Successors: Leadership, Stability and Change in the USSR* (Cambridge: Cambridge University Press, 1980), 166-67.
13. Victor C. Falkenheim, "Political Participation in China," *Problems of Communism* 27, no. 3 (May-June 1978).
14. James Townsend, *Political Participation in Communist China*, new ed. (Berkeley and Los Angeles: University of California Press, 1968), 7.
15. Brzezinski and Huntington, *Political Power*, 196.
16. David M. Lampton, "Advancing Interest in China's Complex Society" (unpublished paper, 1977), 3.
17. Michel Oksenberg, "Occupation Groups in Chinese Society," *The Cultural Revolution: 1967 in Review*, Michigan Papers in Chinese Studies, no. 2 (Ann Arbor: University of Michigan Center for Chinese Studies Publications, 1968), 2.
18. *Interest Groups in Soviet Politics*, ed. H. Gordon Skilling and Franklyn Griffiths (Princeton: Princeton University Press, 1971), 336.
19. See for example, Marc Blecher, "Leader Mass Relations in Rural Chinese Communities: Local Politics in a Revolutionary Society" (Ph.D. diss., University of Chicago, 1977).
20. For a discussion of this point see Victor C. Falkenheim, "Decentralization in Maoist Perspective," *Current Scene* 16, no. 1 (January 1978).
21. Michel Oksenberg, "Methods of Communication within the Chinese Bureaucracy," *China Quarterly*, no. 57 (January-March 1974).
22. Edward Friedman, "The Politics of Local Models, Social Transformation and State Power Struggle in the People's Republic of China: Tachai and Teng Hsiao-ping," *China Quarterly*, no. 76 (December 1978); also "Anhwei Revokes Titles of Fake Taching-style Enterprises," *Foreign Broadcast Information Service* (hereafter FBIS) (21 June 1978): E3.
23. Stephen Andors, "Factory Management and Political Ambiguity, 1961-63," *China Quarterly*, no. 59 (July-September 1974).

24. Mitch Meisner, "Dazhai: The Mass Line in Practice," *Modern China* 4, no. 1 (January 1978): 55.

25. *Peking Review* 21, no. 10 (10 March 1978): 20.

26. "Fully Develop the Enthusiasm for Rural Basic Level Cadres," RMRB (28 April 1979); trans. in FBIS (1 May 1979): L1.

27. *Xinhua* (14 November 1978); trans. in FBIS (17 November 1978): E7.

28. Lucian Pye, *The Dynamics of Chinese Politics* (Cambridge, Mass.: Oelgeschlayer, Gunn & Hain Publishers, Inc., 1981).

29. Tang Tsou, "Prolegomenon to the Study of Informal Groups in CCP Politics," *China Quarterly*, no. 65 (January 1976): 100-101; Nathan, "A Factional Model."

30. Michel Oksenberg, "Economic Policy Making in China: Summer, 1981," *China Quarterly*, no. 90 (June 1982): 181.

31. Gordon Bennett, "Activists and Professionals: China's Revolution in Bureaucracy 1959-1965, A Case Study of the Finance-Trade System" (Ph.D. diss., University of Wisconsin, 1973).

32. Lowell Dittmer, "Bases of Power in Chinese Politics: A Theory and Analysis of the Fall of the Gang of Four," *World Politics* 21, no. 1 (October 1978).

33. For a description of the "system" notion, see A. Doak Barnett, *Cadres, Bureaucracy and Power* (New York: Columbia University Press, 1967).

34. See Victor C. Falkenheim, "Autonomy and Control in Chinese Organization: Dilemmas of Rural Administrative Reform," in *Organizational Behavior in Chinese Society*, ed. Sidney L. Greenblatt, Amy Averbach Wilson, and Richard W. Wilson (New York: Praeger, 1981).

35. Parris Chang, *Power and Policy in China*, rev. ed. (State College: Pennsylvania State University Press, 1979).

36. Thomas Fingar, "Introduction: The Quest for Independence," in *China's Quest for Independence: Policy Revolution in the 1970s*, ed. Thomas Fingar and the Stanford Journal of International Studies (Boulder: Westview Press, 1980).

37. Victor C. Falkenheim, "Political Reform in China," *Current History* 8, no. 476 (September 1982).

38. Richard Lowenthal, "On 'Established' Communist Party Regimes," *Studies in Comparative Communism* 7, no. 4 (Winter 1974).

39. Ibid., 347.

Chapter 2

1. On the concept of interest in Confucian thought, cf. Donald J. Munro, "The Concept of Interest in Chinese Thought" (paper presented at the Workshop on the Pursuit of Political Interest in the PRC, Ann Arbor, Michigan, 10-17 August 1977); see also I-fan Ch'eng, *"Kung* as an Ethos in Late 19th Century China," in *Reform in Nineteenth Century China,* ed. Paul Cohen and John Schrecker, East Asian Monograph, no. 72 (Cambridge, Mass.: Harvard University Press, 1976), 170-81.

2. See Ying-mao Kau, "Urban and Rural Strategies in the Chinese Communist Revolution," in *Peasant Rebellion and Communist Revolution,* ed. John Wilson Lewis (Stanford: Stanford University Press, 1974).

3. James R. Townsend, *Political Participation in Communist China* (Berkeley: University of California Press, 1969), 52-55.

4. See James D. Seymour, "Communist China's Bourgeois-Democratic Parties" (M.A. thesis, Columbia University, n.d.).

5. Mao Zedong, "Some Questions Concerning Methods of Leadership," in *Selected Works of Mao Tse-tung* (Beijing: Foreign Languages Press, 1965), vol. 3, 117-23.

6. Liu Shaoqi (Liu Shao-ch'i), *On the Party* (Beijing: Foreign Languages Press, 1950), 53.

7. John Wilson Lewis, *Leadership in Communist China* (Ithaca: Cornell University Press, 1963), 98-100.

8. Townsend, *Political Participation,* 84-85.

9. Liu Shaoqi, "Some Basic Principles for Organizing the Masses" (1 May 1939), *Collected Works of Liu Shao-ch'i* (Hong Kong: Union Research Institute, 1969), i, 99-115.

10. Liu Shaoqi, "Report" (18 August 1964), as quoted in "Selected Edition on Liu Shao-ch'i's Counterrevolutionary Revisionist Crimes," trans. in *Selections from China Mainland Magazines* (hereafter SCMM), no. 653 (5 May 1969) (Hong Kong: U.S. Consulate General): 27.

11. Liu Shaoqi, "Self-examination" (23 October 1966), in *Liu Shaoqi wenti ziliao juanji* [A special collection of materials on Liu Shaoqi] (Taibei: Institute for the Study of Chinese Communist Questions, 1970), 621-25.

12. Kenneth Lieberthal, *Central Documents and Politburo Politics in China*, Michigan Papers in Chinese Studies, no. 33 (Ann Arbor: University of Michigan Center for Chinese Studies Publications, 1978).

13. A pentrating analysis of Red Guard factionalism may be found in Hong Yung Lee, *The Politics of the Chinese Cultural Revolution: A Case Study* (Berkeley: University of California Press, 1978).

14. See Ronald Suleski, "Changing the Guard in Shanghai," *Asian Survey* 12, no. 3 (September 1977): 886-97.

15. A perceptive analysis of post-Cultural Revolution patterns of participation may be found in Victor C. Falkenheim, "Political Participation in China," *Problems of Communism* 27, no. 3 (May-June 1978): 18-32.

16. See Graham Young, "Party Building and the Search for Unity," in *China: The Impact of the Cultural Revolution*, ed. Bill Brugger (New York: Barnes and Noble, 1978), 35-70.

17. Gu Shutang, Zou Mu, and Tang Zaixin, "The Question of Bourgeois Right and the 'Gang of Four's' Counterrevolutionary Plot," *Hongqi* [Red flag], no. 8 (8 August 1977): 65-70.

18. See Mao Tse-tung (Mao Zedong), *A Critique of Soviet Economics*, trans. Moss Roberts (New York: Monthly Review Press, 1977).

19. Zhang Chunqiao, "On Exercising All-round Dictatorship Over the Bourgeoisie," *Hongqi*, no. 4 (1 April 1975): 3-13.

20. As cited in Gu, "The Question of Bourgeois Right," 65-70.

21. Yao Wenyuan, "On the Social Basis of the Lin Biao Anti-Party Clique," *Hongqi*, no. 3 (1 March 1975): 1-13.

22. Yuan Qing, "An Important Question in the Relations of Production," *Hongqi*, no. 5 (1 May 1975): 8-14.

23. Zhang, "On Exercising All-round Dictatorship," 3-13.

24. Quoted in Zhai Qing, "The Essential Relations Between Man and Man Are Class Relations," *Xuexi yu pipan* [Study and criticism], no. 8 (14 August 1976).

25. Quoted in Li Xin, "Leading Cadres Must Consciously Restrict Bourgeois Rights," *Hongqi*, no. 7 (1 July 1976): 17-21.

26. An Qun, "Resolutely Trust and Rely on the Majority of the Masses," *Hongqi*, no. 3 (3 March 1973): 11-16.

27. Zhang, "On Exercising All-round Dictatorship," 3-13.

28. The Mass Criticism Group of Beijing University and Qinghua University, "Lin Biao and the Doctrines of Confucius and Mencius," *Hongqi*, no. 2 (1 February 1974): 8-16.

29. Yao Wenyuan, "Dictatorship of the Proletariat and the Renegade Lin Biao," *Peking Review* (27 June 1975): 8.

30. Tian Zhisong, "Resist Corruption, Never Be Stained," *Hongqi*, no. 5 (1 May 1973): 15-18.

31. Hong Yuan, "Communists Should Work for the Interests of the Vast Majority of the People," *Hongqi*, no. 11 (1 November 1973): 3-8.

32. Gan Ge, "Do Things According to Party Principles," *Hongqi*, no. 10 (1 October 1972): 34-37.

33. Political Seminar of the Military and Political Cadre School of the Shenyang PLA Units, "Revolution Means Fighting for the Interests of the Masses," GMRB (11 February 1978): 2.

34. "Correspondence on Bourgeois Right," *Xuexi yu pipan*, no. 3 (16 March 1975).

35. Theoretical Group of Beijing Normal University, "Betrayal by the 'Gang of Four' of Chairman Mao's Directive on the Question of Theory," *Hongqi*, no. 2 (3 February 1977): 13-19; see also Theory Group of the Shenyang PLA Units, "Refute the Reactionary Fallacy that There Is a 'Bourgeois Class' Inside the Party," *Hongqi*, no. 11 (7 November 1977): 61-64.

36. Gu, "The Question of Bourgeois Right," 65-70.

37. Ibid.

Chapter 3

1. The author would like to thank Martin Whyte, Jean Oi, Michel Oksenberg, and Andrew Nathan for their careful commentaries on the initial draft of this chapter. The field research on which it is based was funded jointly by dissertation grants from the National Science Foundation, the U.S. Department of Education Fulbright-Hays Fellowship Program, and the Social Science Research Council. Subsequent archival research, and the initial writing, was completed while the author held a post-doctoral fellowship at the Center for Chinese Studies, University of California, Berkeley, in 1981-82. While this financial and intellectual assistance is gratefully acknowledged, the author is

solely responsible for the analysis presented here.

Essential background for this chapter is the author's 1979-80 interview project in Hong Kong, during which seventy Chinese emigrés were interviewed intensively, for a total of 464 hours, about their past industrial work experience. The interview subjects held a wide variety of industrial positions, from top executive posts to temporary worker; thirty-two of them had experience as blue-collar workers in a wide variety of enterprises. Limitations of space prevent a full account of the interview procedures and fuller documentation of conclusions with references to interview transcripts. The author provides this in his book, *Communist Neo-Traditionalism: Work and Authority in Chinese Industry* (Berkeley: University of California Press, 1986).

2. Charles Tilly, *From Mobilization to Revolution* (Reading, Mass.: Addison-Wesley, 1978). Tilly provides a summary framework of group political theory that begins with the formation of groups and specifies the conditions that lead to successful collective action to achieve group goals.

3. Merilee Grindle argues that attempts to influence the implementation of policy, rather than the making of policy, constitute the main course for the pursuit of interests in most Third World nations. See her introductory essay in *Politics and Policy Implementation in the Third World*, ed. Merilee Grindle (Princeton: Princeton University Press, 1979). "Corruption" is just one variety of the kinds of activity that grow under these conditions. See James C. Scott, *Comparative Political Corruption* (Englewood Cliffs, N.J.: Prentice-Hall, 1971).

4. Gordon Skilling, "Groups in Soviet Politics: Some Hypotheses," in *Interest Groups in Soviet Politics*, ed. Gordon Skilling and Franklyn Griffiths (Princeton: Princeton University Press, 1971), 29. Skilling, it should be noted, warned that broad social groups like peasants and workers were too diverse and insufficiently cohesive to behave as "interest groups," as do lower-level elites who occupy a position "between society and decision-makers" (ibid., 29). This stricture, however, has understandably not constrained subsequent writers from applying the notion to mass groups in China that mobilized to pursue their interests in 1966-67 (e.g., Michel Oksenberg, "Occupational Groups in Chinese Society and the Cultural Revolution," in *The Cultural Revolution: 1967 in Review*, Michigan Papers in Chinese

Studies, no. 2 [Ann Arbor: University of Michigan Center for Chinese Studies Publications, 1968]). I describe the approach here simply to offer it as one possible conceptualization of the political activity of Chinese workers.

5. Skilling's capable defense of the interest group model against its critics demonstrates that it cannot be dismissed simply as a misguided application of pluralist theories to Soviet realities. See his "Group Conflict in Soviet Politics: Some Conclusions," in Skilling and Griffiths, *Interest Groups.*

6. Franklyn Griffiths offers a detailed critique of Skilling's interest group theory along these lines in his "A Tendency Analysis of Soviet Policy-Making," ibid., 335-77. In light of the Chinese Cultural Revolution and recent workers' movements in Poland one might be tempted to add that genuine group politics among mass groups occurs only when a communist regime is in a state of crisis or disintegration.

7. Griffiths labels this "tendencies of articulation": group members tend to articulate similar interests separately and individually when opportunities arise.

8. A recent analysis of Hungary, while not citing Griffiths, argues persuasively that workers there have exercised unmistakable influence in precisely this way since the establishment of the "New Economic Mechanism" after 1968. See Charles Sabel and David Stark, "Planning, Politics, and Shop-Floor Power: Hidden Forms of Bargaining in Soviet-Imposed State Socialist Societies," *Politics and Society* 11, no. 4 (1982): 439-75.

9. I leave aside the complex questions that immediately arise about how the clientelist system that encompasses Chinese workers compares with the endless varieties of clientelism that have occurred in all types of political systems. A literature review by James Scott, and the volume of which it is a part, give one an idea of the many questions that should properly be raised in this regard. These questions are beyond the scope of the present chapter. See James C. Scott, "Political Clientelism: A Bibliographical Essay," in *Friends, Followers, and Factions: A Reader in Political Clientelism,* ed. Stephen W. Schmidt, James C. Scott, Carl Landé, and Laura Guasti (Berkeley: University of California Press, 1977), 483-505.

10. My argument here parallels that of Landé about peasant participation in local politics in the developing areas. See

Carl Landé, "Networks and Groups in Southeast Asia: Some Observations on the Group Theory of Politics," in ibid., 75-99, especially the opening pages.

Jean C. Oi has developed an analysis of patron-client politics in the contemporary Chinese countryside that has greatly influenced my own thinking about Chinese workers, although there are major differences in the forms clientelism takes in factory and village. See Jean C. Oi, "State and Peasant in Contemporary China: The Politics of Grain Procurement" (Ph.D. diss., University of Michigan, 1983), esp. chs. 6 and 7; and her "Communism and Clientelism: Rural Politics in China," *World Politics* 37, no. 2 (January 1985): 238-66.

11. This figure includes all blue collar workers employed in all manufacturing and mining enterprises, but excludes those in services, construction, transportation, and administrative organs. These other sectors are excluded because the organization of enterprises and the quality of labor relations may differ significantly from manufacturing, and also because government statistics are organized according to this definition of "industrial." This figure is the total of the five sub-groups enumerated below.

12. The status of a state cadre is determined in part by the size of the enterprise and the level of administration that governs the plant. The director of a large heavy industrial complex under a national ministry may have the rank of vice minister, while the director of a small enterprise may have the rank of a sub-municipal official.

13. *Zhongguo jingji nianjian 1982* (Beijing: Jingji guanli zazhishe, 1982), v-94 (hereafter cited as *Jingji nianjian 1982*). The figures cited here include only employment in commune and brigade enterprises classified as "industrial." It excludes employment in other rural sideline enterprises in transportation, services, and agricultural production. The figure for employment includes all employees and therefore counts managerial personnel, but in these small enterprises the number of supervisors is probably very small. The gross value of industrial output of all these commune enterprises was 58 billion *yuan* in 1981, out of a national total of 540 billion. See Zhonghua renmin gongheguo guojia tongji ju, *Zhongguo tongji nianjian 1981* (Hong Kong: Xianggang jingji daobaoshe, 1982), 134, 208 (hereafter cited as *Tongji*

nianjian 1981).

14. After 1978 many areas of the Chinese countryside began to employ household contracting systems and other practices that changed the organization of collective agriculture, the rationing of grain, and the distribution of the harvest. My account describes practices that were common until 1979.

15. This is dictated by the system of household registration designed to prevent migration to the cities. One's grain rations continue to be drawn at the place of legal registration. Since these workers are not participating in collective agricultural labor, they must "earn" their rations by paying cash to their team.

16. The average cash income of a rural family is a small fraction of that of an urban one. According to 1980 government surveys, the average annual per capita income of urban families was 429 *yuan*, while that of rural families only 179 *yuan*. Only 86 *yuan* of this 179 was actually distributed by the production team, a figure that underscores the importance of any outside wage income. See Xinhuashe, "Jueda duoshu zhigong jiating shouru xianzhu zengzhang," RMRB (31 December 1980): 1; and Xinhuashe, "Nongcun ren junnian zong shouru zengjia dao yibai qishijiu yuan," RMRB (3 January 1981): 1.

17. See William L. Parish and Martin K. Whyte, *Village and Family in Contemporary China* (Chicago: University of Chicago Press, 1978), 59-71.

18. See Dwight Perkins, ed., *Rural Small-scale Industry in the People's Republic of China* (Berkeley: University of California Press, 1977), 216-18; and Oi, "State and Peasant," ch. 4.

19. Parish and Whyte, *Village and Family*, 37, is the source for the half of this statement that refers to brigade headquarters, and my own interviews for the statement about county-level enterprises.

20. The number of temporary workers in Chinese industry is rarely reported in official publications, including the statistical compendia cited elsewhere in this chapter. This may be due, in part, to statistical confusion about how to classify and count them, especially since much of this employment is casual and short-term. It may also be due to official reluctance to openly acknowledge the magnitude of this industrial "underclass," which does not enjoy the wages, benefits, and social security of state sector workers. A recent

State Council document, however, cites a figure of 9.3 million as the total number of rural residents working on a non-permanent basis in urban state-sector enterprises. If we assume that this official figure misses much of the casual and short-term employment of this type, and note that it does not count rural residents' employment in urban collective enterprises, the figure for all rural residents employed temporarily in urban enterprises is probably higher. The 9.3 million figure, however, includes non-industrial employment. If we assume that the undercount of the casual laborers and the excluded urban collective employees roughly balances the number employed in non-industrial state enterprises, then the figure of 9 million is a reasonable estimate of rural temporary industrial employment as defined here. See the document dated 30 December 1981 in *Zhonghua renmin gongheguo guowuyuan gongbao*, no. 374 (10 February 1982): 885.

21. This practice has gained legitimacy since the easing of restrictions on rural side-line enterprise since 1978, but it flourished earlier despite the fact that it was, formally speaking, illegal. Managers I interviewed explained that rural construction teams are preferred to state companies because the state crews are more expensive, work more slowly, and scheduling them is often full of red tape and delays. An additional advantage of the rural teams is that they can be employed without notifying state planning agencies which might object to the expansion or renovation of the plant if they find out beforehand.

22. Despite the strict controls, rural residents can occasionally obtain permanent jobs in an enterprise in a town or small city, and in some cases in larger cities or mining districts in the interior that have been built up rapidly since the 1950s, leaving them short of labor. In general, however, this is tightly restricted, especially in the larger cities where unemployment has been a continuing concern. Despite the controls, a total of some thirteen million rural residents were able to migrate to the cities between 1966 and 1976. See John Emerson, "Urban School-leavers and Unemployment in China," *China Quarterly*, no. 93 (March 1983): 8.

23. This is a rough estimate I have arrived at based on the numbers of urban temporaries my interview subjects commonly reported in their factories, and on fragmentary

statistics dating from the 1950s and 1960s. (See Andrew G. Walder, "The Remaking of the Chinese Working Class: 1949-1981," *Modern China* 10, no. 1 [January 1984]: 3-48.) My original estimate fits very closely with a source cited by Emerson ("Urban School Leavers," 4-5) that states that 6 percent of the urban labor force are temporary workers assigned by labor bureaus, and another 1 to 2 percent are temporaries assigned by street labor service stations. Since officials apparently do not consider rural contract workers to be part of the urban labor force, the number probably applies only to urban resident temporaries. Six percent of the urban labor force as we have defined it yields a figure very close to four million. A precise count is as difficult as a precise definition of this group, since they are often shifted in and out of small neighborhood collective factories when their assignments are made by street organs, and at other times might be counted as unemployed.

24. Trusted temporaries are often hired when an enterprise is given permission to expand its permanent labor force.

25. These are typically people who completed high school but were refused college admission, individuals who have refused or who have resigned from state job assignments given earlier, who have been expelled from state employment for repeated violations of rules or for political or criminal offenses, or people for whom the state simply never found job assignments. Temporary workers receive a small fraction of the insurance and other benefits of permanent employees, and only are entitled to them so long as they are employed.

26. Several of my interview subjects remarked that temporary workers, because of their desire to have their jobs extended, were generally more diligent than permanent employees. In fact, one reason why temporaries are hired for more arduous kinds of work outside the normal production sequence is that permanent workers resist transfers to heavy labor either through outright refusals or calculated slothfulness on the job.

27. Some groups of contract workers from the suburban communes near large cities did raise grievances about the percentage of their wages taken by their communes and other issues regarding their terms of employment. (See Andrew G. Walder, *Chang Ch'un-ch'iao and Shanghai's January Revolution*, Michigan Papers in Chinese Studies, no.

32 [Ann Arbor: University of Michigan Center for Chinese Studies Publications, 1978], 39-46.) But for them the abolition of the contract labor system might take away these lucrative outside sources of income. Unless the migration controls in large cities were abandoned, rural temporaries could not benefit by the abolition of contract labor. Their demands tended to address specific conditions of contracts.

Urban temporaries, on the other hand, pressed the more radical demand for an end to their outcast status in the urban labor force. Theirs was a demand for permanent employment to which they felt entitled as urban residents. They formed the active organization of temporary workers that played a major role in Shanghai's January Revolution and, according to several informants from Shanghai, endured as an organization for several years after 1967. The sharp distinction in interests and orientation of these two groups of temporaries was stressed by several of my Shanghai informants.

28. See Michel Korzec and Martin K. Whyte, "Reading Notes: The Chinese Wage System," *China Quarterly*, no. 86 (June 1981): 261-62.

29. Urban temporary workers had political influence only when they were able to form coalitions across enterprises during the Cultural Revolution. This ability was rapidly suppressed after the formation of revolutionary committees. See Walder, *Shanghai's January Revolution*, 65-83; and Hong Yung Lee, *The Politics of the Chinese Cultural Revolution* (Berkeley: University of California Press, 1978), 296-301.

30. *Tongji nianjian 1981*, 106.

31. Ibid., 203, is the source for the number of urban industrial enterprises.

32. Ibid., 424.

33. According the *Zhongguo baike nianjian 1980* (Shanghai: Zhongguo da baike quanshu chubanshe, 1980), 293 (hereafter cited as *Baike nianjian 1980*), there were 36,412 collective enterprises run by street committees in cities and towns in 1979, out of a total of just under 100,000.

34. *Tongji nianjian 1981*, 134, 208. Total value of industrial output in 1981 was 540 billion *yuan,* of which 77 billion was produced in the urban collective sector, and 58 billion in rural collectives.

35. In the urban collective sector there is 2,000 *yuan* of fixed

capital investment per worker; in the state sector, 10,000 *yuan;* in the rural collective sector, only 950 *yuan.* See *Jingji nianjian 1981,* iv-56; and Feng Lanrui and Zhao Lukuan, "Urban Unemployment in China," *Social Sciences in China,* no. 3 (March 1982): 130.

36. *Tongji nianjian 1981,* 118, 203. According to this source, there were 28.6 million blue-collar workers in state industrial enterprises and 34.1 employees overall.

37. *Tongji nianjian 1981,* 208, 134.

38. Ibid., 424.

39. *Jingji nianjian 1981,* iv-34.

40. Judging from interviews with emigrés, workers most often change jobs when they are young, and the reasons usually have to do with dissatisfaction with their initial job assignment. Workers are also more likely to resign their jobs if they have been punished by the factory leadership or have developed reputations as troublemakers, harming their chances within the enterprise. As the worker grows older and takes on family responsibilities, job resignations become less likely.

41. *Jingji nianjian 1981,* iv-36. There are a total of 84,200 state industrial enterprises in China, according to *Tongji nianjian 1981,* 203. I suspect that the 42,000 figure cited in the first source refers to enterprises under the central budget, while the additional 42,000 excluded by this figure includes those under local budgets (*difang guoying*). Whatever the explanation for the discrepancy, the output figures still illustrate the disproportionate contribution of large enterprises to output figures.

42. I have been unable to determine how many employees work in the elite group of large state enterprises. Chinese statistics released to date do not include breakdowns of enterprises by the number employed in them.

43. These small supplements may at first glance appear insignificant, but they are highly valued by employees. In a situation where most major foodstuffs are rationed, and 57 percent of the average family's budget goes for food, supplementary ration tickets and small subsidies for food are significant benefits (*Tongji nianjian 1981,* 429).

44. After the increase of grain prices in urban areas in 1979, the grain subsidy for state workers reached 7 percent of the wage bill; ibid., 427.

45. These and other benefits are summarized in the following sources: *Laodong gongzi wenjian xuanbian* (n.p.: Fujian sheng geming weiyuanhui, 1973), 317-366; and *Shehui wenjiao xingzheng caiwu zhidu zhaibian*, ed. Caizhengbu, wenjiao xingzheng caiwusi (Beijing: Zhongguo caizheng jingji chubanshe, 1978), 426-43.

46. Zhou Shulian and Lin Senmu, "Tantan zhuzhai wenti," RMRB (5 August 1980): 5.

47. The rents charged to the occupants of these state-owned dwellings do not even begin to cover the costs of their construction (*Jingji nianjian 1981*, iv, 179-83). Expenditures for rent comprise only 1.4 percent of the average urban family's budget, or .53 *yuan* per person each month (*Tongji nianjian 1981*, 429).

48. This is a significant benefit. According to official figures, housing repairs fell behind the deterioration of the housing stock in the two decades after 1956, to the point that over 50 percent of the housing stock was classified as "in poor repair" in 1978 (Zhou and Lin, "Tantan zhuzhai wenti").

49. These figures are the metric equivalents of those cited in *Jingji nianjian 1981*, iv, 182.

50. *Baike nianjian 1980*, 293.

51. Of the thirty-eight enterprises surveyed by Barry Richman in 1965, two stood out as having "by far the largest" proportion of party members, with 20 and 30 percent, respectively. The two having the smallest proportions had 6 and 7 percent. Most enterprises, in other words, have rates of party membership of around 10 to 15 percent, a number that fits with the memories of my emigré interviewees. Whatever the proportion of party members among employees as a whole, the proportion is much higher among leadership personnel than among workers. See Barry Richman, *Industrial Society in Communist China* (New York: Random House, 1969), 761-62.

52. The files are usually thicker for white-collar staff, especially those who are well-educated or who have suspicious family backgrounds. The files of department-level leading cadres and above are kept at a level of administration above the enterprise, at a bureau or company personnel department.

53. My interviewees consistently identified security department personnel as former soldiers, something that is confirmed by Gordon White in his study of the job assignments given to

demobilized soldiers: "The Politics of Demobilized Soldiers from Liberation to Cultural Revolution," *China Quarterly*, no. 82 (June 1980): 196-97.

54. When an employee is placed "under control" (*guanzhi*), the suspect is required to report at regular intervals to the security department and write periodic self-evaluations of his or her improving political consciousness. After a fixed period the worker's progress will be evaluated and a decision made to either discontinue the measure or apply more serious punishments.

55. I describe this dimension of *biaoxian* more fully in Andrew G. Walder, "Organized Dependency and Cultures of Authority in Chinese Industry," *Journal of Asian Studies*, no. 43 (November 1983): 60-63.

56. The link between work performance and reward, however, cannot be made too indirect, or else declining work performance will result. This is in fact what happened in the decade after 1966, when the link between work performance and reward was severed almost completely. This analysis, keep in mind, is of worker political participation and the political control of workers. One cannot assume that a workforce whose political activities are restricted into very narrow channels and who are compliant politically, are also well-disciplined and hardworking. Usually quite the opposite is the case, because a conscious withdrawal of work effort is the chief means of registering discontent.

57. This is not something that is unique about Chinese workers. White collar personnel and students in middle school and college are faced with the same necessity. See Michel Oksenberg, "Getting Ahead and Along in Communist China: The Ladder of Success on the Eve of the Cultural Revolution," in *Party Leadership and Revolutionary Power in China*, ed. John W. Lewis (Cambridge: Cambridge University Press, 1970), 304-47; Ezra Vogel, "Voluntarism and Social Control," in *Soviet and Chinese Communism: Similarities and Differences*, ed. Donald Treadgold (Seattle: University of Washington Press, 1967), 168-84; Susan L. Shirk, *Competitive Comrades: Career Incentives and Student Strategies in China* (Berkeley: University of California Press, 1982); and Jonathan Unger, *Education Under Mao* (New York: Columbia University Press, 1982).

58. See Martin K. Whyte and William L. Parish, *Urban Life in*

Contemporary China (Chicago: University of Chicago Press, 1984), ch. 11.

59. The Chinese enterprise is honeycombed with staff positions in various political and administrative offices that require few specific skills besides literacy. People are often assigned to jobs with vaguely-defined responsibilities in trade union, youth league, and party offices, or in the many non-technical administrative departments — for example, propaganda, sales and supply, or general affairs. Sometimes these people are no more than "helpers" (*ganshi*) to staff members with more skill and experience. These are the plums of the patronage system and they are the kinds of positions eventually attained by the most favored activists.

60. See A. Doak Barnett and Ezra Vogel, *Cadres, Bureaucracy, and Political Power in Communist China* (New York: Columbia University Press, 1967); and John Wilson Lewis, *Leadership in Communist China* (Ithaca, New York: Cornell University Press, 1963).

61. Another kind of favor is sexual. The reward system invites sexual harassment of females, because their male supervisors can flexibly evaluate their *biaoxian*. It is difficult to judge how widespread this problem is, but it is clear from the frequency with which emigrés mention this in passing that it is not uncommon. In the past several years a series of short stories have described the problem (although they referred to the countryside and to the military), and several press articles have reported factory cadres who were punished for abusing their powers of office by favoring mistresses in their work units.

62. Outright bribery, at least by workers, is apparently quite rare. This practice generally involves building up a store of goodwill over a period of time, to be drawn on in future situations. Sometimes the giving of unsolicited gifts, however, occurs so close to the expected favor that it borders on petty corruption. One recent emigrant from China has described vividly how he set out on a systematic campaign of gift giving and visitation in order to secure the permission of his oil refinery's top officials to take the national university entrance exam. This kind of account was repeated many times by my interview subjects. See Liang Heng and Judith Shapiro, *Son of the Revolution* (New York: Knopf, 1983), 253-58.

63. See Morton Fried's study of political and economic institutions in an east China county seat in 1948, particularly his discussion of *ganqing* (*The Fabric of Chinese Society* [New York: Praeger, 1953], 102-4).

64. There are several rhyming couplets that residents of China use to express this. Two examples are: *renqing dayu zhengming* (human sentiments are greater than official certificates), and *yige laoxiang dengyu sange tuzhang* (one [common] home village is worth three official seals).

65. This contention is exacerbated when the national party leadership is split and sends mixed messages to its grass roots units. This was especially the case in the mid-1970s and, of course, during the Cultural Revolution of 1966-68.

66. This has frequently been the fate of highly educated technical personnel with suspicious family backgrounds, who generally stay aloof from workplace politics and concentrate on their work. These are the prototypical victims of past Anti-Rightist campaigns.

67. It follows that much of the work of social control is carried out naturally through these informal networks. The Party's formidable repressive apparatus rarely needs to be employed, because it is a given condition that is rarely tested.

68. This period began after the withdrawal of work teams from institutions where they had been directing the early Cultural Revolution (in factories this was often called the "four cleans" after a campaign that had been carried out earlier in the countryside), and ended with the formation of revolutionary committees, usually under military leadership. This began in some parts of the country as early as October 1966, and ended as late as the end of 1968 in some of the outlying provinces.

69. An obvious corollary of this view is that the movement throughout Chinese society was a straightforward outgrowth of patterns of distribution, opportunity, and social mobility, and of the informal social structure of work and educational institutions. This is a theme stressed in most recent research on the subject, although most accounts currently in print adopt a straightforward "interest group" approach to political mobilization that needs to be modified with a fuller appreciation of the role of vertical networks in shaping orientations (more on this below). See, for example, Lee, *Politics of the Cultural Revolution*. Research on the Red

Guard movement in middle schools, by far the most exhaustively researched corner of the topic, shows quite clearly the relationship of student orientations to broader patterns of social mobility. For the best example of this recent scholarship, see Anita Chan, Stanley Rosen, and Jonathan Unger, "Students and Class Warfare: The Social Roots of the Red Guard Movement in Guangzhou (Canton)," *China Quarterly*, no. 83 (September 1980): 397-446.

70. See Lee, *Politics of the Cultural Revolution*, 134-35. We should note, however, that published membership figures of this sort do not distinguish the active core from more nominal "members" of factions. Membership figures, further, tended to fluctuate considerably after one faction or another "seized power" in local governments and work unit. Workers outside the active core of these organizations tended to flock to the winning side. Membership figures of this sort are therefore most meaningful in the early stages of the movement. Afterwards, it is less clear exactly what these figures mean.

71. Of course, only permanent workers were members of the state-sponsored trade union, and these grass roots union organizations were strongest precisely in the larger state enterprises. See Neale Hunter, *Shanghai Journal: An Eyewitness Account of the Cultural Revolution in Shanghai* (Boston: Beacon, 1969), 177-202; Walder, *Shanghai's January Revolution*, 28-50; and Lynn T. White III, "Shanghai's Polity in Cultural Revolution," in *The City in Communist China*, ed. John W. Lewis (Stanford: Stanford University Press, 1971), 325-70. It is one thing, however, to say that these conservative groups were sympathetic to local power-holders, and quite another to conclude that the power-holders were manipulating them. My own interviews indicate that the extent of manipulation was small, and that these workers were actively defending their status through their defense of the existing power structure.

72. See Hunter, *Shanghai Journal;* Lee, *Politics of the Cultural Revolution*, 130-32; and White, "Shanghai's Polity." My own interviews confirm this unambiguously.

73. See Lee, *Politics of the Cultural Revolution*, 134.

74. This strategy was encouraged in the mass media and was made possible by the immobilization of the party organization caused by the split in the national leadership and the consequent paralysis of plant security departments.

75. In this section, I am drawing directly upon thirty-three oral histories of the Cultural Revolution in factories, which comprised one part of my interviewing project in Hong Kong. We should note here that the topic of discussion is political activity *within* the enterprise, and not the activities outside which were more often publicized and which form the core of most other accounts of workers in the Cultural Revolution. A notable exception is Raymond Wylie, "Shanghai Dockers in the Cultural Revolution: The Interplay of Political and Economic Issues," in *Shanghai: Revolution and Development in an Asian Metropolis*, ed. Christopher Howe (Cambridge: Cambridge University Press, 1981), 91-124.

76. On the other hand, conservative groups more actively recruited this kind of worker.

77. Another important kind of rebel was an activist or low level officeholder within the network of patronage, whose rise had been arrested by a political or other mistake, or by the souring of relationships with higher officials. These "renegades" were often prominent in the rebel leadership (Wang Hongwen, originally a cadre in his factory's security department, is one such example.) Rebels were not necessarily people of bad class background. Workers with the worst kinds of class backgrounds were often too cautious to participate actively in any faction. These class designations were just one kind of mark that could exclude people from patronage networks. For a thorough discussion of these class designations and their consequences, see Richard Kurt Kraus, *Class Conflict in Chinese Socialism* (New York: Columbia University Press, 1981).

78. Lee, *Politics of the Cultural Revolution*, 133, argues that the skilled/unskilled divide separated conservatives and radicals. This distinction is not a clear one, however, since seniority is more important than skill level in determining pay differentials in the Chinese system. The distinction Lee appears to have in mind is subsumed under the large/small enterprise and the young/veteran worker distinctions he makes at the same time.

79. Most of these officials would eventually return to their leading positions, but they usually transferred (quite willingly) to other enterprises if they had suffered public humiliation in this way, permanently losing face in the enterprise.

80. The characteristics of the fabled leaders of city-wide worker organizations bear out this characterization of the rebel core. Pan Guoping, Chen Ada, and Geng Jinzhang, all prominent leaders of rebel workers' organizations in Shanghai, were repeatedly characterized by my Shanghai informants as young workers in their early twenties who "really had guts," and who "weren't afraid of anybody." Wang Hongwen differed from them in that he was not a worker, but a staff member in a factory security department, and he was in his upper twenties at the time. But like the prototypical rebel, Wang suffered from low status and black marks on his record—widely rumored among Shanghainese to be due to sexual misbehavior. Wang also differed from these other rebel leaders in that he actively cooperated with Zhang Chunqiao's efforts to demobilize the workers' movement in early 1967, while the others either resisted or fell from grace.

    A Hangzhou informant had worked before the Cultural Revolution in the same factory as Weng Senhe, later to become the leader of the city's rebel organization. He was described as a young, skilled worker who "didn't know how to keep his mouth shut." His forthright complaints about pay and working conditions earned the leadership's enmity and he was later transferred to another factory as an ordinary worker.

81. The result was to make the membership characteristics of the two factions more similar through time, masking the sharp distinctions between their original active cores. Another implication of this phenomenon is that we should not take the published figures of rebel and conservative groups' strength too seriously.

82. This is also the period during which workers were to learn the most about the files. They became secret documents once again soon after the establishment of revolutionary committees beginning in 1967.

83. See Andrew Walder, *Communist Neo-Traditionalism*, ch. 6.

84. See Andrew Walder, "Industrial Reform in China: The Human Dimension," in *The Limits to Reform in China*, ed. Ronald Morse (Boulder, Colo.: Westview, 1983).

85. See Andrew Walder, "Wage Reform and the Web of Factory Interests." Paper presented at the Conference on Policy Implementation in Post-Mao China, Ohio State University, June 1983.

86. Ibid., and Susan L. Shirk, "Recent Chinese Labour Policies and the Transformation of Industrial Organisation in China," *China Quarterly*, no. 88 (December 1981): 579-84.
87. Walder, "Wage Reforms," contains a fuller analysis of the case presented here in abstract form.

Chapter 4

1. A brigade (*shengchan dadui*) is a rural residence and production unit of several thousand people. Brigades are divided into production teams (*shengchan xiaodui*), and are grouped together to form communes. See n. 16, below.
2. Data for the chapter include the national and provincial press, in Chinese and in English translation, the few collections of internal documents available in the West, traveler's reports, and interviews with twenty-five former residents of rural China, mostly peasants and rusticated youths, conducted in Hong Kong in 1975-76, and supported by a grant from the Social Science Research Council. The data base necessarily restricts the scope of the chapter. Because I rely heavily on the reports of informants, who remember best more recent events, the chapter focuses on post-1962 participation patterns, a period of relative organizational stability in the countryside. My informants were better able to report on local village activities, and thus the discussion is largely confined to peasant political participation in production teams and brigades.
3. Samuel Huntington and Joan Nelson, *No Easy Choice: Political Participation in Developing Countries* (Cambridge, Mass.: Harvard University Press, 1976), 3.
4. For a discussion of Chinese elite attitudes to opposition and dissent, see Peter R. Moody, *Opposition and Dissent in Contemporary China* (Stanford: Hoover Institute Press, 1977), 37-51.
5. For definitions of the various class labels see "Decisions Concerning the Differentiation of Class Status in the Countryside" (issued by the Government Administration Council of the People's Republic of China on 4 August 1950) in *The People's Republic of China: A Documentary History of Revolutionary Change*, ed. Mark Selden (New York: Monthly Review Press, 1979), 218-25.
6. *New China News Agency* (hereafter NCNA), 13 September

1953 in *Survey of China Mainland Press* (hereafter SCMP), no. 651 (Hong Kong: United States Consulate General): 12.

7. *Renmin ribao*, 3 May 1953, in SCMP, no. 581 (30 May-1 June, 1953): 31.

8. Liu Shaoqi (Liu Shao-ch'i), "Report on the Draft Constitution of the People's Republic of China (1955)," in James R. Townsend, *Political Participation in Communist China* (Berkeley: University of California Press, 1969), 68.

9. Radio Jiangxi, 20 November 1964, in *News from Chinese Provincial Radio Stations* (hereafter NFCPRS) (Hong Kong: British Information Service), no. 84 (26 November 1964): 16.

10. NMI. This citation and others, such as CN and KP, refer to informants, former residents of China, interviewed in Hong Kong from May 1975 to October 1976. NM indicates a peasant informant, CN a sent-down youth, and KP, a cadre.

11. C. S. Chen and Charles Price Ridley, *Rural People's Communes in Lien-chiang* (Stanford: Hoover Institute Press, 1969), 114.

12. Mao Zedong (Mao Tse-tung), "On the Correct Handling of Contradictions Among the People," *Selected Readings from Mao Tse-tung* (Beijing: Foreign Languages Press, 1967), 350-88.

13. Mao Zedong, "Analysis of the Classes in Chinese Society," *Selected Readings*, 11-20.

14. RMRB, 28 December 1955, in SCMP 1206 (12 January 1956): 16.

15. Chen and Ridley, *Rural People's Communes*, 101.

16. For the relevant regulations governing the operation of communes, brigades, and teams for the 1961-78 period, see "Regulations on the Work of the Rural People's Communes (Revised Draft)," September 1962 (the so-called "Sixty Articles") in Union Research Institute, *Documents of the Chinese Communist Party Central Committee, September 1956-April 1969* (Hong Kong: Union Research Institute, 1971), vol. 1, 695-725. For the period after 1978, see "Regulations on the Work in the Rural People's Communes (Draft for Trial Use)," 22 December 1978 (the so-called "New Sixty Articles") in *Issues and Studies* 15, no. 8 (August 1979): 100-12 and 15, no. 9 (September 1979): 104-15. For secondary accounts of rural organization, see Frederick Crook, "The Commune System in the People's Republic of China, 1963-1974," in *China: A Reassessment of the*

Economy, ed. the Joint Economic Committee, Ninety-fourth Congress (Washington, D.C.: U.S. Government Printing Office, 1975), 366-407; Steven Butler, *Agricultural Mechanization in China: The Administrative Impact* (New York: East Asian Institute, Columbia University, 1978); John Pelzel, "Economic Management of a Production Brigade in Post-Leap China," in *Economic Organization in Chinese Society,* ed. W. E. Willmott (Stanford: Stanford University Press, 1972), 287-414; William Parish and Martin King Whyte, *Village and Family in Contemporary China* (Chicago: University of Chicago Press, 1978); Benedict Stavis, *People's Communes and Rural Development in China* (Ithaca: Rural Development Committee, Cornell University, 1974); and Gordon Bennett, *Huadong: The Story of a Chinese People's Commune* (Boulder, Colo.: Westview Press, 1978).

17. According to a 1961 report, peasants in one Fujian brigade were attending party branch meetings, expanded cadre-member meetings, meetings of the youth league, women's federation and the militia, meetings of "positive elements," propaganda personnel discussion meetings, and mass meetings. See Chen and Ridley, *Rural People's Communes,* 174-75.

18. NM4.

19. CN5L-1-9. The right to have private plots is explicitly recognized in both the "Sixty Articles" and the "New Sixty Articles," although how this land is to be distributed is not specified.

20. See John P. Burns, *Political Participation in Rural China,* ch. 5 (forthcoming).

21. Regulations for election to county people's congresses are, however, available. The Sixty Articles (1962): articles 18 and 38 require that peasants elect the production team head, accountant, a control committee member, a supervisor, and management committee members for one year terms. The New Sixty Articles (1978): article 9 requires that team elections be called every two years. Apart from these general requirements, I am aware of no other regulations governing elections at this level.

22. See Chen and Ridley, *Rural People's Communes,* 217, 235-36, and 288, where it is indicated that peasant reluctance to assume cadre duties was widespread enough in some places for the term "refusing to act as a cadre" to be

included on the same team cadre evaluation form used by the brigade as "other abuses" such as theft, speculation, decadent behavior, and "bad work attitude."

23. Parish and Whyte, *Village and Family*, 106-11.
24. CN11A, B, C.
25. The evidence for this assertion is presented in John P. Burns, "Peasant Interest Articulation and Work Teams in Rural China: 1962-1974," in *China's New Social Fabric*, ed. Godwin C. Chu and Francis L. K. Hsu (Honolulu: University of Hawaii Press, 1983), 143-74.
26. CN11D-3.
27. Ibid.
28. See Richard Baum, *Prelude to Revolution: Mao, the Party and the Peasant Question, 1962-1966* (New York: Columbia University Press, 1975) for details of the Four Clean-Ups Campaign.
29. See "The Organizational Rules of Poor and Lower-Middle Peasant Associations (Draft)," June 1964, in Richard Baum and Frederick C. Teiwes, *Ssu-ch'ing: The Socialist Education Movement of 1962-1966* (Berkeley: Center for Chinese Studies, University of California, 1968), 95-101.
30. NM5B-6.
31. NM4D-1.
32. Kay Ann Johnson, "China Trip Notes," May-June 1978.
33. NCNA, 14 September 1975, in *China News Summary* (Hong Kong), no. 584 (24 September 1975).
34. See cases in interview files, CN5B-3, 6 and CN5J-21.
35. CN5B-5.
36. CN5A-10.
37. Ibid.
38. See Maurice Freedman, *Chinese Lineage and Society: Fukien and Kwangtung* (London: Athlone Press, 1971) where it is noted that lineage ties are stronger in south China.
39. Ezra Vogel, "Land Reform in Kwangtung: 1951-1953," *China Quarterly*, no. 38 (April-June 1969): 46.
40. William Parish, "China—Team, Brigade, or Commune," *Problems of Communism* 25, no. 2 (March-April 1976): 51-65.
41. *The Politics of the Chinese Red Army: A Translation of the "Bulletin of Activities" of the People's Liberation Army*, ed. Chester Cheng (Stanford: Hoover Institute Press, 1966), 11-14, 200, 234, 284, 320, 475 and 613-14.

42. CN5H-8, 9.
43. NM3B-5.
44. CN5F-16.
45. CN5K-16.
46. CN5G.
47. NM4C-14.
48. CN2.
49. CN5.
50. See Falkenheim, "Political Participation in China," *Problems of Communism* 27 (May-June 1978): 18-32, for a different list of modes of participation: written participation, meetings, lobbying, and quasi-legal participation. See Marc Blecher, "Leader-Mass Relations in Rural Chinese Communities: Local Politics in a Revolutionary Society" (Ph.D. diss., University of Chicago, 1978) for another list of modes: meetings, informal discussions, local grapevine, contacting, big character posters, mass organizations, local elections, interviews, and work and investigation teams. With regard to the written modes, the "Constitution of the People's Republic of China (1954)," chapter 3, article 97, and the revised Constitution (1975), chapter 3, article 27, acknowledge the right of citizens to lodge written or oral complaints with authorities. See *Selected Legal Documents of the People's Republic of China*, ed. Joseph Wang (Arlington: University Publications of America, 1976), 54 and 86, respectively.
51. *Nanfang ribao* [Southern daily] (hereafter NFRB), 8 January 1965. For recent evidence of a renewed interest in letter publishing, see RMRB, 24 February 1978. Also see Godwin Chu, *Radical Change Through Communication in Mao's China* (Honolulu: University of Hawaii Press, 1977), 238 for an analysis of 182 letters to the editor which appeared in *People's Daily* in 1967-68.
52. Baum, *Prelude to Revolution*, 114-15.
53. NM4E-2.
54. Chu, *Radical Change*, 232-38.
55. See the Li Yizhe *dazibao*, "Concerning Socialist Democracy and the Legal System," translated in *Issues and Studies* 12, no. 1 (January 1976): 116, where it is stated that the 'right' to post big character posters was suppressed in Guangzhou by "City Political Appearance Cleaning and Sweeping Teams," organized by the Guangzhou Municipal Party Committee and equipped with water hoses and brooms to

remove at any time big character posters appearing on any street or alley. Mao then issued "Document 18" giving legitimacy to the use of these posters. In 1980, however, the constitution was revised, deleting from the document the "four big freedoms," one of which was the right to post big character posters.

56. See Interview File CN5L-29.
57. Steven Butler, personal communication (Hong Kong, Universities Services Centre, November 1977).
58. Chu, *Radical Change*, 238.
59. CN8A-11.
60. Burns, *Political Participation in Rural China*, ch. 5.
61. For a different conclusion see Chu, *Radical Change*, 235-38.
62. See Parish and Whyte, *Village and Family*, 47-73.
63. CN5K-16.
64. NM6H-10. See also Interview File, CN4B-6, and Parish and Whyte, *Village and Family*, 47-73.
65. Office of the CCP, Bao'an (Pao-an) County Party Committee, *Pao-an Bulletin*, translated in *Union Research Service*, ed. Union Research Institute 27, nos. 7, 8, 9 (24 and 27 April and 1 May 1962): 128.
66. NM4D-8.
67. Radio Guiyang, Guizhou (21 March 1979), in *Summary of World Broadcasts* (hereafter SWB) FE/6079/B11/14 (29 March 1969): 14. Reports from Guangdong, Shandong, Hunan, and Sichuan are included in the same issue of SWB.
68. Radio Xi'an (Sian) (14 January 1965), in NFCPRS, no. 91 (21 January 1965): 37-38. Some may question whether this is actually corruption. Peasants were reported to have replied that it was simply local custom to invite people for meals. But Radio Xi'an asked why those invited were always cadres. The broadcast concluded that this was "far from being a small matter."
69. RMRB, 23 June 1975, in SCMP, no. 5901 (24 July 1975): 142.
70. CN8A-11.
71. NM4C-15.
72. CN5L-19.
73. CN5F-18.
74. NM8E-2.
75. "A Factual Account of an Investigation Conducted at T'ao-yuan," in *Zheng-fa gong-she* (Commune of the College of

Political Science and Law) 17 (7 April 1967), in SCMP, no. 3958 (13 June 1967): 11.

76. NCNA (Beijing), 7 July 1980.
77. CN5K-12-14.
78. *New York Times*, 9 August 1979, A3.
79. NCNA dispatch in *Ta Kung Pao* (Hong Kong), 21 October 1979.
80. See the "New Sixty Articles," 100-12.
81. See discussion of the 1953 Electoral Law in Townsend, *Political Participation*, 118.
82. Richard Kraus, "The Evolving Concept of Class in Post-Liberation China" (Ph.D. diss., Columbia University, 1974), 316-17.
83. See "Mobilizing All Positive Factors," *Beijing Review*, no. 7 (16 February 1979): 4-5.
84. NFRB, 15 December 1962, in SCMP, no. 2924 (21 February 1963): 11.
85. Radio Hubei, 16 July 1965, in NFCPRS, no. 116 (22 July 1965): 13.
86. Ch'en and Ridley, *Rural People's Communes*, 103.
87. Liu Shaoqi, "Report," in Townsend, *Political Participation*, 68.
88. *Xinhua ribao*, 20 June 1953, in *SCMP Supplement*, no. 677 (27-28 October 1953).
89. RMRB, 26 January 1970, in SCMP, no. 4597 (16 February 1970): 7.
90. RMRB, 15 November 1953, in SCMP, no. 689 (17 November 1953): 21.
91. Radio Henan, 22 October 1963, in NFCPRS, no. 24 (24 October 1963): 4.
92. Radio Henan, 12 September 1963, in NFCPRS, no. 24 (19 September 1963): 28.
93. G. William Skinner and Edwin A. Winckler, "Compliance Succession in Rural Communist China: A Cyclical Theory," in *A Sociological Reader on Complex Organizations*, ed. Amitai Etzioni (New York: Holt, Rinehart and Winston, 1969), 410-38.
94. See A. Doak Barnett, *Cadres, Bureaucracy, and Political Power in Communist China* (New York: Columbia University Press, 1967), and Michel Oksenberg, "Methods of Communication Within the Chinese Bureaucracy," *China Quarterly*, no. 57 (January-March 1974): 1-39.

95. Ch'en and Ridley, *Rural Peoples' Communes.*
96. Editorial, "Give Play to the Leadership Role of Basic Level Organizations," RMRB, 19 February 1982, in FBIS 41 (2 March 1982): K8-K11.
97. See, for example, RMRB, 30 March 1982.
98. For discussions of the 1979-81 county people's congress elections, see Brantley Womack, "The 1980 County-Level Elections in China: Experiment in Democratic Modernization," *Asian Survey* 22, no. 3 (March 1982): 261-77; and Barrett L. McCormick, "Election Campaign in Nanjing: The Center, Local Cadres, and the People" (paper prepared for the Association of Asian Studies Annual Meeting, March 1982). For a discussion of the commune-level elections, see John P. Burns, *Political Participation in Rural China,* ch. 5.

Chapter 5

1. Helpful suggestions on earlier drafts were received from Victor Falkenheim, Thomas Fingar, Hua Di, Eugene Lewis, Linda Lubrano, Denis Simon, and Donald Sutton. I am grateful to the Hoover Institution for support during the preparation of the manuscript.
2. Tang Tsou, "Prolegomenon to the Study of Informal Groups in CCP Politics," *China Quarterly,* no. 65 (January 1976): 98-113.
3. Andrew Nathan, "A Factionalism Model for CCP Politics," *The China Quarterly,* no. 53 (January-March 1973): 34-66.
4. J. Bruce Jacobs, "A Preliminary Model of Particularistic Ties in Chinese Political Alliances: *Kan-ching* and *Kuan-hsi* in a Rural Taiwanese Township," *China Quarterly,* no. 78 (June 1979): 237-74.
5. Peter L. Berger and Thomas Luckmann, *The Social Construction of Reality* (Garden City, N.Y.: Doubleday, 1966).
6. Chester I. Barnard, *The Functions of the Executive* (Cambridge: Harvard University Press, 1978).
7. Mancur Olson, *The Logic of Collective Action* (Cambridge: Harvard University Press, 1977).
8. Ibid., 48-50.
9. Albert O. Hirschman, *Exit, Voice and Loyalty* (Cambridge: Harvard University Press, 1970).
10. I have argued elsewhere that the periodic effort to radicalize

science is a reflection of competing visions of what scientific development and the role of science in society were all about. Richard P. Suttmeier, *Research and Revolution* (Lexington, Mass.: Lexington Books, 1974).

11. Michel Crozier, *The Bureaucratic Phenomenon* (Chicago: The University of Chicago Press, 1964).

12. Jeremy Boissevan, "Patronage in Sicily," in *Political Corruption*, ed. Arnold Heidenheimer (New Brunswick, N.J.: Transaction Books, 1970), 138-52.

13. Martin King Whyte, *Small Groups and Political Rituals in China* (Berkeley: University of California Press, 1974).

14. For details, see Richard P. Suttmeier, "Chinese Scientific Societies and Chinese Scientific Development," *The Developing Economies* 11, no. 2 (June 1973): 146-63.

15. Ibid.

16. "Numerous Contradictions Within the Ranks of the Scientific Circle," *New China News Agency* (hereafter NCNA), 30 April 1957, in U.S. Consulate General, Hong Kong, *Survey of the China Mainland Press* (hereafter SCMP), 1541.

17. Ibid.

18. "Criticisms and Suggestions Made by Scientists at Department Meetings of Department Committee of the Academy of Sciences," RMRB, 27 May 1957, in U.S. Consulate General, Hong Kong, *Current Background* (hereafter CB), 460.

19. "Academy of Sciences Convenes Forum for Peking Scientists to Discuss Contradictions Within Their Ranks," China News Agency, 3 May 1957, in SCMP, 1541.

20. "Numerous Contradictions Within the Ranks of the Scientific Circle," ibid., 9.

21. "Criticisms and Suggestions Made by Scientists," ibid., 10.

22. Zhou Enlai, "On the Question of Intellectuals," in *Communist China 1955-59: Policy Documents with Analysis*, ed. Robert R. Bowie and John K. Fairbank (Cambridge: Harvard University Press, 1965), 141.

23. Ibid., 141.

24. Ibid., 141-42.

25. Daniel S. Greenberg, *Politics of Pure Science* (New York: New American Library, 1967).

26. "July 23 Forum of Scientists," NCNA, 23 July 1957, in SCMP, 1594.

27. Guo Moro, "Opening Address to the Second Plenum of the

Department Committees, Chinese Academy of Sciences,"
RMRB, 24 May 1957, in CB, 460.

28. Ibid.
29. "Criticisms and Suggestions Made by Scientists," ibid., 10.
30. "Scientists Continue to Hit Back at Rightists," NCNA, 16 July 1957, in SCMP, 1581.
31. Guo Moro, "Closing Address at the Second Plenum of the Department Committee," RMRB, 31 May 1957, in CB, 560.
32. Ibid.
33. *China News Analysis*, no. 193 (16 August 1957): 3.
34. Ibid.
35. An incomplete English version of this was released by NCNA on 8 June, 1957. See SCMP, 1562.
36. "Duiyu yuguan wo guo kexue tizhi wenti de jidian jian," GMRB, 9 June 1957, 3.
37. Ibid.
38. Departmentalism was disruptive of the post-graduate system. Non-CAS departments hated to lose their bright young people and consequently went to great lengths to frustrate the transfer.
39. "Duiyu yuguan wo guo kexue tizhi wenti de jidian jian," ibid., 3.
40. Ibid.
41. Ibid.
42. Guo Moro, "In Refutation of an Anti-Socialist Scientific Program," speech to the Fourth Session of the First National People's Congress, 5 July 1957, RMRB, 6 July 1957, in CB, 467.
43. "Academy of Sciences Convenes Forum for Peking Scientists to Discuss Contradictions within Their Ranks," China News Agency, 3 May 1957, in SCMP, 1541.
44. Guo Moro, "In Refutation," ibid., 11.
45. Ibid.; *China News Analysis*, 193.
46. "Scientists Meet to Criticize Anti-Socialist Scientific Program," NCNA, 14 July 1957, in SCMP, 1574.
47. Chu-yuan Cheng, *Scientific and Engineering Manpower in Communist China, 1949-1963* (Washington: The National Science Foundation, 1965), 175.
48. Private communication.
49. Private communication.
50. Suttmeier, "Chinese Scientific Societies," 146-63.
51. Zhou Jingfu, "For the Liberation of Thought and the

Determined Follow Through of the Main Party Line Concerning the Construction of Socialism in the Tasks of Science," RMRB, 7 June 1958, in U.S. Department of Commerce, *Joint Publications Research Service* (hereafter JPRS), DC 472.

52. See Suttmeier, *Research and Revolution*, 96, 117 n. 51.

53. See Sanford A. Lakoff, "Scientists, Technologists and Political Power," in *Science, Technology and Society*, ed. Ina Spiegel-Rosing and Derek de Solla Price (London and Beverly Hills: Sage Publications, 1977), 374-79.

54. For interpretations of these trends see Merle Goldman, "Teng Hsiao-ping and the Debate over Science and Technology," *Contemporary China* 2, no. 4 (Winter 1978): 46-49; Kenneth Lieberthal, *Central Documents and Politburo Politics in China* (Ann Arbor: University of Michigan Center for Chinese Studies Publications, 1978); Thomas Fingar, "Domestic Policy and the Quest for Independence," in *China's Quest for Independence in Policy Evolution in the 1970s*, ed. Thomas Fingar (Boulder: Westview Press, 1980), 23-89; Richard P. Suttmeier, "Recent Developments in the Politics of Chinese Science," *Asian Survey* 12, no. 4 (April 1977): 375-92; and Richard P. Suttmeier, *Science, Technology and China's Drive for Modernization* (Stanford: The Hoover Institution Press, 1980), ch. 1.

55. Goldman, "Teng Hsiao-ping," 43.

56. According to one report, scientists were less involved in preparing the outline report than in publicizing and propagating it once Hu Yaobang prepared it. "Preliminary Analysis of Hu Yaobang and China's Future," *Dongxi fang* (Hong Kong), 10 July 1980, in JPRS, 76427.

57. See Suttmeier, "Recent Developments."

58. See *The Chinese Academy of Sciences: A Brief Introduction* (Beijing: CAS, 1981).

59. See Tong Yi, "The Democratic Parties in Action," *Beijing Review*, no. 45 (7 November 1983): 22-28.

60. Personal communication.

61. Xinhua (Beijing), 22 and 23 February 1980, in FBIS (25 February 1980); Xinhua (Beijing), 28 February 1980, in FBIS (29 February 1980).

62. Xinhua (Beijing), 3 November 1980, in JPRS, 76922.

Chapter 6

1. Much of the early material in this article is drawn from my book *China's Intellectuals: Advise and Dissent* (Cambridge, Mass.: Harvard University Press, 1981).
2. Frederick Wakeman, "The Price of Autonomy: Intellectuals in Ming and Qing Politics," *Daedalus*, no. 2 (Spring 1972).
3. David Nivison, "Ho Shen and His Accusers," in *Confucianism in Action*, ed. David Nivison and Arthur Wright (Stanford: Stanford University Press, 1959), 221.
4. William T. de Bary, "Chinese Despotism and the Confucian Ideal," in *Chinese Thought and Institutions*, ed. John K. Fairbank (Chicago: University of Chicago Press, 1957), 197.
5. Andrew Nathan, "Liang Qichao's New Style of Writing and Late Qing Propaganda" (paper delivered at the Association for Asian Studies Conference, 25-27 March 1977).
6. James Polachek, "Institutional Background of Qingyi Rhetoric in Late Qing" (paper delivered at the Association for Asian Studies Conference, 25-27 March 1977).
7. See Lucian Pye, "Communications and Chinese Political Culture," *Asian Survey* 28, no. 3 (March 1978): 221-46.
8. See Charles Hucker, "The Donglin Movement in the Late Ming Period," in Fairbank, *Chinese Thought*, 61; also Wakeman, "The Price of Autonomy."
9. Vera Schwarcz, *The Chinese Enlightenment: Intellectuals and the Legacy of the May Fourth Movement of 1919* (Berkeley: University of California Press, 1985).
10. Hualing Nieh, *Literature of the Hundred Flowers* (New York: Columbia University Press, 1981), 1:47.
11. Roderick MacFarquhar, *The Hundred Flowers* (New York: Praeger, 1960), 51.
12. Liaison Center of the Chinese University of Science and Technology, Red Guard Congress, 10 June 1967, "Counterrevolutionary, Revisionist Peng Zhen's Towering Crimes," in SCMP, no. 639, 8-9.
13. It was charged in the Cultural Revolution that he had been dismissed because he had not published Mao's speech of 12 March 1957 before the Propaganda Department and his 27 February 1957 speech, "On the Correct Handling of Contradictions Among the People."
14. *Wenyi bao*, no. 819 (1964): 17-18.
15. Timothy Cheek, "Deng Tuo: Culture, Leninism and

Alternative Marxism in the Chinese Communist Party,"
China Quarterly, no. 87 (1981): 486.

16. Deng Tuo, "Welcome 'The Miscellaneous Scholar,'" in
Yanshan yehua heji [Evening chats at Yanshan] (Beijing:
Beijing chubanshe, 1963), 9-11.

17. Louis Barcata, *China in the Throes of the Cultural Revolution*
(New York: Hart Publishing Co., 1968), 216.

18. Ibid., 214.

19. Yao Wenyuan, "On 'Three Family Village' – The Reactionary
Nature of 'Evening Chats at Yanshan' and 'Notes from
Three Family Village,'" *Chinese Literature*, no. 7 (1966): 43.

20. Zhang Chunqiao, "Destroy the Bourgeois Idea of Right,"
RMRB, 13 October 1958, 2; see also Parris Chang, *Radicals
and Radical Ideology in China's Cultural Revolution* (New
York: Research Institute of Communist Affairs, Columbia
University, 1973).

21. Wu Zhunji, RMRB, 1 October 1958.

22. Guan Feng, "On the Problem of Struggle Between Materialism and Idealism," GMRB, 6 June 1958, in *Chinese Studies
in History and Philosophy* 2, no. 4 (Summer 1969): 32.

23. Guan Feng and Lin Yushi, "The Use of the Class Viewpoint
and Historicalism in Historical Research," *Lishi yanjiu*, 15
December 1963, in SCMM, no. 409, 15.

24. Guan Feng, "Philosophical Research Must Turn Its Face
toward the Current Class Struggle," *Honqi*, 26 February
1964, in SCMM, no. 410, 34.

25. Li Feng, "Insist on the Integration of Theory with Practice
and Strengthen Scientific and Technical Research," RMRB,
19 November 1972, in SCMP, no. 5267, 208.

26. The Educational Revolutionary Group of Beijing University,
"Make a Success of Teaching Theoretical Subject of National
Science," *Hongqi*, no. 9 (1972), in SCMM, no. 737-738, 59.

27. Zhou Peiyuan, "Some Views in Educational Revolution in the
Science Faculties of Universities," GMRB, 6 October 1972, in
SCMP, no. 5238, 120.

28. Ibid., 121.

29. RMRB, 13 January 1977, 2.

30. *Chinese Literature for the 1980s*, ed. Howard Goldblatt
(Armonk, N.Y.: M.E. Sharpe, Inc., 1982), 56-57.

31. *Chishi niandai* [The seventies] (monthly Hong Kong), no. 1
(1980).

32. Leo Ou-fan Lee, "Technique as Dissidence: A Perspective of

Contemporary Chinese Fiction" (paper delivered at the Conference on Contemporary Chinese Literature, St. John's University, New York, 28-31 May 1982).

33. Goldblatt, *Chinese Literature*, 107.
34. Liu Binyan, "People or Monsters?" in *People or Monsters?*, ed. Perry Link (Bloomington: Indiana University Press, 1983), 26.
35. Ibid., 43.
36. Zhou Yang, "Examination of Several Theoretical Questions about Marxism," RMRB, 16 March 1983, 5.
37. Li Honglin, "Socialism and Opening to the Outside World," RMRB, 15 October 1984, 5.
38. RMRB, 8 December 1984, 1.
39. China News Agency, special correspondent Liu Nan, 7 January 1985; FBIS (10 January 1985): K12.
40. Liu Binyan, "Creative Freedom," *Jing bao*, 2 February 1985, 7.
41. Ke Ling, "Concentrate on Rooting Out Stubborn 'Leftist' Disease," RMRB, 31 December 1984, 7; FBIS (9 January 1985): K9.
42. RMRB, 3 January 1985, 1.
43. Li Honglin, "From 'One Person Alone has the Say' to 'Everybody has a Say,'" RMRB, 22 April 1985; FBIS (30 April 1985): K14.
44. Ibid., K16.
45. He called for protections for journalists in *Xinwen Jizhe* [Journalist], 1 (1985). *Zhengming* (Hong Kong) (1 June 1985); FBIS (6 June 1985): W6.
46. Hu Yaobang, "On the Party's Journalism Work" given on 8 February 1985, RMRB, 14 April 1985; FBIS (15 April 1985): K1.
47. Ibid., K8.
48. Ibid., K9.
49. Ibid., K3.
50. Ibid., K14.

Chapter 7

1. Sheldon Wolin, *Politics and Vision* (Boston: Little, Brown, 1960), for example page 434, the last page of text.
2. The classic statement is Robert A. Dahl, *Who Governs? Democracy and Power in an American City* (New Haven: Yale

University Press, 1961), for example page 325, the concluding page. See also Samuel P. Huntington, *Political Order in Changing Societies* (New Haven: Yale University Press, 1968).

3. Robert A. Dahl, *Modern Political Analysis* (Englewood Cliffs: Prentice-Hall, 1963), 40.

4. Elaboration on the difference between political and administrative levels is in Lynn T. White III, "Shanghai's Polity in Cultural Revolution," in *The City in Communist China*, ed. John W. Lewis (Stanford: Stanford University Press, 1971), 368.

5. James R. Townsend includes "all those activities through which the individual consciously becomes involved in attempts to give a particular direction to the conduct of public affairs, excluding activities of an occupational or compulsory nature." Actually, Townsend only excludes participation "independent of the normal content" of occupations – and this gets closer to the notion here, if "normal content" is regarded restrictively. (James R. Townsend, *Political Participation in Communist China* [Berkeley: University of California Press, 1967], 4). This is the premier book on participation in China. The Soviet scholars have taken somewhat longer, but Theodore H. Friedgut, *Political Participation in the USSR* (Princeton: Princeton University Press, 1979), 18-19, refers to Townsend's definition and moves part way toward the version given here. For Huntington and Nelson, participation is "usually avocational." See n. 76.

6. See John P. Hardt and Theodore Frankel, "The Industrial Managers," in *Interest Groups in Soviet Politics*, ed. H. Gordon Skilling and Franklyn Griffiths (Princeton: Princeton University Press, 1971), 193-94.

7. Albert Hirschman, *Exit, Voice, and Loyalty: Responses to Decline in Firms, Organizations, and States* (Cambridge: Harvard University Press, 1970).

8. This slogan is occasionally cited; for example, see A. Doak Barnett, with a contribution by Ezra Vogel, *Cadres, Bureaucracy and Political Power in Communist China* (New York: Columbia University Press, 1967), 551.

9. Franklyn Griffiths, "A Tendency Analysis of Soviet Policy-Making," in Skilling and Griffiths, *Interest Groups*, 335-77.

10. Parks Cobel, Jr., *The Kuomintang and Shanghai Capitalists, 1927-37* (Cambridge: Harvard University Press, 1980), and

Qunzhong [Masses] (Shanghai) 1, no. 5 (3 June 1946): 6.

11. See John Gardner, "The *Wu-fan* Campaign in Shanghai: A Study of the Consolidation of Urban Control," in *Chinese Communist Politics in Action,* ed. A. Doak Barnett (Seattle: University of Washington Press, 1969), 477-539.

12. SHGSZL 3, no. 97 (6 December 1962): 5798.

13. JFRB, 16 October 1950.

14. SN, 24 and 30 November 1950.

15. The aides were *xieshui* workers; the groups were called *huju zu;* and the systems were called *jiti baojiao zhidu.* SHGSZL 3, nos. 29, 31-33 (12, 16, 20, 23 April 1952): 1939, 2015, 2116, 2119.

16. GMRB, 8 September 1953.

17. RMRB, 3 March 1954.

18. An early example is in RMRB, 26 May 1951.

19. DGB, 5 January 1952; and JFRB, 5 February 1952.

20. NCNA, 15 July 1953, gives these examples.

21. Interview in Hong Kong, February 1970.

22. XWRB, 1 November 1956.

23. Not all enterprises, however, are legal. See Lynn T. White, "Low Power: Small Enterprises in Shanghai, 1949-67," *China Quarterly,* no. 73 (March 1978): 45-77.

24. LDB, 8 September 1950.

25. LDB, 9 September 1952, reports that only 40,000 of the Shanghai children passing middle-school exams that year were from worker or peasant backgrounds. On the U.S.S.R., see David Granick, *The Red Executive* (New York: Doubleday, 1960), 137.

26. XDRB, 10 December 1969.

27. SHGSZL 3, no. 93 (22 November 1952): 5609; and RMRB, 11 May 1953.

28. Robert Loh, *Escape from Red China* (New York: Coward McCann, 1962), 114-16.

29. SHGSZL 2, no. 37 (9 May 1951): 1344.

30. Month-by-month figures are given in the source immediately above and in NCNA (Beijing), 31 October 1951.

31. Examples involving the rubber industry can be found in NCNA, 30 November 1955. These issues will be best treated in a recent book by Dorothy Solinger, *Chinese Business Under Socialism* (Berkeley: University of California Press, 1985).

32. XWRB, 29 August 1955.

33. LDB, 16 February 1957.

34. The shops were the Luzhiguan and the Leiyunshang. XWRB, 27 August 1955.
35. "Waide caiban renyuan," XWRB, 15 November 1956, particularly mentions luxury goods, "high-shelf goods" (*gaodang huo*).
36. NCNA, 12 March 1958.
37. JFRB, 25 September 1954.
38. Calculation from NCNA, 2 February 1955.
39. Calculated from NCNA, 12 January, 1955. The trades were cloth, native cloth, sundries, sugar, coal, and tobacco.
40. NCNA, 25 November 1955.
41. JFRB, 28 April 1955.
42. NCNA, 21 November 1955.
43. DGB (Tianjin), 29 October 1955.
44. XWRB, 23 September 1955.
45. NCNA, 27 May 1956.
46. XMB, 21 January 1957.
47. WHB, 17 January and 27 February 1957; XWRB, 16 February 1957; and two interviews in Hong Kong.
48. JFRB, 21 February 1957.
49. XWRB, 4 May 1957.
50. Barry M. Richman, *Industrial Society in Communist China* (New York: Random House, 1969), 481-82, shows this tendency in the Shanghai Truck Factory and the Shanghai Steel Corporation.
51. This distinction is owed to a comment by Michel Oksenberg.
52. A "special production responsibility" is a *teshu shengchan renwu*, as an interviewee reports.
53. See also Joseph Berliner, *Factory and Manager in the USSR* (Cambridge: Harvard University Press, 1957), 72-76.
54. DGB (Beijing), 3 January 1964.
55. Richman, *Industrial Society*, 269 and 579-80; and NCNA, 26 April 1966.
56. This can be computed from raw data in Richman, *Industrial Society*, table 3-13, 154-56.
57. The two kinds are called, respectively, *tiaotiao* and *kuaikuai* leaderships. Interview referring to the mid-1960s; also Franz Schurmann, *Ideology and Organisation in Communist China* (Berkeley: University of California Press, 1966).
58. See Lynn T. White III, "Leadership in Shanghai," in *Elites in the People's Republic of China,* ed. Robert A. Scalapino (Seattle: University of Washington Press, 1972), 302-77.

59. XWRB, 2 March 1963. This speech related interestingly to the concurrent rise of Zhang Chunqiao in Shanghai's cultural affairs. At this time both Cao and Zhang were calling for more party control in their respective but separate fields. Mayor Ke Qingshi clearly supported them both, although they became Shanghai's main rivals at the beginning of the Cultural Revolution.

60. XWRB, 9 May 1964.

61. Richman, *Industrial Society*, 716.

62. XWRB, 23 July 1964, gives examples in the Shanghai Weaving Machine Factory.

63. XWRB, 30 March 1965.

64. Bruce MacFarlane, "Notes on China Trip" (unpublished ms., 1968), interview of 20 April 1968, on previous commercial procedures.

65. Richman, *Industrial Society*, table 9-2, 792-94.

66. See RMRB, 14 April 1966, for an example referring to the Political Department of the Shanghai Silk Mill.

67. Interview with an ex-engineer in a large factory, Berkeley, California, June 1973.

68. For example, see WHB, 29 April 1967.

69. See NCNA, Shanghai, 25 February and 18 May 1970, for examples.

70. A good example in WHB, 25 September 1968.

71. Examples are in JFRB, 1 August 1968; XDRB, 11 October and 23 December 1968; and Shanghai Radio, 31 January 1969.

72. See RMRB, 14 January 1967; *Asahi Shimbun*, 16 January 1967; and *Agence France Presse*, 17 February 1967, both for praises of "worker management" and for rejection by Zhou of its excesses in Shanghai.

73. An illustrative book—but many could be cited—is *Gonghui zai qiye guanli zhong de zuoyong* [The function of trade unions in business management] (Beijing: Gongren chubanshe, 1981). One of the most prominent new business schools is in the city of Dalian.

74. Useful examples are: *Chen Yun's Strategy for China's Development: A Non-Maoist Alternative*, ed. Nicholas R. Lardy and Kenneth Lieberthal (White Plains: M.E. Sharpe, 1983); *China's Economic Reforms*, ed. Lin Wei and Arnold Chao (Philadelphia: University of Pennsylvania Press, 1982); and *Economic Reform in the PRC: In Which China's Economists*

Make Known What Went Wrong, Why, and What Should Be Done about It, ed. and trans. George C. Wang (Boulder: Westview Press, 1982).

75. Andrew Walder, "Industrial Reform in China: The Human Dimension," in *The Limits of Reform in China,* ed. Ronald A. Morse (Boulder: Westview Press, 1983), 58-59.

76. Samuel P. Huntington and Joan M. Nelson, *No Easy Choice: Political Participation in Developing Countries* (Cambridge: Harvard University Press, 1976). See especially page 4.

77. Ibid., 5.

Chapter 8

1. This chapter is a revised version of a paper presented at the Workshop on the Pursuit of Political Interest in the People's Republic of China, sponsored by the Joint Committee on Contemporary China of the Social Science Research Council and the American Council of Learned Societies, and held at the University of Michigan in August 1977. I appreciate the suggestions and criticisms that the participants in the workshop offered on that early draft. In the course of revising the paper for publication, I have also benefitted greatly from the detailed comments provided by Victor Falkenheim, Harlan Jencks, Harvey Nelsen, Michel Oksenberg, and Dorothy Solinger.

2. This echoes Parris Chang's conclusion: "What is most striking of [sic] the PLA intervention in Chinese politics is that the scope, objective, and domain of the intervention have been structured largely by the civilian leaders, and by Mao in particular." See Parris H. Chang, "Mao Tse-tung and His Generals: Some Observations on Military Intervention in Chinese Politics," in *Comparative Defense Policy,* ed. Frank B. Horton III, Anthony C. Rogerson, and Edward L. Warner III. (Baltimore: Johns Hopkins University Press, 1974), 122.

3. For a further comparison of the Soviet and Chinese armies along these lines, see Jonathan R. Adelman, "The Soviet and Chinese Armies: Their Post-Civil War Roles," *Survey* 24, no. 1 (Winter 1979): 57-81.

4. This point should not, of course, be overstated. Clearly there was some division of labor between military and civilian leaders, and personal tensions and rivalries may well have existed at a comparable period between the party center and

some of the field commanders. Nonetheless, when compared with the situation that existed in the Soviet Union, party-army relations in China were harmonious and cooperative.

5. See John Gittings, *The Role of the Chinese Army* (London: Oxford University Press, 1967).

6. The PLA's representation on the Eighth Central Committee (elected in September 1956) was 19 percent; on the Ninth Central Committee (elected in April 1969, during the Cultural Revolution), 45 percent; on the Tenth Central Committee (elected in August 1973), 32 percent; on the Eleventh Central Committee (elected in August 1977), 29 percent; and on the Twelfth Central Committee (elected in September 1982), 19 percent. (*China: A Look at the 11th Central Committee* [Washington: National Foreign Assessment Center, Central Intelligence Agency, October 1977]; Hong Yung Lee, "China's Twelfth Central Committee: Rehabilitated Cadres and the Technocrats," *Asian Survey* 23, no. 6 [June 1983]: 679.) The military's representation on the Politburo ranged from four to six members between the Eighth Party Congress in 1956 and the Ninth Congress in 1969. It rose to thirteen (eleven full members and two alternate members) at the Ninth Congress, fell to seven (five full members and two alternates) with the purge of Lin Biao and his followers in 1971, rose to ten after the fall of the Gang of Four, and with the Twelfth Party Congress, has now fallen back to eight (seven full members and one alternate).

7. See Parris H. Chang, "Research Notes on the Changing Loci of Decisions in the CCP," *China Quarterly*, no. 44 (October-December 1970): 181-94; and Kenneth G. Lieberthal, *A Research Guide to Central Party and Government Meetings in China, 1949-1975* (White Plains: International Arts and Sciences Press, 1976).

8. The reduction in the number of vice premiers announced in 1982 means that the military no longer has routine representation at this level of government. But a leading PLA officer, Yu Qiuli, remains a member of the party secretariat.

9. Ying-mao Kau, "The Role of the Military in Transition: The Politics of Mao's Army Building," in *Proceedings of the Fifth Sino-American Conference on Mainland China* (Taipei: Institute of International Relations, 1976), 605-54.

10. Mao Zedong, "Problems of War and Strategy" (1938), in

Selected Works of Mao Tse-tung (Peking: Foreign Languages Press, 1967), vol. 2, 224.

11. These mechanisms are described in Gittings, *Role of the Chinese Army;* Harvey Nelsen, *The Chinese Military System: An Organizational Study of the People's Liberation Army*, 2d ed. (Boulder: Westview, 1981); and Harlan W. Jencks, *From Muskets to Missiles: Politics and Professionalism in the Chinese Army, 1945-1981* (Boulder: Westview, 1982).

12. Nelsen, *Chinese Military System*, 151.

13. Jencks, *Muskets to Missiles*, 176.

14. See Paul H. B. Godwin, "The Party and the Gun in China," *Problems of Communism* 29, no. 3 (May-June 1980): 75-80.

15. The best short survey of these cleavages appears in A. Doak Barnett, *Uncertain Passage: China's Transition to the Post-Mao Era* (Washington, D.C.: Brookings, 1974), 91-109.

16. On bureaucratic cleavages within the Chinese armed forces, see William W. Whitson, "Organizational Perspectives and Decision-Making in the Chinese High Command," in *Elites in the People's Republic of China*, ed. Robert A. Scalapino (Seattle: University of Washington Press, 1972), 381-415; and Joseph J. Heinlein, Jr., "China's Force Posture: Factors in the Policy Process," in Horton, *Comparative Defense Policy*, 326-39.

17. Jencks, *Muskets to Missiles*, ch. 6.

18. Harvey Nelsen, "Regional and Paramilitary Ground Forces," in *The Military and Political Power in China in the 1970s*, ed. William W. Whitson (New York: Praeger, 1972), 135-52. Until recently there were eleven military regions. That number was reduced to seven in mid-1985.

19. Harvey Nelsen, "Military Forces in the Cultural Revolution," *China Quarterly*, no. 51 (July-September 1972): 444-74.

20. Ellis Joffe, *Party and Army: Professionalism and Political Control in the Chinese Officer Corps, 1949-1964*, Harvard East Asian Monograph, no. 19 (Cambridge: East Asian Research Center, Harvard University, 1967); and William W. Whitson, *The Chinese High Command: A History of Communist Military Politics, 1927-71* (New York: Praeger, 1973), ch. 10.

21. On the relationship between commanders and commissars in the Soviet Red Army, see Timothy J. Colton, *Commissars, Commanders, and Civilian Authority: The Structure of Soviet Military Politics* (Cambridge: Harvard University Press,

1979).

22. Whitson, *Chinese High Command,* ch. 9.

23. On the role of factions in Chinese politics generally, see Lucian W. Pye, *The Dynamics of Chinese Politics* (Cambridge: Oelgeschlager, Gunn, and Hain, 1981). On factions in the PLA, see Whitson, *Chinese High Command;* William Parish, "Factions in Chinese Military Politics," *China Quarterly,* no. 56 (October-December 1973): 667-99; Allen S. H. Kong, "Comradeship in Arms: An Analysis of Power Through Associations in the CPLA—February 1970 to February 1974," *Asian Survey* 14, no. 7 (July 1974): 663-77; and Nelsen, *Chinese Military System,* 150-57.

24. Nelsen, *Chinese Military System,* 147-57; and Jencks, *Muskets to Missiles,* 223-31.

25. Paul H. B. Godwin, "Civil-Military Relations in China: The Guerrilla Experience," *Studies in Comparative Communism* 11, no. 3 (Autumn 1978): 265-77.

26. This discussion of the interests of the PLA has benefited from the analyses of organizational interests in Graham T. Allision, *Essence of Decision: Explaining the Cuban Missile Crisis* (Boston: Little, Brown, 1971); Colton, *Commissars, Commanders, and Civilian Authority;* Anthony Downs, *Inside Bureaucracy* (Boston: Little, Brown, 1967); Morton H. Halperin, *Bureaucratic Politics and Foreign Policy* (Washington: Brookings, 1974); Eric Nordlinger, *Soldiers in Politics* (Englewood Cliffs: Prentice-Hall, 1977); and *Interest Groups in Soviet Politics,* ed. H. Gordon Skilling and Franklyn Griffiths (Princeton: Princeton University Press, 1971).

27. Michel Korzec and Martin King Whyte, "Reading Notes: The Chinese Wage System," *China Quarterly,* no. 86 (June 1981): 248-73.

28. *Zhengming,* no. 53 (March 1982): 16-17.

29. Gittings, *Role of the Chinese Army,* 394; Ellis Joffe, "The Chinese Army Under Lin Piao: Prelude to Political Intervention," in *China: Management of a Revolutionary Society,* ed. John M. H. Lindbeck (Seattle: University of Washington Press, 1971), 343-74; and Harry Harding, *Organizing China: The Problem of Bureaucracy, 1949-1976* (Stanford: Stanford University Press, 1981), 217-23.

30. One Hong Kong periodical even reported that a group of demobilized servicemen, dissatisfied with their assignments in the countryside, had kidnapped the party secretary and

the government magistrate in one county near Canton, and attacked the public security bureau. Official Chinese sources denied the details of the report, but acknowledged that there had been a "minor demonstration" by former servicemen. See *Zhengming*, no. 50 (December 1981): 33-34; and *South China Morning Post*, 12 December 1981, 8.

31. Nelsen, *Chinese Military System*, 147-57; and Jencks, *Muskets to Missiles*, 223-31.

32. For a good short discussion of the corporate interests of military organizations, see Nordlinger, *Soldiers in Politics*, 47-53.

33. For further details on the controversy between Luo and Lin, see Harry Harding and Melvin Gurtov, *The Purge of Lo Jui-ch'ing: The Politics of Chinese Strategic Planning*, R-548-PR (Santa Monica: The Rand Corporation, 1971).

34. On the 1950s, see Joffe, *Party and Army;* on the 1970s, see Harry Harding, "The Domestic Politics of China's Global Posture, 1973-1978," in *China's Quest for Independence: Policy Evolution in the 1970s*, ed. Thomas Fingar and the *Stanford Journal of International Studies* (Boulder: Westview, 1980), 93-146.

35. On the debates of 1955, see Alice Langley Hsieh, *Communist China's Strategy in the Nuclear Era* (Englewood Cliffs: Prentice-Hall, 1962). On the debates of 1965, see, *inter alia*, Harding and Gurtov, *The Purge of Lo Jui-ch'ing*. On the debates of 1977-78, see, *inter alia*, Harding, "Domestic Politics of China's Global Posture." Further sources on all of these time periods are provided in the section on the changing roles of the PLA, below.

36. Alan P. L. Liu, "The 'Gang of Four' and the Chinese People's Liberation Army," *Asian Survey* 19, no. 9 (September 1979): 817-37.

37. Lynn T. White III, "The Liberation Army and the Chinese People," in *Political Participation Under Military Regimes*, ed. Henry Bienen and David Morell, Sage Contemporary Social Science Issues, no. 26 (Beverly Hills: Sage Publishers, 1976), 115-35.

38. This conclusion echoes that in Jencks, *Muskets to Missiles*, 126.

39. Gerald Segal cautions us, however, not to overestimate the role of the PLA in Chinese foreign policy-making. See his "The PLA and Chinese Foreign Policy Decision-Making,"

International Affairs 57, no. 3 (Summer 1981): 449-66.

40. See Thomas M. Gottlieb, *Chinese Foreign Policy Factionalism and the Origins of the Strategic Triangle,* R-1902-NA (Santa Monica: The Rand Corporation, 1977); and Harding, "Domestic Politics of China's Global Posture."

41. Ibid.

42. Robert A. Dernberger, "Communist China's Industrial Policies: Goals and Results," in *Mainland China's Modernization: Its Prospects and Problems, Proceedings of the Tenth Sino-American Conference on Mainland China* (Taipei: Institute of International Studies, 1981), 122-63.

43. See RMRB, 7 January 1957, in *Current Background,* no. 452 (31 May 1957): 1-3.

44. On PLA uneasiness about liberalization in post-Mao China, see *Nanfang ribao,* 4 April 1981, in FBIS (13 April 1981): P1-2.

45. *Zhengming,* no. 53 (March 1982): 16-17.

46. Jencks, *Muskets to Missiles,* 6.

47. *Dongxiang,* 16 April 1981, in FBIS (20 April 1981): W1-4.

48. On the various roles that an army can play in civilian politics, see Colton, *Commissars, Commanders, and Civilian Authority;* S. E. Finer, *The Man on Horseback: The Role of the Military in Politics,* 2d ed. (Harmondsworth: Penguin, 1976); Robert C. Fried, *Comparative Political Institutions* (New York: MacMillan, 1966); Roman Kolkowicz, "The Military," in *Interest Groups in Soviet Politics,* ed. Skilling and Griffiths, 131-70; and Nordlinger, *Soldiers in Politics,* 21-29.

49. For a list of these conferences through 1975, with an index to reports and speeches on military matters, see Lieberthal, *Research Guide to Meetings.*

50. For analyses of some allegorical and analogical articles from the 1960s and 1970s, see Harding and Gurtov, *Purge of Lo Jui-ch'ing;* and Harding, "Domestic Politics of China's Global Posture."

51. Just before the Lushan Plenum, the Soviet Union formally announced that it was repudiating its agreement to assist China in the development of nuclear weapons. If this was intended to assist Peng Dehuai, however, it was counterproductive, for it gave rise to charges of collusion between Peng and Khrushchev.

52. On the PLA's lobbying in the mid-1950s, see Hsieh, *China's Strategy in the Nuclear Era;* Roderick MacFarquhar, *The*

Origins of the Cultural Revolution, Vol. 1: Contradictions Among the People, 1956-1957 (New York: Columbia University Press, 1974); and Gregory J. Terry, "The Debate on Military Affairs in China, 1957-59," *Asian Survey* 16, no. 8 (August 1976): 788-813.

53. On the Peng Dehuai affair, see Philip Bridgham, "Factionalism in the Central Committee," in *Party Leadership and Revolutionary Power in China,* ed. John Wilson Lewis (Cambridge: Cambridge University Press, 1970), 203-35; David A. Charles, "The Dismissal of Marshal P'eng Teh-huai," in *China Under Mao: Politics Takes Command,* ed. Roderick MacFarquhar (Cambridge: MIT Press, 1966), 20-33; Ellis Joffe, *Between Two Plenums: China's Intraleadership Conflict, 1959-1962,* Michigan Papers in Chinese Studies, no. 22 (Ann Arbor: The University of Michigan Center for Chinese Studies, 1975); J. D. Simmonds, "P'eng Te-huai: A Chronological Re-examination," *China Quarterly,* no. 37 (January-March 1969): 120-38; and Frederick C. Teiwes, *Politics and Purges in China: Rectification and the Decline of Party Norms, 1950-1965* (White Plains: M.E. Sharpe, 1979), ch. 9.

54. On the purge of Luo Ruiqing, see Harding and Gurtov, *The Purge of Lo Jui-ch'ing;* and Michael Yahuda, "Kremlinology and the Chinese Strategic Debate, 1965-66," *China Quarterly,* no. 49 (January-March 1972): 32-75.

55. On the PLA's demands for modernization and professionalization in the late 1970s, see Paul H. B. Godwin, "China's Defense Dilemma: The Modernization Crisis of 1976 and 1977," *Contemporary China* 2, no. 3 (Fall 1978): 63-85; Ellis Joffe and Gerald Segal, "The Chinese Army and Professionalization," *Problems of Communism* 27, no. 6 (November-December 1978): 1-19; and Ellis Joffe, "Defense Modernization and Civil-Military Relations in China," *International Political Science Review* 2, no. 3 (1981): 317-26.

56. The views of the PLA on these socioeconomic and political issues can be found in DGB, 27 January 1981; *Dongxiang,* 16 January 1981, in FBIS (5 February 1981): U1; *Dongxiang,* 16 April 1981, in FBIS (20 April 1981): W1-4; and *Nanfang ribao,* 4 April 1981, in FBIS (13 April 1981): P1-2. A summary of military opinion can be found in the statement by June Teufel Dreyer in U.S. Ninety-seventh Congress, First Session, Senate Committee on Foreign

Relations,   *The   Implications   of*   *U.S.-China   Military   Cooperation* (Washington, D.C.: U.S. Government Printing Office, 1981), 5-18.

57. Thus, military spending, which rose immediately after the purge of the Gang of Four, fell during the early 1980s. The official Chinese figures, in billions of current *yuan,* are given below:

	1978	1979	1980	1981	1982	1983	1984	1985
Budgeted								
billion *yuan*		20.23[a]	19.33[b]	16.67[c]	17.87[d]	17.87[f]	17.87[g]	18.67[h]
% of total budget		18.10	16.90	15.80	15.80	14.20	13.10	11.90
Actual								
billion *yuan*	16.78[a]	22.27[b]	19.38[c]	16.80[d]	17.64[e]	17.71[g]	18.07[h]	
% of total spending	15.10	17.50	16.00	15.50	15.30	13.70	11.90	

Sources: a. *Beijing Review*, 20 July 1979, 17–24; b. FBIS, Supplement No. 76, 23 September 1980, 16–29; c. *Beijing Review*, 11 January 1982, 14–23; d. *Beijing Review*, 31 May 1982, 16–19; e. *Beijing Review*, 11 July 1983, vi-viii; f. *Beijing Review*, 17 January 1983, 13–17; g. FBIS, 4 June 1984, K1–9; h. *Beijing Review*, 29 April 1985, i-iii.

58. On the role of the PLA in the early 1950s, see Harding, *Organizing China,* ch. 2; and Ezra Vogel, *Canton Under Communism: Programs and Politics in a Provincial Capital, 1949-1968* (Cambridge: Harvard University Press, 1969), ch. 2.

59. On the role of the PLA in the Cultural Revolution, see Jürgen Domes, "The Cultural Revolution and the Army," *Asian Survey* 8, no. 5 (May 1968): 349-63; Jürgen Domes, "The Role of the Military in the Formation of Revolutionary Committees, 1967-68," *China Quarterly,* no. 44 (October-December 1970): 112-45; Angus M. Fraser, *The Changing Role of the PLA Under the Impact of the Cultural Revolution,* P-524 (Arlington: Institute of Defense Analyses, 1969); John Gittings, "Army-Party Relations in the Light of the Cultural Revolution," in *Party Leadership and Revolutionary Power,* ed. John W. Lewis, 373-403; Ellis Joffe, "The Chinese Army After the Cultural Revolution: The Effects of Intervention," *China Quarterly,* no. 55 (July-September 1973): 450-77; Harvey Nelsen, "Military Forces in the Cultural Revolution," *China Quarterly,* no. 51 (July-September 1972): 444-74; Harvey Nelsen, "Military Bureaucracy in the Cultural Revolution," *Asian Survey* 14, no. 4 (April 1974): 372-95; and Thomas W. Robinson, "The Wuhan Incident," *China Quarterly,* no. 47 (July-September

1971): 413-38.

60. According to U.S. Government estimates, the Chinese military budget increased from about 22 billion *yuan* in 1965 to approximately 40 billion *yuan* in 1971. See Ronald G. Mitchell and Edward P. Parris, "Chinese Defense Spending, 1965-78," in U.S. Ninety-sixth Congress, First Session, Joint Economic Committee, *Allocation of Resources in the Soviet Union and China—1979* (Washington, D.C.: Government Printing Office, 1979), pt. 5, 66-72. U.S. Government estimates of Chinese defense spending are usually about twice the official Chinese figures.

61. On the role of the PLA on the eve of the Cultural Revolution, see Byung-joon Ahn, *Chinese Politics and the Cultural Revolution* (Seattle: University of Washington Press, 1976); John Gittings, "The 'Learn from the PLA' Campaign," *China Quarterly*, no. 18 (April-June 1964): 153-59; Joffe, "The Chinese Army Under Lin Piao"; Ralph L. Powell, "Commissars in the Economy: The 'Learn from the PLA' Movement in China," *Asian Survey* 5, no. 3 (March 1965): 125-38; and Ralph Powell, "The Increasing Power of Lin Piao and the Party Soldiers, 1959-1966," *China Quarterly*, no. 34 (April-June 1968): 38-65.

62. On the role of the PLA in the 1970s, see Ellis Joffe, "The PLA in Internal Politics," *Problems of Communism* 24, no. 6 (November-December 1975): 1-12; Harding, "Domestic Politics of China's Global Posture"; and Harry Harding, "China After Mao," *Problems of Communism* 26, no. 2 (March-April 1977): 1-19.

63. Reassignments in early 1967 included the purge of Marshal He Long, a vice chairman of the Military Affairs Committee; the reorganization of the PLA's Cultural Revolution Group; and the appointment of eleven new military district and region commanders. See Jencks, *Muskets to Missiles*, 93-95.

64. Nelsen, *Chinese Military System*, 75-77.

65. Defense spending was 14.9 billion *yuan* in 1977; 16.78 billion *yuan* in 1978; and was budgeted to be 20.30 billion *yuan* in 1979: a 36 percent increase over two years. Because of the Sino-Vietnamese War, actual spending in 1979, at 22.27 billion *yuan*, was even higher than budgeted. See *Beijing Review*, 20 July 1979, 17-24. U.S. Government estimates show similar trends, but are about twice these official Chinese figures. See *Chinese Defense Spending, 1965-1979*

(Washington, D.C.: National Foreign Assessment Center, Central Intelligence Agency, July 1980).

66. On the Lin Biao affair, see Philip Bridgham, "The Fall of Lin Piao," *China Quarterly*, no. 55 (July-September 1973): 427-29; Harding, *Organizing China*, ch. 10; Joffe, "The Chinese Army After the Cultural Revolution"; and *The Lin Piao Affair: Power Politics and Military Coup*, ed. Michael Ying-mao Kau (White Plains: International Arts and Sciences Press, 1975).

67. The reforms of mid-1985 are discussed in, *inter alia*, DGB, 12 June 1985 in FBIS (12 June 1985): W1-2; *Wenhuibao* (Hong Kong), 12 June 1985, in FBIS (12 June 1985): W2-3; and *Wenhuibao*, 14 June 1985, in FBIS (14 June 1985): W1.

68. For a similar viewpoint, see Godwin, "Civil-Military Relations in China."

INDEX

A

Academy of Sciences, "Outline Summary Report of," 150; Philosophy and Social Science Department of, 165, 170
administrative organs (*xingzheng dan wei*), 202
Aeronautics and Ordnance, Ministry of, 222
Al Qing, 170
All-China Federation of Journalists, 169; *see also* All-China Journalists' Association
All-China Federation of Literature and Art, 165
All China Federation of Scientific Societies, 128, 131, 134
All-China Journalists' Association, 167; *see also* All-China Federation of Journalists
An Ziwen, 228
Anti-Rightist Movement, 21, 136, 138, 140, 143, 152, 164, 170, 175, 176, 177, 178, 197, 200
Association for the Dissemination of Scientific and Technological Knowledge, 128
Association of Science and Science Technology Policy Studies (ASSTPS), 152

B

Ba Jin, 170
Bai Hua, 177, 186
Bai Hua Campaign, 180
Bao'an County, 108
baohuang pai ("royalists"), 82

D

E

F

X

Y